AMERICA AS STORY

Historical Fiction for Middle and Secondary Schools

Second Edition

Rosemary K. Coffey / Elizabeth F. Howard

American Library Association
Chicago and London
1997

Project editor: Louise D. Howe

Cover designer: Richmond Jones

Text designer: Charles Bozett

Compositor: Clarinda in Galliard on a Penta DeskTopPro

Printed on 50-pound Lakewood White, a pH-neutral stock, and bound in 10-point coated cover stock by BookCrafters.

The paper used in this publication meets the minimum requirements of American National Standard for Information Sciences—Permanence of Paper for Printed Library Materials, ANSI Z39.48-1992∞

Library of Congress Cataloging-in-Publication Data

Coffey, Rosemary K.
    America as story: historical fiction for middle and secondary
schools / Rosemary K. Coffey, Elizabeth F. Howard. — 2nd ed.
        p.   cm.
    Rev. ed. of: America as story / Elizabeth F. Howard. 1988.
    Includes index.
    ISBN 0-8389-0702-4
    1. Historical fiction, American—Bibliography.   2. Young adult
fiction, American—Bibliography.   3. United States—History—
Juvenile fiction—Bibliography.   4. High School libraries—United
States—Book lists.   5. Junior high school libraries—United States—
Book lists.   I. Howard, Elizabeth Fitzgerald.   II. Howard,
Elizabeth Fitzgerald. America as story.   III. Title.
Z1232.H68   1997
[PS374.H5]
016.813'08108'00835—dc20   96-43453

Printed in the United States of America.

01 00 99 98 97   5 4 3 2 1

For Megan, Susan, and
James Coffey

For L. C. H. again

Contents

II. *The American Revolution and the New Nation*   17

III. *The Civil War and Reconstruction*   47

IV. *Westward Expansion and the Native American Response*   88

V. *Immigration, Industrialization, Urbanization*   123

VI.   *The Jazz Age and the Depression*   152

Introduction

THE NEED AND A SOLUTION

The introduction to the 1988 edition of *America as Story* began with some familiar student laments on studying history such as "Who cares about . . . anyway?" and "It's so-o-o bo-o-o-ring!" That introduction also noted the concern of social studies teachers that students acquire a deeper appreciation of history beyond memorizing dates and battles, that they develop a critical sense, a spirit of inquiry, some historical understanding and even enthusiasm. "Try fiction first" was the solution offered by this handbook, with its annotations, comments, and suggested follow-up activities.

THE RESPONSE

The response to the first edition from reviewers, teachers, and librarians was overwhelmingly positive. Clearly, *America as Story* filled a gap. Now, eight years later, with a surge in the publishing of historical fiction for young readers, it is time for a new edition and for some changes.

TEXTBOOKS AND OTHER MATERIALS

As was stated in the first introduction, it may be assumed that, for the foreseeable future, the textbook will continue to be the foundation for teaching American history in most school systems. But more and more middle and junior high schools are moving toward the use of primary and secondary sources giving a true flavor of the period under study. Reading historical fiction in conjunction with both textbooks and associated sources helps students to see history as the story of real people with feelings, values, and needs to which they themselves can relate, based on their own experiences and interests. This feeling of connection, of participation in the story, is crucial if students are to find history as exciting and stimulating as it actually is.

STARTING WITH STORY

So again, start with story. It is recommended that teachers consider assigning an appropriate novel (or novels) at the beginning of each new unit. By plunging vicariously into the experiences of fictional young people—building a sod house on the Nebraska prairie, following the North Star with a bold band of escaping slaves, traveling in steerage from rural Russia to urban America, or parachuting into enemy territory after a B-17 has been shot down—students will find history coming to life. Hard data in the textbook or quaint formulations in primary sources will have more meaning. Moreover, students will be able to contribute to class discussions insights derived from their individual reading.

Through this method of revitalizing history, it is expected that students will develop increased comprehension of their country's past. Once they begin to see history as story, related to the destinies of "ordinary" people like themselves, teachers may then find it possible to lead students to develop that critical sense and spirit of inquiry so important for real understanding. Some may ultimately be led to read historical fiction for pleasure as well.

THE REVISION

Although the 1988 edition included a large percentage of books for middle and junior high schools, its subtitle, *Historical Fiction for Secondary Schools,* may have been misleading to teachers and librarians. Since American history is widely taught in grades 5 and 8, as well as in the junior or senior year of high school, it was decided both to change the subtitle to stress the middle school emphasis and to increase the number of books included for younger readers.

The 1988 edition of this book, which was substantially shorter, included annotations of a number of lengthy novels written in the early part of the twentieth century. In the revised edition, these have been replaced by more than twice as many recent historical novels for young people, reflecting the explosion of interest in this field. Nearly all the books new to this edition came out in the 1990s.

SELECTION GUIDELINES

The approximately 200 books in this annotated compilation have been chosen and arranged to present aspects of American history through story. While actual events such as Civil War battles are important to the content in many of the books, in others the emphasis is on ordinary people living ordinary lives in a historical context. It is this idea, that history is the story of individual lives, which is considered most important for students to grasp.

The books, which are arranged in eight broad chronological and topical categories, are listed alphabetically by title within each category. An author-title index is also provided. Each section concludes with a list of briefly annotated *More Challenging Books for Advanced Readers,* which were fully annotated in the first edition. These encompass many classics of American historical fiction.

It is important to note that this is a highly selective list, as space restraints have necessitated omission of other worthwhile books. Local librarians will be able to recommend substitutes if specific volumes are not available.

In the selection of books, most of which have been published since 1970, the following guidelines were used:

1. *Time and place.* The time period covered in these books ranges from the beginning of the colonial era in the late 1500s to contemporary times. The setting is what is now the United States, except for a few entries dealing with immigration, or with wars in the twentieth century where some of the action takes place in Europe or Asia.

2. *Reading level.* The symbol (1) following the citation signifies books recommended for upper-level students (grades 11–12) or

younger students reading at a higher-than-grade level; the symbol (2) indicates a mid-range (grades 8–10); and the symbol (3) denotes books appropriate for middle school students reading at grade levels 5/6–8). Many are coded with more than one of these numbers, indicating their suitability for more than one grade level. The symbols are provided to guide the teacher or librarian in recommending books to individual students. The brief annotations at the end of each section refer to more challenging books that are significantly longer and/or more sophisticated than the others.

3. *Quality.* Historical fiction in the style of romantic pot-boilers or swashbuckling adventure stories has not been included. This handbook focuses on books of literary quality which present not only history carefully researched and accurately recounted, but also characters with whom young readers can identify and situations which provide for thoughtful involvement. Most were drawn from respected bibliographies of recommended books; others were suggested by knowledgeable experts in the field of American history.

4. *Content of entry.* Each entry contains three parts. First, there is a short annotation introducing the plot. Although this volume is intended primarily for teachers and librarians, the annotations are designed to arouse interest and may be used to promote the books with prospective readers. A second paragraph provides a comment on historicity, i.e., an indication of what a reader might learn about historical events or the ways of living, customs, attitudes, and values of the time. (Instances of sexual explicitness and strong language are noted in books for younger readers.) The third part, Suggestions for Reports or Activities, lists some ideas for possible follow-up to the reading. At least one question or activity is based on historical events described or referred to in the story; others may deal with historical, literary, or affective considerations. Many call for the student to do additional research related to the content of the book, and some invite the reader to imagine or extend specific elements of plot or character. Parents of children who are being schooled at home may find this last section of particular value. But these are suggestions only; teachers, librarians, and students themselves may, of course, devise their own activities as well.

ARRANGEMENT BY HISTORICAL PERIODS

The same chronological and topical arrangement as in the first edition has been used, except that the final section has been divided into two, with one focusing on "The United States and World War II" and the other on "America in the Modern World." The sections on "The American Revolution and the New Nation" and "The Civil War and Reconstruction" have been substantially expanded, as those are areas on which middle school social studies teachers tend to concentrate. The list of books related to immigration has also been considerably extended, with special attention paid to the contributions of Asians and Latin Americans to the story of America.

I. *Colonial America.* This period stretches from the late sixteenth century when Europeans initially began to settle the New World until the early 1770s. Books in this section deal with such topics as the voyage of the Pilgrims, the disappearance of the Roanoke colony, the growth of Plymouth, the Puritans and their way of life, the Salem witch trials, and early relationships with the Indians. Several portray how young whites captured by the Indians grew to prefer their new lives.

II. *The American Revolution and the New Nation.* The novels in this section take place in the period beginning in the mid-1770s, when tensions peaked between the British government and the colonists, and continue through the American Revolution and the ratification of the Constitution to the early days of the new nation. Readers will learn of contrasting views of loyalists and self-styled patriots and the unglamorous aspects of war. Other topics include the slave trade, Shays' Rebellion, shipboard life crossing the Atlantic, and conflicts over land grants between settlers of different states.

III. *The Civil War and Reconstruction.* Books in this section are set generally from the 1830s through the 1870s. Exceptions include some multigenerational chronicles whose most important action takes place during the Civil War, but which may begin earlier or extend beyond the Reconstruction period. Covered in this section are the issue of slavery, life in the South, the Underground Railroad, the action of the war, and the experiences of Reconstruction. A number of the books are written from a slave's point of view.

IV. *Westward Expansion and the Native American Response*. The westward movement in its varied aspects has provided rich materials for novelists. The period covered is the nineteenth century until the closing of the frontier. Included are the explorations of Lewis and Clark, glimpses of the ruggedness of pioneer life, the transfer of East Coast orphans to new homes in the Midwest, frontier justice, and portrayals of conflicts with the Indians. Current fiction reflects changing attitudes toward Native Americans, conveying appreciation for Indian peoples and culture and acknowledgment of wrongdoing on the part of the European-American newcomers.

V. *Immigration, Industrialization, Urbanization*. These books are set in the period from the mid-nineteenth century through World War I and cover such interrelated topics as the life of the working poor, the rise of the new-moneyed class, and the "Gilded Age." Stories about immigrants deal with those coming from Sweden, China, Russia and Eastern Europe, Ireland, and Italy, and with blacks moving from the South to the North and West. The hardships for immigrants arriving by ship and the struggle to find the elusive "streets of gold" are described. Several classics of American literature are listed at the end of this section.

VI. *The Jazz Age and the Depression*. The period covered extends from 1918 through the 1930s. Books set in the 1920s depict the life of the leisure class and the "Jazz Age." Themes in the 1930s concentrate on the Great Depression itself and the plight of blacks in the era of Jim Crow, complicated by the competition between blacks and whites for the few jobs available. Attention is given to the reasons why many unemployed men deserted their families and to the increasingly adult responsibilities assumed by quite young children.

VII. *The United States and World War II*. This period overlaps occasionally with the previous one, as it includes stories set in the 1930s but reflecting the movement toward another world war. The novels feature tales of Jewish immigrants starting a new life in North America, Japanese families interned during the war and then returning home, youngsters eager to go to war till they actually get there and see what it is like, children on the home front dealing with shortages, rationing, and anxiety about family members overseas, and the impact on Americans of the atomic bombing of two Japanese cities.

VIII. *America in the Modern World*. From mid-century to the present, this period encompasses the Korean and Vietnam wars, Asian and Latin American immigration, and the civil rights movement in the United States. A young man chooses Canada over the draft, while others participate in a war they do not understand, and a Vietnamese immigrant recalls the pain the war brought to his family. Southern youngsters, black and white, try to comprehend why there are so many restrictions on acceptable behavior. Three young men who are in Mississippi to register black voters are caught in the tension of the times and lose their lives. A group of illegal immigrants from El Salvador reaches Chicago safely only to realize that someone has to go back for their baby sister.

Acknowledgments

The revised edition retains about three-fourths of the entries published in the 1988 edition. Thus our gratitude to all those persons mentioned in the previous acknowledgments continues, along with our indebtedness to the bibliographical sources listed. Additional works consulted for the new edition include the National Council for the Social Studies bibliography compiled by Fran Silverblank, *An Annotated Bibliography of Historical Fiction for the Social Studies, Grades 5 through 12* (Kendall-Hunt, 1992), and *Understanding American History Through Children's Literature: Instructional Units and Activities for Grades K–8*, by Maria A. Perez-Stable and Mary Hurlbut Cordier (Oryx, 1994). Barbara Elleman, formerly editor of *Book Links*, was most helpful, as, of course, were various issues of *Book Links*. Dallas Clautice, Head, Children's Department, Carnegie Library of Pittsburgh, offered valuable suggestions. An e-mail request for possible titles was fruitful. *Horn Book Magazine, School Library Journal*, and the lists of "Notable Trade Books in the Social Studies" from *Social Education* were also useful resources, as were H. W. Wilson's *Senior High School Catalog, Junior High School Catalog*, and *Children's Catalog*. We also consulted with members of the Board of the National Council for the Social Studies.

Patrick Hogan, editor with ALA Editions, offered his encouragement, advice, and reassurance at appropriate intervals, all of which were greatly appreciated.

ROSEMARY K. COFFEY
ELIZABETH F. HOWARD

I   *Colonial America*

Beyond the Burning Time   Kathryn Lasky
New York: Scholastic, Blue Sky, 1994. 272p. (1, 2)

Twelve-year-old Mary Chase, living in Salem Village, Massachusetts, in 1692, wonders what is really going on when several of her friends start having fits and visions. Soon the villagers begin to look for witches as the cause of the girls' strange behavior. One by one the suspects are named by the stricken girls, beginning with a disreputable older woman and a slave but going on to include some of the most respectable residents of Salem. Many are convicted and hanged, while Mary and her older brother Caleb try frantically to save their widowed mother from a similar fate.

Comment

This retelling of the story of the Salem "witches" raises alternative explanations for the intense persecution of members of certain families by members of other families. The desire of young people for attention; the insecurity caused by a previous governor's revocation of the colony's charter (which protected titles to land); the role of old grudges, jealousy, and money; and other considerations are revealed to be factors encouraging the hysteria and superstition.

Suggestions for Reports or Activities

1. In 1752 Salem Village was incorporated as the town of Danvers. Consult a history of the state of Massachusetts to explore what happened in Danvers in later years.

2. What do you think became of Sarah Good's little daughter Dorcas after her mother was hanged? Tell what the life of an orphaned girl at this time may have been like.

3. Read Arthur Miller's play *The Crucible* and compare it to this book. How did the explanations for what happened differ in the two accounts? Which characters had the major roles?

Calico Bush   Rachel Field
New York: Macmillan, 1931. 201p. (2, 3)

It seems hard to believe that only a year ago she was in her beloved France, happy and loved. Now everything is changed, even her name. The delicate Marguerite Ledoux, who loved to dance and could sew fancy little stitches, is now Maggie, the Sargents' bound-out servant. Marguerite, Grand'mère, and Uncle set sail for America with hopes for a shiny new future. But Uncle died, and then Grand'mère's illness and subsequent death left Marguerite a penniless orphan. The Sargent family took her in, and now they are moving to the wilderness of Maine. Maggie is brave and resourceful, gets along well with the children, and is eager to please. The family is ill-prepared for frontier life and faces many dangers. Hostile Indians and wild animals are tough foes, but the bitter cold is even harder to bear. Although hardship and tragedy mark Maggie's thirteenth year, her trials strengthen her as she begins to grow toward womanhood.

Comment

Details such as the breaking of sod to plant crops and the weaving of cloth to make clothing make this portrayal of the early American frontier realistic. Maggie's experience with anti-French prejudice is informative: the clash between English and French settlers led to eventual war. Readers will gain a real sense of what it meant to leave "civilization" to settle in a wilderness area.

Suggestions for Reports or Activities

1. Imagine that you are going to move to an unsettled wilderness region, as Marguerite had to do. You can take only ten items. Decide what to take and explain your choices.

2. Consider the items that the Sargents decided to take to Maine. Write a rationale explaining the wisdom or ignorance that they exhibited in deciding to transport those specific items.

3. Find out what you can about the early settlement of Maine. Compare your discoveries with the information provided in the novel.

4. What were the reasons for anti-French prejudice?

Calico Captive   Elizabeth George Speare
Boston: Houghton Mifflin, 1957. 274p. (2, 3)

At her very first dancing party Miriam discovers that she and Phineas Whitney have a bond between them, but the next morning her whole world is changed. Indians attack her family's cabin. Miriam, along with her sister Susanna, her brother-in-law James, and their children, are captured and forced to march toward an uncertain fate. Miriam is terrified but learns that the Indians do not intend to harm them. Rather, they will most likely be sold to the French. Susanna gives birth to a baby girl, whom she names Captive, and has to stay behind with the Indians. Miriam is transported north to become a servant in a wealthy French home in Montreal. There she meets dashing, romantic Pierre, who almost makes her forget Phineas Whitney.

Comment

This book is an interesting look at the tensions building up between the English and the French over land rights in North America. Readers will become aware of Indian-French cooperation against the English, including the Indian practice of capturing English settlers and selling them to the French. Montreal is described as a cultured, urbane place. This book is valuable in casting some light on the connections between Canadian and U.S. history.

Suggestions for Reports or Activities

1. What were the causes of the French and Indian Wars? What was the conclusion?

2. The story is based on actual fact. English settlers were captured by the Indians and sold to the French. Can you find any more information about this practice in a reference source?

3. At the end of the story Miriam thinks that New Englanders believe that Montreal is a "place of wickedness, like the ancient cities of Sodom and Gomorrah." Why would the New England colonists have such an opinion?

Constance: A Story of Early Plymouth   Patricia Clapp
New York: Lothrop, Lee & Shepard, 1968. 255p. (2, 3)

From the moment land is first sighted from the *Mayflower*, Constance Hopkins is determined to hate America. In her journal she records the fear and excitement of landing and beginning to build the

Plymouth community, the sparsely furnished cabin she must now call home, the tentative friendship with nearby Indians, the terrible sickness which in those first months took the lives of half of the brave band. She describes the cold, the drought, the hunger, and the anguish of the loss of loved ones. But she records the good times, too—the joy in the times of plenty, the feasting, and the flirting. This is a lively account of an adolescent's concern for herself and for her relationships with others: father, stepmother, and the young men who take an interest in her. Constance gradually accepts this strange new place.

Comment

The formidable task of eking out a living from the barren shores of New England is realistically portrayed. Within the context of a very engaging story, Clapp provides readers with solid historical background on such topics as the agreement between the *Mayflower* group and their sponsors, which led to the establishment of the Plymouth colony, changing methods of government and land allotment, the diversity of the group (not all were members of the church), the peaceful trading with the Indians, the means of disciplining people who did not follow the rules of the community. Through the reflections of Constance, fourteen years old in the beginning and twenty at the end, the growing pains of Plymouth and those of a high-spirited maturing young adult are intertwined.

Suggestions for Reports or Activities

1. What can you discover in the book about the reasons for the establishment of the Plymouth colony?

2. What was the role of women at Plymouth? Did they play any part in making policy for the colony?

3. People from different cultures have often complained about how other people look, dress, smell, talk, and so forth. Can you think of instances today where some people are bothered by personal or physical attributes of others? What can you say about the value of discussing this point?

A Country of Strangers   Conrad Richter
New York: Knopf, 1966. 169p. (2, 3)

Fifteen-year-old Stone Girl, once known as Mary Stanton, reluctantly leaves her Indian husband and flees to another Ohio village with her young son. This seems to be her only chance to avoid being returned to the white family from which she was kidnapped ten years earlier and which she scarcely remembers. When her husband fails to come after her, Stone Girl is ultimately led to her father's home. However, Captain Stanton refuses to accept her, and she has come too far from her Indian village to return by herself. Her dilemma is resolved only after the death of her son, Otter Boy.

Comment

Told from the point of view of a young white woman who wants to stay with the Indians, this story offers an unusual perspective on the terrible experience suffered by many settlers on the frontier, namely, losing a child to the alien and greatly feared Indians whose land they had appropriated. By articulating the emotional ties which many of these children developed with their captors, the author makes plausible the idea that not all were glad to return to their families and to the white way of life.

Suggestions for Reports or Activities

1. Check some of the historical accounts of the colonial period in Ohio and Pennsylvania for information on the Indians' return of their white captives. Are there any details of real children who were reluctant to go back?

2. Imagine the history of the other girl who claimed to be Mary Stanton. Who was she? Where did she come from? How did she manage to persuade Captain Stanton that she was his real daughter?

3. Think about Captain Stanton's reasons for refusing to recognize Stone Girl as his daughter. How valid were they? Could you have countered his arguments any better than his mother did? What would you have said?

I Am Regina   Sally M. Keehn
New York: Philomel, 1991. 237p. (1, 2)

In 1755, eleven-year-old Regina watches helplessly as two armed Indians kill her father and older brother. Then she and her sister Barbara are taken captive and carried off to two separate villages. For the next nine years Regina, given the name of Tskinnak (Blackbird), struggles to remember her family and her life on a Pennsylvania farm, even as she becomes more and more a part of her adoptive family and their way of life. By the time the Swiss Colonel Bouquet forces her return to colonial civilization, she can no longer speak her native language or recognize the mother of her dreams.

Comment

This fictionalized narrative is based on a true story; in fact, Regina's tombstone stands in a cemetery near present-day Stouchsburg, Pennsylvania. It is a moving account of inhumanity on both sides of the long struggle between the first inhabitants of the Americas and the European settlers who challenged them. Regina suffers unforgivable losses as a colonial child, and then suffers again as the white men destroy the Indian village she has come to call home and kill or harass people who have comforted and befriended her in her despair. The impact of war upon the innocents of all sides becomes unforgettably clear.

Suggestions for Reports or Activities

1. Who was Colonel Bouquet? Find out what he was doing in Pennsylvania and what his historical role was in returning the Indian captives to their families.

2. Read a historical account of the return of the captive children in 1764. Did many of them resist leaving their Indian families? What happened to them?

3. In this book Regina tells her own story up to the time she and her mother found each other. Write another two to three pages, in Regina's voice, telling what happened to her and Quetit after they reached the new cabin. What was strange to her? What was familiar? How long did it take her to learn to speak German again?

4. Imagine the reunion between Regina and her sister Barbara. How did they communicate? What did they have to say to each other? Where do you think Barbara had been for the five years since her escape? (See if your library can locate Barbara's own story in *Pennsylvania Archives,* Series II, Volume 7, pp. 428–38.)

The Light in the Forest   Conrad Richter
New York: Knopf, 1953. 117p. (3)

True Son is angry. As part of an agreement to keep peace, whites are insisting that captives who have been living with the Indians be returned to their white settlements. True Son, fifteen years old, has lived with the Delaware tribe since being captured as a baby. He resents his real parents and the alien ways of whites: their strange smell, restrictive clothing, tasteless food. He grows to love his little brother, Gordie, but some of his relatives have had unhappy experiences with Indians and nurse a deep hatred. When Little Crane is found murdered by True Son's uncle, True Son decides to return to his Indian family. While taking part in a retaliatory ambush, he realizes that his loyalties are split. Where does True Son belong?

Comment

Although True Son was born into a white family, his point of view is Indian. Historical records show that many white captives preferred to remain with the Indians. By emphasizing True Son's identification with his Indian captors, the author provides readers an alternate view of colonial society, and encourages the appreciation of Indian culture. He makes clear that to the Indians the Europeans were the barbarians, a view which Europeans could not even imagine.

Suggestions for Reports or Activities

1. Check into some actual accounts of whites who were captured by the Indians and became acclimated to Indian ways, preferring to stay with the Indians. Write a short paper about one of these people.

2. What are some of the comparisons True Son made between the life of the Indians and the life of the white settlers? Write an imaginary letter from True Son to his biological parents explaining why he does not wish to return to them.

3. Find out about relationships between the Indians of Pennsylvania and the early settlers. How did the Quakers, Pennsylvania's first European settlers, regard the Indians?

Mercy Short: A Winter Journal, North Boston, 1692–93
Norma Farber
New York: Dutton, 1982. 138p. (2, 3)

When her family was massacred in an Indian raid, fifteen-year-old Mercy was taken captive and lived most of a year in an Indian village. Now, after two years as an indentured servant with a family in Boston, Mercy seems plagued by memories of her experience. The young Reverend Cotton Mather, with a reputation for exorcism, is trying to cure her of what he says are demons. He suggests that Mercy keep a journal to record her bouts with the devil. In her journal Mercy tells of the massacre, of the forced march, and of her life. But her reminiscences of the Indians are largely gentle; she records with tenderness giving birth to a short-lived half-Indian child. After some months of recording what Reverend Mather directs, Mercy seems to be cured, but she can see devils when she thinks Reverend Mather wants her to. However, she knows she must appear well, now that the handsome chorister with cornflower blue eyes is seeking permission to court her.

Comment

The author has developed Mercy's story from a few lines about her in the writings of Cotton Mather, noted minister from Puritan Boston. Included are lively descriptions of the bustling seaport of Boston and absorbing details of routines (housekeeping, food preparation, clothing, worship, courtship) and of the restrictive Puritan code (no merrymaking, no dancing, no celebration at Christmas, endless hours in church, constant reflection on sin, and so forth). Mercy records her appreciation of the wisdom and ways of the Indians who captured her, comparing them with the presumably more civilized English settlers. There is a forceful picture of the zealous Reverend Mather. Readers will empathize with a young woman who is trying to find a place for herself, questioning her own English-Christian civilization for its ideas about Indians, slaves, and religious practices.

Suggestions for Reports or Activities

1. Who was Cotton Mather? What were his contributions to the cultural and religious life of his time? What can you find out about his interests in science and medicine?

2. Mercy states that some of the colonists who were captured by the Indians came to prefer Indian life to their own. Can you find any evidence for this statement?

3. The Salem witch trials are mentioned in this story. Do you think the reports from Salem influenced either Mercy or Cotton Mather? Explain.

4. Mercy reads some poetry by Anne Bradstreet. Who was she?

Roanoke: A Novel of the Lost Colony   Sonia Levitin
New York: Atheneum, 1973. 213p. (2, 3)

To escape his cruel master, orphan William Wythers decides to leave England. He becomes a colonist headed for adventure in the

New World. To his dismay, the voyage is miserable, the captain dishonest and cruel, and the colonists disorganized and argumentative. They are forced by the captain to land in Roanoke, Virginia, instead of Chesapeake. William befriends and learns from the Indians and eventually falls in love. When the colony is attacked and massacred, William is saved by his new friends.

Comment

The Roanoke colonists became one of America's early mysteries when all traces of them disappeared. The main historical facts as portrayed in this book are accurate. They are woven into a believable narrative about what life might have been like for the lost colony. The settlers' attitudes toward the native "savages," the disease and barbaric treatment brought by the colonists themselves, and the greed, death, and suffering marking that first winter are described.

Suggestions for Reports or Activities

1. Research information about the lost colony. What are some of the explanations given for its disappearance? How do these explanations fit with the one offered by the book?

2. We are told about William's letter to his nine-year-old sister Bessie, who is still in London, but we do not read his text. Write William's letter, telling Bessie about the New World in a positive way.

3. *Roanoke* is told from William's point of view. However, the Indians were already settled in the area when the colonists arrived. Why did one tribe react in a friendly manner while the other one attacked? How did they accept the colonists' God?

Saturnalia   Paul Fleischman
New York: Harper & Row, 1990. 112p. (2)

It is 1681 in Boston, and young William, a captured Indian turned printer's apprentice, struggles to remember his past even while proving a clever student of the Bible and classical authors under the guidance of his master, Mr. Currie. His path crosses those of many other city dwellers: the menacing tithingman, the pompous wigmaker, the wicked eyeglass maker, the guilt-ridden woodcarver, the suspicious night watchman, a deceitful telescope exhibitor, and assorted other apprentices and captives. Meanwhile, the printer, his family, and his servants plan for a Saturnalia festival in line with Roman tradition to mark the winter solstice. Finally, William finds himself forced to choose: shall he return to what is left of his people, the Narragansets, or shall he stay with the warmhearted Curries until he has served out his time?

Comment

It is clear from this book that both the English settlers and the surrounding Indians had genuine grievances against each other. Many innocents were killed on both sides, and the survivors found it hard to forgive. Yet genuine attempts to move beyond past hurts were made by some, holding out hope for a multiethnic society some time in the future. The dependence of English society on class distinctions between master and servant is also illuminated by the many relationships described herein; in fact, this dependence is suggested as a major reason for the raids against the Indians who were sought by colonists desperate for help in their homes and fields.

Suggestions for Reports or Activities

1. Read about the Narraganset Indians in colonial times. How long did they remain neutral? What can you find out about the Great Swamp fight of December 19, 1675?

2. What exactly were tithingmen supposed to do? The author says that there was one for every ten families in Boston at the time: do you think they were all like Mr. Baggot? Why would anyone want to be a tithingman?

3. Mr. Tut makes some money enticing people to look through his telescope at the sky. When was the telescope invented? Find out what happened to the Italian astronomer and physicist Galileo (1564–1642) when he tried to use the telescope to support the theory of Copernicus that the earth revolved around the sun.

The Sign of the Beaver   Elizabeth George Speare
Boston: Houghton Mifflin, 1983. 135p. (2, 3)

Matt and his father have finished building their cabin in the Maine wilderness. Now Matt will be alone for about six weeks, guarding the house and weeding the garden while waiting for his father to return with his mother and sister and the new baby. Matt is apprehensive, but he manages well, even after a wily stranger steals his gun.

When a bear ransacks the cabin, food is scarce, but Matt is resourceful. However, trying to get honey, Matt is attacked by bees and nearly dies. He is helped by Attean and his grandfather, from a nearby Indian tribe. Attean's grandfather decides that Matt will teach Attean to read in return for being supplied with enough rabbits and squirrels to eat. The boys are reluctant at first, but after a while a close friendship develops. Parting is painful for both of them.

Comment

This story is full of information on living as newcomers to the American wilderness learned to do. The kinds of responsibilities which young people in colonial America were expected to assume are shown in the task which Matt's father leaves with him. Attean's communication of Indian ideas (sharing the land, killing game only for food, respecting others, carefully using the gifts of the forest) and his comments on the white settlers' killing his parents afford today's readers an opportunity to consider the European use of land from an Indian point of view.

Suggestions for Reports or Activities

1. What did Matt learn from Attean? After you have listed some of the survival skills that Attean taught Matt, consider the Indians' values that Matt learned. How were some of these ideas and values communicated to Matt?

2. Matt's new house was in Maine. His old house was in Quincy, Massachusetts. Look at a map of New England. Pick a possible location in Maine for Matt's cabin. What present-day cities lie along the road that went through the wilderness to Maine? Did any of these towns already exist in Matt's time?

The Stratford Devil   Claude Clayton Smith
New York: Walker, 1984. 192p. (2, 3)

Ruth Paine, adopted daughter of an elderly widow, is different from the other girls in Stratford, Connecticut, in the middle of the seventeenth century. She is more inquisitive, more independent, and braver, as well. From the age of twelve, when she has an adventure with wolves and local Indians—both greatly feared by the townspeople—to her brutal and sudden death at twenty-three, Ruth goes her own way. Deserted by the father she has just come to know, she is made a scapegoat by people who did not understand her, and thus disliked her.

Comment

Basing his story on a true happening (the hanging of a young woman as a witch in Stratford nearly fifty years before the famous witch trials in Salem, Massachusetts), the author creates a cast of characters and a series of incidents to illustrate how this unusual circumstance might have come about. As the plot develops, the reader comes to a greater understanding of the values and motivations of the Puritans, their relationships with neighboring Indians, and their fear of the world of nature.

Suggestions for Reports or Activities

1. From a careful reading of this book, select the values that appear to govern the Stratford Puritans. How do these resemble, or differ from, the values of a contemporary religious group of your choice?

2. Why was it so important to the Widow Paine that the townspeople believe she was the biological mother of Ruth?

3. Reconstruct the incidents that led the residents of Stratford to accuse Ruth of witchcraft. Why did she not defend herself? Why did she "confess" in the end?

4. Research the relationship of the Stratford residents and the Indians in the surrounding area during the first part of the seventeenth century. What happened?

This New Land   G. Clifton Wisler
New York: Walker, 1987. 124p. (2, 3)

Narrated by twelve-year-old Richard Woodley, this story tells of the voyage of the Pilgrims to the New World. In July of 1620, a band including both Pilgrims (known as the "Saints") and other English citizens (known as the "Strangers") sets sail on the *Mayflower*, headed for the Virginia Colony. After sixty-six days at sea, the group lands far north of Virginia near Cape Cod. Gradually, the 100 passengers dwindle to half that number, as the lack of food, shelter, and sanitation takes its toll. As virtually every family suffers the loss of a loved one, the survivors begin to wonder why they came. Were their sacrifices worth it?

Comment

This version of the Pilgrims' adventure emphasizes the courage, initiative, and skill needed by the colonists to survive. It shows, moreover, their dependence on the Indians for seed corn, for instruction in planting, harvesting, and hunting, and for trading. Youngsters will be interested to see how the food shared at the first Thanksgiving compares with what has become traditional in the U.S.

Suggestions for Reports or Activities

1. Imagine the coming of the settlers from the point of view of one of the Native Americans whom they glimpsed from time to time but never met. If one of them had been able to write down his thoughts, what would they have been?

2. The Indians Samoset, Squanto, and Massasoit are historical characters, as are Miles Standish and John Alden. Find out more about them and write a paragraph on each in your own words. Is their portrayal in this story accurate?

3. Near the end of the book the author describes the harvest meal shared by the Pilgrims and the Indians. What did they eat? Which of those foods are still eaten for Thanksgiving today, and which are not? Find out when Thanksgiving became a national holiday.

Tituba of Salem Village   Ann Petry
New York: Crowell, 1964. 254p. (2, 3)

Slaves in Barbados, Tituba and her husband John are suddenly sold to a minister, who moves to Salem Village. There Tituba cares for the minister's invalid wife, daughter, and niece. Salem Village proves to be cold and dismal, and Tituba's master greedy and self-seeking. Tituba, too capable at her duties and not fitting the community's standards, eventually is accused of witchcraft by the niece and other village girls. Tituba and two other women are proclaimed to be witches, suffer through a trial, and are then imprisoned.

Comment

Petry has captured the hysteria and fear surrounding the witch trials. She builds the evidence against Tituba in such a clear, logical manner that the reader empathizes with and fears for Tituba. At the same time, Petry realistically pictures a struggling community that can accept success or difference only as the result of an alliance with the devil. The unfairness of the trial is frustrating to the modern reader even as it reflects the tone and mood of the times.

Suggestions for Reports or Activities

1. Tituba, Sarah Good, Sarah Osburne, and others were brought to trial on charges of witchcraft. What happened to these people? Where did Tituba go? Who were the other people involved?

2. Who were some of the famous judges who presided at the Salem witch trials? Why do you think they believed that the accused were witches?

3. Write several journal entries from Abigail's point of view. Why would she accuse Tituba of witchcraft? What are Abigail's feelings during the trial?

4. Draw a map depicting Tituba's journey from Barbados to Boston and then to Salem Village. Note the various means of transportation that she used.

The Witch of Blackbird Pond   Elizabeth George Speare
Boston: Houghton Mifflin, 1958. 249p. (2, 3)

Adjusting to the strict and solemn ways of Puritan Connecticut is difficult for Kit, who has grown up in the easygoing life of high-church Barbados. But her cousins Mercy and Judith are welcoming and friendly, and there are some interesting young men. Kit learns to be useful with the endless household tasks, and joins Mercy in conducting a dame school. Despite her uncle's prohibition, she persists in her friendship with Hannah Tupper, the Quaker outcast whom the townspeople have declared a witch. She also manages some secret reading lessons for little Prudence, who has been thought too backward to learn. But then comes the sickness and with it the fear that witchcraft is the cause. In an exciting rescue, Kit manages to get Hannah to safety, but Kit is forced to stand trial.

Comment

Life in a small New England town in the time of Puritan dominance is serious. But readers will also discover that the colonists were quite human. There are rich details of daily life, such as the meager meals, styles of dress, religious practices, schools, courtship patterns, and ways of healing the sick. The demand for conformity and suspicion of people who were different are compelling. Kit's audaciousness and Hannah Tupper's fortitude are in sharp contrast to accepted patterns of behavior.

Suggestions for Reports or Activities

1. How are Kit and Hannah Tupper alike? Describe how they were treated by the people of Wethersfield. What can you learn about the early colonists' attitudes toward people who were different? Can you suggest any reasons for these attitudes?

2. The people of Connecticut were concerned about their charter from the king. Find out about this charter. What rights were granted to the settlers? Why were they worried?

3. This book describes many of the activities and practices in the day-to-day lives of Kit and her Connecticut cousins. Select one of these activities, such as preparation of meals, making of clothing, caring for the sick, educating the children, worshipping God. Research your topic. Prepare an oral report for class.

4. Why was Wethersfield an important settlement?

Witches' Children: A Story of Salem   Patricia Clapp
New York: Lothrop, Lee & Shepard, 1982. 160p. (1, 2, 3)
Told years later from the point of view of Mary Warren, who had been a bound girl in the house of John and Elizabeth Proctor, a strange and sad tale of fear, superstition, terror, and skewed justice unfolds. Mary notes that Tituba, the slave from Barbados, had been reading palms and foretold that something frightening would take place. Abigail Parris, who had been complaining about her boring life, begins to have screaming fits, and other girls, including Mary, follow her lead. The villagers believe that the girls are possessed by the devil and that the devil must have helpers. Tituba and two other women are arrested as witches, and as the fits continue many other persons are accused. Those who, under lengthy questioning, confess that they are witches are exonerated, but before the madness ends, twenty people are put to death.

Comment

This is a gripping story of the Salem witch trials and the circumstances that precipitated them, the hysteria of several young girls and the superstition and ignorance of the adults who could not understand what was happening. The pressure on the girls to name "witches," and on the accused to confess that they were guilty, as well as the use of "spectral evidence" in the trials, all afford a view of the Puritan theocratic system of justice. The story also provides a picture of daily life and work (such as farming, food preparation, making clothing, managing an inn) in a colonial town.

Suggestions for Reports or Activities

1. Check in an encyclopedia or other source for additional information about the reasons for the Salem witch trials and the outcome. Discuss how accurately the author has reported.

2. Write a newspaper article describing the events in the story. Whom would you interview? How would their stories differ?

3. What do you think is Tituba's role in the affair? Do you believe that she bears any responsibility for what happened? Explain.

4. Try to assess the responsibility for the witch trials, listing the people, the events, and the beliefs that helped to force the situation. Assign a value to each item you list: very important, somewhat important, not very important.

MORE CHALLENGING BOOKS
FOR ADVANCED READERS

The Forest and the Fort   Hervey Allen
New York: Rinehart, 1943. 344p.

A white youngster kidnapped by the Indians chooses to identify with his white parentage after relearning how to speak English. He is engaged as a personal manservant to Captain Simeon Bouyer, who is charged with protecting Fort Pitt from Indian attack and bolstering two forts farther east.

Lusty Wind for Carolina   Inglis Fletcher
New York: Bobbs-Merrill, 1944. 509p.

A French Huguenot family tries to build a new life in the New World, safe from the religious persecution encountered in the Old. In North Carolina they confront Indians, hurricanes, long-distance governance from England, planters divided into political factions, pirates, and their own disappointments.

II *The American Revolution and the New Nation*

April Morning Howard Fast
New York: Crown, 1961. 184p. (2, 3)

Adam Cooper has a little brother who annoys him and a father who fails to appreciate him. Still a boy at fifteen, yet yearning to be a man, Adam dares to sign the muster roll of the Lexington militia on April 19, 1775. His father, although surprised, does not interfere. Thus Adam is standing with the rest of the local farmers and shop-keepers when the British army marches by on its way to Concord, where the ammunition is said to be stored.

Comment

Told from the point of view of a boy who has to become a man in a matter of hours, the story emphasizes the astonishment of the Massachusetts farmers at finding themselves suddenly at war with the British. Made vivid and authentic for the reader are: Adam's outrage at the British decision to fire; his agony at seeing his father die; his disillusionment at the powerlessness of words when confronted with bullets; and his maturation in the course of the rest of the events of that long and memorable day.

Suggestions for Reports or Activities

1. Try to find a British account of the Battle of Lexington. Why did the British fire at men whose guns weren't even cocked? What were their orders? What happened to the British later at Concord? How many made it back to Boston?

2. Read Henry Wadsworth Longfellow's narrative poem "Paul Revere's Ride." Could Revere have been the one who alerted the

Lexington farmers? What does the poem say about what happened afterwards? Compare Longfellow's account with Fast's.

3. Imagine the battle and the other events of the day from the point of view of Levi, Adam's little brother. How much did he see? How much could he only guess at? Write an entry from Levi's journal telling his reactions.

The Bloody Country
James Lincoln Collier and Christopher Collier
New York: Macmillan, 1976. 181p. (2, 3)

Ben Buck tells this story of his father's stubborn determination to find his own life in the Pennsylvania wilderness. Not enough people are planting grain to keep their mill busy, but Daniel Buck refuses to be forced to live as a hired man on his brother's Connecticut farm. So he accepts a good offer of a mill and some acreage 200 miles west near Wilkes-Barre, Pennsylvania. This land is part of a disputed grant, fought over by Connecticut settlers and Pennsylvanians. Indians, British soldiers, and Tories join in cruel tactics to drive out the newcomers, but Ben's father refuses to leave, even after his wife and son-in-law are massacred. Throughout the story Ben has a difficult time trying to reconcile his father's passion for the freedom to live his own life with his equally passionate inability to consider freedom for Joe Mountain, the half-Indian, half-black youth whom he has reared as a virtual brother to Ben, but as a slave, nonetheless.

Comment

This book shows how the colonists fought bitter battles among themselves over land ownership. The authors describe the suffering of hard-pressed farm families who after years of building and working were summarily evicted by official decree or even by crafty speculators. People are pictured as tough and determined. Through Ben's eyes readers can sense the internal struggle of a young person questioning his father's seemingly paradoxical ideas of right and justice.

Suggestions for Reports or Activities

1. How did environmental issues contribute to the movement of settlers from eastern colonies into the wilderness?

2. Ben's father wanted to be free from his brother's domination, yet he could not even consider Joe Mountain's desire for freedom. Discuss this apparent contradiction.

3. The struggle for survival in the wilderness made bitter enemies. Can you justify the actions of the Pennamites in trying to force the settlers from Connecticut to leave?

The Captive   Joyce Hansen
New York: Scholastic, 1994. 192p. (2, 3)

In the midst of an annual ceremony honoring the king, Kofi, youngest son of the Ashanti chief Kwame, is captured and sold to slavers from the Coast. Despite his attempts to escape, he finds himself on a ship bound for Boston and bondage. The friendship that develops between him and Joseph, a slave boy, and Tim, an English indentured servant, helps him survive the storm and the smallpox that kill most of the captives and the crew. Once the three boys are settled with a Puritan couple on a Salem farm, Kofi begins to learn English as a way to help him regain his freedom and return to his village and his family.

Comment

The first third of this book concentrates on the rich culture from which Kofi is removed, thus contradicting the common picture of Africans as "savages." Moreover, as Kofi experiences slavery from the inside, he develops an empathy for the slave owned by his Ashanti family, even though it was he who betrayed them to the slave catchers. The setting in New England, nearly eighty years before the Civil War, offers readers an unusual perspective on slavery in the United States.

Suggestions for Reports or Activities

1. Find out what laws Massachusetts had around 1790 related to slavery and the slave trade. How did these differ from the laws regarding indentured servants such as Tim?

2. When Kofi arrives at the Brownes' house he notices many differences from his Ashanti home. Make a table of comparisons including such items as furniture, clothing, climate, marriage customs, religion, eating habits, men's and women's work, and so on.

3. What is known today about the Ashanti people and their culture? Tell something about their customs, the period in which they were powerful, and the countries in which they now live.

Conceived in Liberty: A Novel of Valley Forge   Howard Fast
New York: Signet, 1966. 196p. (1, 2)

In 1777 Allen Hale is one of nine New Yorkers surviving from a regiment of 300 men. After two years of losing battles, what's left of the Continental Army is about to settle in near Valley Forge, about twenty miles from Philadelphia, where the British Army is billeted. It is the coldest winter on record; the men have no shoes, coats, or blankets, and very little food. Allen watches his companions die one by one until he and two others decide to desert. When they are caught, two are sentenced to twenty lashes of the whip, and the third is to hang, despite being defended by Alexander Hamilton.

Comment

This moving book offers an opportunity to learn about the condition of soldiers during the Revolutionary War from their point of view. Readers will gain new insights regarding the relationship of the men to their officers, and of the men from different states to each other. The role of women as camp followers is also explored. The ragged army of farmers and tradesmen fighting for their freedom is contrasted with the British soldiers in their red coats and polished shoes. George Washington and Alexander Hamilton, among others, come alive as human beings torn by conflicting responsibilities and loyalties.

Suggestions for Reports or Activities

1. Find out more about one of the historical figures featured in the book: Generals Anthony Wayne and Charles Lee, Baron von Steuben, the Marquis de Lafayette, Colonel Alexander Hamilton. Does the author's characterization of that figure seem to be accurate?

2. The book ends with the battle of Monmouth (New Jersey). How did the actual battle turn out? Who is said to have won? Try to find accounts of the battle written by an American and by an Englishman and compare what they say.

3. The women in this book are all "camp followers." What does that mean? Write a sketch of Bess's character, noting her good points and bad points. What kind of person was she?

4. What do you think happened to Allen after he reenlisted? List some of the battles in which he might have fought and speculate as to what he would have found when he finally returned to his home in New York when the war was over.

The Fifth of March: A Story of the Boston Massacre
Ann Rinaldi
New York: Harcourt Brace, Gulliver, 1993. 321p. (1, 2)
The year is 1770, and fourteen-year-old Rachel Marsh, an indentured servant, is caring for the children of John and Abigail Adams. The restless inhabitants of Boston are hostile to King George of England, who has sent soldiers to act as "peacekeepers" among them. One of the soldiers, young Matthew Kilroy, takes up sentry duty outside the Adamses' home; he and Rachel become friends. As time goes on, Rachel has to make many decisions regarding what kind of person she is and where her loyalties belong. When John Adams agrees to defend the British soldiers charged with murder in the "massacre," Rachel's dilemma grows sharper than ever.

Comment

This book offers a fresh perspective on the bloody riot known to Americans as "the Boston Massacre." Readers will encounter alternate descriptions, for instance, of the mulatto Crispus Attucks, regarded by many as the first martyr of the American Revolution, and the silversmith Paul Revere, immortalized in Longfellow's famous poem. The British soldiers are portrayed as individuals with their own fears and concepts of integrity, and even the holders of famous names of the period—John Hancock, Henry Knox, Josiah Quincy—appear torn and indecisive when forced to choose sides.

Suggestions for Reports or Activities

1. Do you see any parallels between what happened to the British soldiers in Boston and what has happened more recently in such places as Somalia or Bosnia—or even Los Angeles after the acquittal of the police officers in the Rodney King case? What happens when a mob takes over and everyone becomes afraid?

2. Miss Alice Pattishell, a Quaker woman, helped make Rachel's visits to Matthew in jail go smoothly; then she helped her get a new job in Philadelphia. What can you find out about the history of

Quakers in Boston? Why were they considered "heretics"? What happened to many of them during colonial times?

3. We hear about two letters in this book, but we do not know exactly what is in them. Write Matthew's letter to his mother, telling her what happened in Boston and why he is in prison. Or write Rachel's letter to the Adamses, explaining why she decided at the last minute not to take her dowry with her.

The Fighting Ground   Avi
New York: Lippincott, 1984. 157p. (3)

In twenty-four hours spanning two April days, thirteen-year-old Jonathan changes his mind about war. He has been so anxious to fight. His father has returned home with a wounded leg. His older brother is a soldier; why not he? Early in the morning the bell tolls, and Jonathan goes to find out the news. A corporal says that some of the enemy are nearby. Jonathan admits that he knows how to fire a gun, and so he joins the little group of men. No one seems to know what the war is all about. Suddenly they confront several Hessian troops, and a skirmish takes place. Jonathan's interest in fighting begins to wane at the sight of blood; but now he is committed.

Comment

This short but quickly moving story points out to young readers that there is nothing pleasant about war. In his brief experience as a "soldier," Jonathan learns important lessons. The Hessians were enemies, but they could still be kind and gentle. The corporal whom he revered as a leader was also capable of viciousness. And his father was above all concerned for Jonathan's welfare.

Suggestions for Reports or Activities

1. You have probably read about the Hessian soldiers in your history text. What information does this story give you about the Hessians? Can you list some adjectives used to describe the Hessians in the story?

2. What were some of the events during that twenty-four-hour period that led Jonathan to change his mind about wanting to be a soldier?

3. Why did Jonathan break up the tavernkeeper's gun?

4. Jonathan's older brother is away fighting in the war. Write a letter that Jonathan might have written to his brother, telling about his experiences that day and how he now feels about being a soldier.

Freelon Starbird   Richard E. Snow
Boston: Houghton Mifflin, 1976. 209p. (2, 3)

Freelon Starbird is an accidental soldier in the American Revolution. He has read Thomas Paine's tract *Common Sense* and has listened to his friend Jib's bold statements about signing up, but he has also heard his father's and uncle's protestation—why get involved in a foolhardy and doomed enterprise? But on the night celebrating the Declaration of Independence, an overindulgence in brandy leads Freelon to put his signature on a roll of recruits. He and his equally inexperienced companions drill, learn how to use their borrowed or makeshift firearms, and finally march off, soon finding out that they do not know much about fighting. Alternatively brave or terrified, advancing or retreating, always ill-clad, hungry, cold, and often confused, the ragtag group crosses the Delaware to join George Washington.

Comment

The American Revolution may have been experienced by most of the unwitting recruits to the Continental army in this way—caught up in the excitement of the moment, not sure what the fighting was about, and unprepared. Readers will feel the uncertainties over enlisting, the occasional triumph, the urge to desert, and the harshness of winter (as formidable an enemy as the British). The author excels in evoking the feelings of personal and bodily stress on the field of battle.

Suggestions for Reports or Activities

1. Freelon is impressed by Thomas Paine's arguments in his book *Common Sense*. Read the book and paraphrase Paine's points. According to your text and other sources, what was the effect of Paine's writing on the colonists' feelings about the war?

2. In the beginning of the book Freelon complains about the common view expressed after the war, that the American Revolution was destined to be successful. John Adams wrote that the war was "only an effect and a consequence of it [the Revolution]. The Revolution was in the minds of the people, and this was effected . . .

before a drop of blood was drawn at Lexington." If this is true, why was the war necessary?

A Gathering of Days: A New England Girl's Journal, 1830–1832   Joan Blos
New York: Scribner, 1979. 144p. (2, 3)

Catherine Hall, age thirteen, begins her journal of a year and a half on her family's New Hampshire farm. Her mother is dead; she and her sister Matty live with their father. Next door live Cassie Shipman, Catherine's best friend, and her brother Asa. Catherine writes of ordinary happenings—chores, school, church, and occasional celebrations. Some excitement is experienced when a "phantom" (a runaway slave) leaves a note in the woods and the children have to make some decisions on their own. Two significant personal events are recorded, the remarriage of her father to a woman with a son Catherine's age and the sudden death of Cassie. But life goes on, and a new adventure awaits Catherine as her journal ends.

Comment

The story depicts everyday life and annual events such as maple syrup gathering, spring planting and cleaning, berry picking, and quilting. Thanksgiving and Fourth of July celebrations are described. Stories, jokes, verses, and recipes from the time help to bring the period to life. School life is vividly portrayed. The incident with the runaway slave shows how the major issue of the times, slavery, reached even this remote New England farmland.

Suggestions for Reports or Activities

1. Describe life on a New England farm in the 1830s.

2. What can you find out about the impact of slavery on the attitudes of New Englanders during the 1830s?

3. Catherine and her friends attended a one-room schoolhouse. How were these schools organized? What was life like for a teacher in such a school? Are there still one-room schoolhouses in the United States today?

4. For a group activity, plan an almanac for a year's farming in New England. Include phases of the moon, equinoxes, solstices, snow-

falls, rainfalls, droughts. Include recommendations for planting, harvesting, syrup making, etc.

George Midgett's War   Sally Edwards
New York: Scribner, 1985. 138p. (2)

It is early 1778 when fourteen-year-old George and his father, fishermen from Okracoke on the Outer Banks of North Carolina, learn that General Washington's men at Valley Forge are desperate for supplies. Angry at the British because their raiders have murdered a beloved villager, they decide to defy the embargo and take their bargeful of much-needed goods through hundreds of miles of treacherous waterways to the Revolutionary army. Along the way George discovers the true origins of his recurrent nightmare of being drowned at sea.

Comment

This short but demanding story depicts the special way of life of the residents of the Outer Banks, separated from Portsmouth Town on the mainland by open water. It also offers insight into the reasons why people choose sides in a conflict, having less to do with the merits of the respective positions than with accidents and happenstance. Characterizations of the Okracoke inhabitants and the people whom the Midgetts meet on their journey are vivid and memorable. Both the appeal of the sea and its dangers are made clear.

Suggestions for Reports or Activities

1. Mention is made of Roanoke Island. Read about the "lost colony" in an encyclopedia or history of colonial America. Describe some of the different ideas about what happened to the colonists.

2. Find out more about barges. Exactly what are they? How are they propelled? Why do they sometimes need to be pulled by mules on the shore? What are they used for today?

3. What do you think happened to George after this adventure? Do you think he took the place in Farrow's boat as his father wished? Why or why not?

4. In the course of this story the villagers of Okracoke make a lot of decisions on behalf of the entire community. Majority appears to rule. List some of these decisions, naming those who opposed them

(if any). Do you know of any communities today (anywhere in the world) where decisions are made in this way?

Guns for General Washington: A Story of the American Revolution Seymour Reit
New York: Harcourt Brace, Gulliver, 1990. 98p. (2, 3)

The British gunboats have laid siege to Boston Harbor. George Washington's army lacks the artillery necessary for a successful attack, so the Bostonians are starving and freezing in the bitter winter of 1775–76. Despite the odds, the young colonel Henry Knox persuades General Washington to give him a dozen men and some funds in order to traverse the 300 miles of mountain wilderness between Boston and Fort Ticonderoga in New York to bring that fort's artillery to Boston. But there are no roads or bridges, and ice storms and heavy snow are inevitable. Henry's teenage brother Will joins Henry in the great adventure.

Comment

The subject of this book is a little-known event of the American War for Independence that should rank for dramatic effect with Paul Revere's midnight ride or the winter crisis at Valley Forge. Some of the information on which this story is based comes from a factual account written by a young boy named John P. Becker who took part in the cannon trek and admired Will Knox.

Suggestions for Reports or Activities

1. Find out more about the attack on Fort Ticonderoga (May 1775) by Benedict Arnold, Ethan Allen, and the "Green Mountain Boys." Who were all these people and how did they capture the fort?

2. The heroes of this story are Will Knox and his older brother Henry. What became of the Knoxes after this adventure? Did they both survive the war? If so, did they go on to accept important responsibilities in the new government?

3. On an outline map that includes New York and Massachusetts, trace the journey of the artillery from Fort Ticonderoga to Boston. Include information regarding the form of transportation used, the approximate dates and duration of each stop, and the nature of the challenges or obstacles that arose at each stage of the trip.

4. Select your favorite portion of the journey and write a letter that Colonel Knox might have sent to his wife, Lucy, at that time telling her what was going on and how he felt about it.

The Hessian   Howard Fast
New York: Morrow, 1972. 192p. (2, 3)

A chain of events—a twist of circumstances—ends in apparently unavoidable tragedy. A squadron of Hessian soldiers—sixteen men and a drummer boy—are joined on their march by a dim-witted villager, carrying his slate and chalk. A spy? The Hessians think so and hang the man. Outraged, the townsfolk plan revenge and ambush the group, killing all but one. Hans Pohl, the sixteen-year-old drummer boy, is wounded, but he escapes and finds a hiding place at the farm of a Quaker family, the Heathers. Sally Heather, their teenage daughter, nurses Hans back to health, and the two fall in love. At length his whereabouts is discovered, and a trial is held.

Comment

This book calls attention to the role of the Hessian mercenaries in the American Revolution. The accidental nature of so much of the tragedy of war and the inevitability of unfairness are highlighted. The disdain with which the Quakers and the Roman Catholics were regarded is evident. The starkness of the military trial, with its unyielding adherence to principle, is in harsh contrast to the tenets of Christian love expressed by the Quakers and Dr. Feversham.

Suggestions for Reports or Activities

1. Who were the Hessians? Where did they come from? What was their role in the American Revolution? Can you uncover any information on whether some of the Hessians remained in America after the war?

2. Can you imagine a way in which Hans' life could have been saved? Write a different concluding chapter for this story.

3. Most readers identify with Hans and feel that he was wrongfully hanged, and this is what the author intends. What is the argument advanced by Squire Hunt? Write a short paper in which you justify his position.

I'm Deborah Sampson: A Soldier of the American Revolution
Patricia Clapp
New York: Lothrop, Lee & Shepard, 1977. 176p. (2, 3)

Since her mother cannot afford to keep her, Deborah Sampson is "bound" at the age of ten to a good family with several sons. Deborah learns to run, plant, chop wood, and shoot as well as any boy her age. As she grows up, she falls in love with Robbie, one of the sons. Their romance is ended when Robbie goes off to fight for the Rebels and is killed. Wishing to "do something for Robbie," Deborah tucks her hair under her hat and enlists in the Continental army. The often amusing adventures of a woman serving in a man's army add a light-hearted flavor to the sometimes grim accounts of the hardships of war.

Comment

Readers will feel involved in events leading to the war such as the taxes and restrictive laws enforced by the British. Specific events are mentioned, including the Boston Tea Party, the Boston Massacre, the battles of Lexington and Concord, and the formation of the Continental Congress. Some important figures appear. The book conveys a sense of people uniting for a common cause as well as giving a feeling for the ordinary life of farmers during the 1770s.

Suggestions for Reports or Activities

1. Deborah Sampson was a real person. Can you find out about her in an encyclopedia or other source? What can you learn about her life after the war ended? Does the account agree with the information in Clapp's book?

2. Deborah was a rather unusual young woman for her time. What can you discover about the role of women during the American Revolution?

3. The book describes some of the hardships suffered by soldiers during the Revolutionary War. Check in your textbook and in some reference sources to find out about day-to-day life in the Continental army.

John Treegate's Musket   Leonard Wibberley
New York: Farrar, Straus & Cudahy, 1959. 188p. (2, 3)

John Treegate's musket had seen proud service on the side of England in the French and Indian Wars. And now, years later, with colonists' discontent mounting and talk of revolution in the air, Treegate remains fiercely loyal and vows that his musket will never be fired against the king. He sets off to England on business, leaving his son Peter presumably safely apprenticed to a barrel-stave maker in Boston. But shortly after, Peter finds himself accused of a murder and escapes aboard a merchant vessel bound for the French Indies. Shipwrecked off the coast of the Carolinas and suffering from amnesia, he is rescued and cared for by a Scottish hermit. Four years later, with his memory restored, he returns to Boston, to his father's great joy. But father and son find themselves on opposite sides in the growing revolutionary ferment until events cause the intractable John Treegate to change his mind. Joining with Peter, he shoulders his beloved musket and stands with the Patriots at the Battle of Bunker Hill.

Comment

Readers will sense the conflict of loyalties within a family and the buildup of tension in Boston. Peter's experiences aboard the *Maid of Malden* shed light on the colonists' efforts to find trade outlets and circumvent the restrictions imposed by the British. The poverty of the people of Boston during the British blockade is described. Important events such as the Boston Massacre, the Boston Tea Party, and the early battles of the war are part of the story.

Suggestions for Reports or Activities

1. What might have been some reasons for John Treegate's loyalty to England? Why might it have been easier for Peter to side with the Patriots?

2. Check in a reference source for more information on the plight of Boston merchants during the British blockade. Is the story of the *Maid of Malden* plausible?

3. What events led John Treegate finally to change his mind about his musket?

4. Who was Sam Adams? What was his role in the buildup of sentiment toward revolution?

Johnny Tremain   Esther Forbes
Boston: Houghton Mifflin, 1943. 238p. (1, 2)

Silversmith apprentice Johnny Tremain is becoming skilled at his craft; his future is assured. He will marry one of his master's daughters and acquire half of the business. But an accident with hot, molten silver severely damages his hand. With no prospects for a livelihood, the desperate Johnny is befriended by Rab, a printer's helper. Rab helps him get a job delivering the *Boston Observer,* a publication of the Sons of Liberty, the Patriot leaders who are protesting England's treatment of the colonies. Johnny finds a role in the developing struggle. He is proud to join in the protest with the Sons of Liberty, and helps dump the tea in Boston Harbor. After the Battle of Lexington, when Rab is killed, Johnny learns that his hand is not hopelessly disabled and that he may be able to return to his trade. For now, most importantly, he can use it to fire Rab's musket in the Patriots' cause.

Comment

This story is a look into the everyday life of the upper classes, the merchants and artisans, and the lowly apprentices of colonial Boston. It is also an exciting picture of the city in ferment just before and in the early days of the Revolution. Samuel Adams, Paul Revere, Dr. Warren, and other figures in our history emerge as real people, and even British soldiers are human. The Boston Tea Party and the battles of Lexington and Concord are portrayed from the viewpoints of ordinary people involved in the events.

Suggestions for Reports or Activities

1. Johnny had hoped to become a silversmith. What other trades were possible careers for young people in Boston at the time? If you had been a young boy then, which of these might you have selected? What would you need to do to learn your craft?

2. It seems that not much was expected of young girls besides becoming proficient in household tasks. Is this true? What can you find out about the part played by women in Revolutionary Boston?

3. We don't read much about Paul Revere aside from his famous ride in Longfellow's poem. What can you find out about his role in history? (Or select one of the other members of the Sons of Liberty to investigate.)

Jump Ship to Freedom
James Lincoln Collier and Christopher Collier
New York: Delacorte, 1981. 198p. (2, 3)

Part two of the Arabus Family Saga, this book focuses on Daniel, a slave belonging to Captain Ivers. Daniel and his mother plan to buy their freedom with the soldier's pay notes from the American Revolution earned by Daniel's father. The father, however, dies on a sea voyage, and Mrs. Ivers takes the notes away from Daniel's mother. Daniel manages to steal back the notes, but Captain Ivers forces him onto a ship bound for the West Indies, where he will be expected to work in the cane fields. Daniel now must find a hiding place for the notes. When the ship docks in New York because of a storm, Daniel escapes to Sam Fraunces' tavern. From there he plots to retrieve the notes in order to buy his and his mother's freedom. (For other stories involving some of the same characters, see *War Comes to Willie Freeman* and *Who Is Carrie?* below.)

Comment

Daniel's misadventures involve the reader in the debate and compromise in the Constitutional Convention over the issue of slavery. The pay notes also play an important role, as Daniel deals with famous historical personages over the question of whether the individual states or the government to be formed by the Convention should be responsible for paying them off.

Suggestions for Reports or Activities

1. Why was Daniel so upset about becoming a slave in the cane fields in the West Indies? Research the conditions in which slaves lived and worked there in this time period.

2. Read about the Constitutional Convention's quandary regarding slavery. What was the Connecticut Compromise? Write a short speech in which you try to convince the members of the Convention to abolish slavery altogether in the new nation.

3. Imagine that you are Daniel. Write an epitaph for Birdsey.

My Brother Sam Is Dead
James Lincoln Collier and Christopher Collier
New York: Four Winds, 1974. 216p. (2, 3)

Tim Meeker tells the story of his family as it becomes involved in the American Revolution. Each family member has a different role and viewpoint. Tim's brother Sam, for instance, leaves his studies at Yale to become a "rebel" soldier. His father objects to all war and wishes to have no part of it. Tim's mother worries about her family's involvement in the Revolution, while Tim's own views change as he witnesses war's death and destruction. After his father disappears, the news of Sam's death and the problems of daily survival serve to confuse the remaining family members further as they seek to determine their ultimate loyalties.

Comment

The Meeker family's uncertainties mirror those of the conflict through which the United States was born. The authors contrast the views of the "rebels" revolting against oppression with those of the Loyalists fighting for their king and country. Both sides are portrayed as human; both sides make mistakes that cost lives. The book helps the young reader understand that there are many versions of what is right.

Suggestions for Reports or Activities

1. Many of the people and events mentioned here were real, as were all of the places. There even was a Meeker family in Redding. Select a person or event and research the historical accuracy of the version given here.

2. As the Meeker family is torn apart by opposing views, Tim realizes that there are more than two sides to the question. Write several pages from a journal Tim might have written as his loyalties changed.

3. Sam never loses his idealism, even when learning about the hardships of war. Imagine that you are Sam and write letters to Betsy Read describing your feelings about being a part of the American Revolution.

Ruffles and Drums   Betty Cavanna
New York: Morrow, 1975. 222p. (2, 3)

Sarah Devotion Kent witnesses the start of the American Revolution at the battle in Concord, Massachusetts. Sarah is sixteen, patriotic without reservation, and filled with longing to be a part of the action. She even becomes engaged to her childhood friend Tom because he is going off to war. After Sarah's father and brother join the rest of the neighbors to fight the British, reality sets in. Sarah and her mother must nurse a wounded British officer; life on the farm turns harsh without the help of the men; and to Sarah's consternation, she begins to change her unfavorable opinion of James, the British officer.

Comment

The American Revolution is depicted here through the feelings and reactions of a young girl. Readers will share the initial excitement of a country fighting for a cause, followed by the unromantic drudgery of daily life involved in running a farm, winding cartridge papers for the soldiers, and coping with shortages of food and clothing. Although Sarah still believes in freedom, as she matures she realizes that the reality of revolution is much less glamorous than the idea of it.

Suggestions for Reports or Activities

1. Research the origin of the American flag. What did the first flag look like? Draw a picture of the flag that Sarah would have seen in the 1770s.

2. Imagine that you are Sarah. Write several letters to a friend in which you describe your feelings about the war, Tom, and James.

3. Do further reading and research about the beginning of the American Revolution. Is the book accurate in its historical details? Make a chart with two columns. In the first column list the historical facts presented in the book. In the second column add new facts that you found in your research.

Sarah Bishop   Scott O'Dell
Boston: Houghton Mifflin, 1980. 230p. (2, 3)

Sarah Bishop's father is outspoken in his loyalty to King George. He dies after renegade rebels set fire to his house and barn, and torture him with tar and feathers. Sarah tries to locate her brother Chad, who has signed up to fight on the Patriots' side, but after weeks of searching she finds that he too has died. Wrongfully accused by the British of setting a major fire and threatened by a ne'er-do-well fellow who has offered her a ride, she flees to the wilderness, where through bitterness, stubbornness, and inventiveness she makes her home in a cave. Living with a beaver and a bat for company, but cheered by the occasional visit of an Indian family, Sarah shuns people, seeking aid only when she needs to earn money for supplies. After being declared innocent of a charge of witchcraft, she does appear tentatively to reach out again to human society.

Comment

Ordinary people became innocent victims during the American Revolution. Being on the wrong side—or causing any suspicion— could result in being vandalized or murdered by one's neighbors. The war is depicted as being a civil war between Americans of opposing viewpoints as well as a war against English injustice. Sarah is shown as an example of the fortitude and independence of which colonial women were capable.

Suggestions for Reports or Activities

1. Different types of people are considered weird or peculiar in different periods of history. Do you think that Sarah Bishop would be considered an unusual person today? Would you like to have her for a friend? Explain.

2. We sometimes have been given the impression in our history books that the Patriots were the "good guys" and the Loyalists, or Tories, were the "bad guys." What have you found in this book that either supports or contradicts this idea?

3. Textbooks often portray the Revolutionary War strictly as a fight between the Americans and the British. How does this narrative alter this picture?

Second Daughter: The Story of a Slave Girl

Mildred Pitts Walter
New York: Scholastic, 1996. 214p. (2)

Aissa and Fatou, known to their masters as Lizzie and Bett, live as slaves in the Colony of Massachusetts at the time of the Revolutionary War. Even though Bett's husband is a free man, he is not permitted to buy his wife's freedom; their daughter automatically takes the status of her mother, so she too is a slave. Headstrong Aissa, who refuses to acknowledge her slave name and is frequently in trouble with the spoiled and petulant mistress, longs for freedom and the right to be herself. Finally, Bett's close attention to the conversations in the master's drawing room lead her to believe that slavery is unconstitutional in Massachusetts. Since women cannot sue in Massachusetts courts, she looks for a man to join her in her suit.

Comment

In 1781 a slave named Mum Bett sued her owner for her freedom under the Massachusetts Constitution. The court papers mentioned that she had a sister and a husband, but both were nameless. In this book the sister acquires a name and a distinct personality as she, too, struggles for her freedom. That even a master who intends to be kind may treat his slaves capriciously and cruelly is shown to be almost inevitable in a system that permits one human being to own another.

Suggestions for Reports or Activities

1. Consult a history of the Commonwealth of Massachusetts to find out when slavery in that state was declared unconstitutional. Is there any mention of specific cases that led to this decision? When were all the slaves in Massachusetts actually told that they were free?

2. Josiah and other black men in this story join the Continental army to fight for freedom from Britain. Find out when blacks were first allowed to join and in what capacity. Did those who survived the war receive any special treatment from the new government?

3. Read about some of the controversies surrounding the language used in the Declaration of Independence. What was said about black people? Was there any agitation to outlaw slavery in the new country?

4. Imagine Aissa's life after freedom. What kind of work did she do "in the home of a well-to-do merchant"? Who were some of the women who might also have lived in her boardinghouse? Why was she learning to speak Fulfulde, and who was teaching her?

1787   Joan Anderson
San Diego: Harcourt Brace Jovanovich, 1987. 200p. (2, 3)
The summer of the Constitutional Convention in Philadelphia is brought to life through the eyes of Jared Mifflin, a Princeton student assigned as an aide to James Madison. Jared's job is to facilitate the smooth running of the proceedings by taking care of details such as having sufficient candles, controlling traffic in the State House area, and keeping the press away. It is quite a summer. Jared, who is from an upper-class family, makes two new friends: William, a servant of Benjamin Franklin, and Henry, the slave of a delegate from Georgia. Because of them he finds himself concerned about the new Constitution's provisions for the common man and for slaves. The most pleasing development of this most exciting summer is his growing fondness for Hetty Morris, an affection which she returns.

Comment

Against the backdrop of the love story of Jared and Hetty, the author has woven the story of the Convention, introducing the major actors and discussing the highlights and the main areas of debate, such as how to satisfy small and large states' concerns for adequate representation. Washington, Madison, Hamilton, Franklin, and others are shown in debate or at leisure. The life of the city is also described, as Jared moves from the State House to the docks, to a slave auction, to the market, to a fox hunt, and to a grand ball. The Constitutional Convention comes to life as a vibrant event.

Suggestions for Reports or Activities

1. After coming to know Henry and William, Jared found himself more concerned that the Constitution protect the rights of all citizens. What were the provisions of the Constitution regarding slavery? How was the Constitution amended to provide for individual rights?

2. What was the role of James Madison in framing the Constitution?

3. Why did the members of the Convention feel that it was necessary to keep the proceedings secret? Take both sides of the debate— the position of Weaver, the newspaper editor, and of James Madison— and list arguments for and against this policy.

4. Select a state and imagine that you are one of its delegates. Write a letter home to your constituents after the momentous signing of the Constitution.

The Sign Painter's Secret: The Story of a Revolutionary Girl
Dorothy and Thomas Hoobler
Englewood Cliffs, N.J.: Silver Burdett, 1991. 52p. (3)

When the British capture Philadelphia in 1777, five of their officers move into the large house occupied by the MacDougal family. Annie, her little brother Brian, and their mother move up to the empty servants' bedrooms on the third floor, while Mother serves as the officers' cook and maid. For a long time Annie cannot understand why Mother is so cheerful, given that Father is away from home trying to raise money for the Revolution, and older brother Rob is fighting in the Revolutionary army. Later she learns that she has a special role to play in helping General George Washington stay informed about the British plans.

Comment

This easily read story provides a counterpoint to the more common focus on the Revolutionary army's season at Valley Forge. Told from the point of view of civilian Patriots forced to feed and quarter enemy soldiers, it shows that rebellion may take different forms. Contemporary readers may be intrigued by the use of children as spies and by the suggestion that Martha Washington was with her husband during that long, cruel winter.

Suggestions for Reports or Activities

1. What do you think Annie's father was doing in Charleston (South Carolina) all this time? Find out what role Charleston played in the Revolutionary War in the winter of 1777–78.

2. Imagine that Annie was captured by the British on her way to General Washington's camp. Tell how she might have managed to escape and return to her family.

3. Follow the directions at the end of the book and make a silhouette of a friend or family member. Write an explanation of how you did it.

The Slave Dancer Paula Fox
New York: Bradbury, 1973. 176p. (2, 3)

Jessie Bollier is kidnapped near the New Orleans docks in 1840 and forced aboard a ship heading for West Africa. He finds conditions intolerable. The crew is a scurvy bunch, cruel to each other and led by a brutish captain. Food is bad, water is scarce, sleeping quarters are dark and cramped, and Jessie is miserable. When the ship arrives in Africa and takes on its human cargo, Jessie finds out why he is there: to play his fife in order to "dance the slaves." This is a method of providing some exercise so that slaves can be kept in somewhat better health for the marketplace. Jessie is degraded by this role and sickened by the lot of the blacks, quartered on top of each other in the stench-filled hold. Many become ill, die, and are thrown overboard. The ship withstands a challenge by a British antislavery vessel, but then it is wrecked in a fierce storm; almost everyone is lost.

Comment

This story depicts how the slave trade worked, the rationale of necessity and profit which made it seem legitimate, and how the trade continued long after Congress had outlawed it. Appalling conditions aboard ship are graphically described, including both the inhuman nature of the lives of the sailors (men who were scarcely more than slaves themselves) and the despicable treatment of the blacks on the voyage. Jessie's reaction to his plight gives readers a view from a sensitive young person exposed to the horrors of such a voyage.

Suggestions for Reports or Activities

1. Find out about the British attitude toward the slave trade. What actions did the British navy take against slave ships? Does the account in the story seem plausible, based on what you have learned from other sources?

2. New Orleans was a bustling shipping center in the mid-nineteenth century. Read about the port of New Orleans. Write a report describing the commercial activities taking place there.

3. In the book Ras is helped to escape north to freedom. Invent a story of his journey.

Time Enough for Drums   Ann Rinaldi
New York: Holiday House, 1986. 249p. (2)

Jemima Emerson, high spirited and opinionated, is impatient with her strict and demanding tutor, John Reid, who appears to be a Tory spy. By the time she finds out he is working for the Americans, Jemima knows that he is in love with her, and the sentiment is mutual. The war is reaching close to home: Jemima discovers that her mother, unbeknownst to her father, is the secret author of letters to the newspapers seeking support for the Continental army, and her brother Daniel enlists. Then the British occupy Trenton, her father is killed, and her mother appears to descend into an incurable depression. This story tells of one family's efforts to continue their lives in spite of the hardship and heartache of war.

Comment

Through the everyday life of a quite prosperous family during the time of the battle of Trenton, the story shows how opinions differed over the rebels' (Patriots) cause. The British troops occupying the town are portrayed as reasonable, but the Hessians are stereotyped as uncouth ruffians. The somewhat contrived love story will not interfere with readers' gaining some understanding of the vicissitudes of war and its effects on ordinary people.

Suggestions for Reports or Activities

1. Jemima's mother had an unusual job for a woman of those times. What was the role of women during the American Revolution? Can you discover information about the activities of any specific woman or women of the period?

2. What famous work was written to arouse enthusiasm for the Revolution? Research the role of the press in creating needed support among the rebels (or Patriots).

3. There is a famous painting called *Washington Crossing the Delaware*. Try to find a reproduction of this painting, and write a short paper describing what might have been the feelings of the men in the picture.

4. What was the importance of the battle of Trenton for the outcome of the war?

The True Confessions of Charlotte Doyle   Avi
New York: Avon, 1990. 232p. (2)

Charlotte Doyle, thirteen years old in 1832, stays behind in England to finish out the school year while the rest of her family establish their new home in Providence, Rhode Island. The trans-Atlantic crossing, which could take one to two months depending on the weather, is to occur during the summer holidays on a ship owned and operated by her father's firm. Charlotte looks forward to the voyage, never dreaming that it will be on a vessel managed by a murderous captain, run by a mutinous crew, threatened by a hurricane, and subject to various other disasters, including a charge that Charlotte herself has murdered the first mate. Charlotte undergoes many changes in character and outlook as she tries to survive in the face of hitherto unimagined challenges.

Comment

A rousing sea story set at a time when captains had total control of their ships and their crews, this narrative raises many questions about the assumptions that may govern our lives and behavior and lead us into difficulties. Readers may learn a lot about sailing ships, but they will also explore gender roles, parent-child relationships, the limits of personal responsibility, and shifting definitions of friend and foe. Charlotte evolves from a dutiful daughter of the middle class into an independent young woman who makes her own life choices, most of which young readers will applaud while admiring her courage.

Suggestions for Reports or Activities

1. Imagine a different ending for the story: What if Charlotte had stayed with her family? What sort of person would she have become? Describe her life in Providence over the next ten years or so.

2. Read an account of shipboard rules in the mid-nineteenth century. Was there any legal way to bring an unjust captain to account? What usually happened to the challenger?

3. Compare the voyage made by the *Seahawk*—which took nearly two months—with a contemporary trans-Atlantic crossing in terms of route, length of passage, size of ship, number of crew members needed, powers of the captain, etc. Look for information related to a freighter rather than a passenger ship.

War Comes to Willie Freeman
James Lincoln Collier and Christopher Collier
New York: Delacorte, 1983. 178p. (2, 3)

Willie Freeman is a thirteen-year-old free black girl. Her father was granted his freedom when he enlisted in the militia to fight the British. After witnessing her father's death in the battle of Fort Griswold (Connecticut), Willie learns that the British have taken her mother as a prisoner. Pretending to be a boy, Willie sets off on a journey to New York hoping to find her mother. This trip is especially dangerous because she is black; she has to avoid not only the war around her but also the possibility of being seized as a runaway slave. The story tells of Willie's adventures in New York, still posing as a boy. She finds some help at Sam Fraunces' Tavern in New York and later plays a role in a landmark New Haven court case that guarantees the freedom of Connecticut former slaves who fought in the Revolution. (For other stories involving some of the same characters, see *Jump Ship to Freedom,* above, and *Who Is Carrie?* below.)

Comment

The American Revolution is seen here through the eyes of a strong, intelligent girl who personally experiences the hardships of war and observes its effects on the people around her. The story recalls an actual incident, the famous court case of *Arabus v. Ivers.*

Suggestions for Reports or Activities

1. Blacks played a significant part in the American Revolution and the birth of this country. How is this important fact illustrated by this story? What additional information can you find in your text or other sources about blacks in the American Revolution?

2. What role did women play in society during this time period? Why did Willie have to pretend to be a boy? How did her friend Horace react when he discovered she was really a girl? How did his actions and attitudes change?

3. Draw a map of the British colonies in America during the Revolution. Trace Willie's journey on the map. Be sure to include Fort Griswold and the various important places she visited on the way to New York.

Who Comes to King's Mountain?   John and Patricia Beatty
New York: Morrow, 1975. 287p. (1, 2)

As the Revolutionary War heats up in western South Carolina in 1780, fourteen-year-old Alexander MacLeod is an unquestioning "king's man," despite Scots-born grandparents who are open rebels. In the course of this story, Alec changes his mind, and his allegiance, several times, torn by conflicting loyalties. He rides first with the Loyalists, led by a neighbor; then with Patriots commanded by Francis Marion, the "Swamp Fox"; then, reluctantly, with another band of Loyalists headed by a Scot. Alec's excursions as a spy make him suspect to everyone he meets. His grandmother, known to some as a witch, predicts many of his adventures but is unable to save her own husband from his fate.

Comment

The familiar categories of "Patriot" and "Loyalist" fall apart in this narrative. The Highland Scots in South Carolina faced many choices, exemplified by the paths taken by several of the characters.

Readers may begin to understand the ambiguities and contradictions confronting people who found it difficult to support wholeheartedly one side or the other. The British could be as suspicious of declared Loyalists as of Patriots. Often families were divided. The impact of the war on farmers and tradesmen may remind readers of more recent conflicts where the distinction between soldier and civilian has, for many purposes, broken down.

Suggestions for Reports or Activities

1. Consult a map and a history of South Carolina. On an outline map of the state mark the location of Charles Towne (Charleston), Camden, Ninety-Six, the Pee Dee and Santee rivers, and King's Mountain. Mark also the places in South Carolina named after some of the historical characters in this book (Sumter, Marion) and explain when and why they got their names.

2. Describe the battle at King's Mountain. Why had Major Ferguson decided to make a stand there? Why didn't it work out? Given the title of the book, who, indeed, came to King's Mountain and won the battle?

3. Have you ever been in a situation where one member of your family advised you to do one thing, and another member wanted you to do something else? Describe the situation, the advice you got, and the reasons you decided to do what you did. Do you see any parallels with Alec's dilemma?

Who Is Carrie?   James Lincoln Collier and Christopher Collier
New York: Delacorte, 1984. 158p. (3)

Part three of the Arabus Family Saga, this story centers around a kitchen slave named Carrie. A curious young person, Carrie is always getting into mischief, partly because of her inquisitiveness about her unknown personal history. She works in Sam Fraunces' famous tavern, which enables her to become part of the history of the post-Revolutionary era. For example, when she is pursued by Captain Ivers, who wants to prove she is his slave, she hides by working in President George Washington's kitchen. Eventually, Carrie pieces together a plausible account of her own background. (For other stories involving some of the same characters, see *War Comes to Willie Freeman* and *Jump Ship to Freedom,* above.)

Comment

Carrie becomes involved in various historical events. She witnesses Washington's inauguration and eavesdrops on conversations held by Thomas Jefferson and Alexander Hamilton. These experiences permit the modern reader a glimpse of our forefathers through the eyes of an ordinary young person living at that time, before history had judged them great.

Suggestions for Reports or Activities

1. Write an advertisement for the lost-and-found section of the newspaper calling for additional background information on Carrie. Be sure to include the important known clues about Carrie's identity.

2. Write a letter from Carrie to Willie in which Carrie tells Willie about their possible relationship. Remember to include the tone of excitement that Carrie feels when she learns who she may be.

3. Find out more about the period when the nation's capital was located in New York City. Why was New York chosen? What problems did the choice create? Why was the seat of government moved? Where did it go, and when?

The Winter Hero   James Lincoln Collier and Christopher Collier
New York: Macmillan, 1978. 152p. (3)

Justin looks up to Peter, his sister's husband, because he was a hero in the Revolution, and Justin would like to be a hero, too. But Peter is ready to fight again. Like other farmers in the area he is heavily in debt. They cannot pay the high taxes levied by the General Court, and the sheriff takes their plows, horses, or oxen. Peter is enraged when his oxen are seized and held by Mattoon, a wealthy landowner who has loaned him money. He decides to join Captain Daniel Shays' scheme to protect the farmers' property rights. Peter gets Justin a houseboy's job at the house of Mattoon, supposedly to earn back the oxen but actually to be able to spy for Shays' "Regulators." Justin has several chances to show his bravery, to fight, and even to save Peter's life twice. But he learns that being a hero is not without cost.

Comment

Shays' rebellion was the organized effort of citizens of several Massachusetts towns to shut down the courts to prevent the hearing of foreclosure cases. The authors have expanded on this incident to show an example of the growing pains of the new nation. Justin sees at first only the excitement of being allowed to join in a man's job, but discovers that even a small war brings hurt and pain.

Suggestions for Reports or Activities

1. Read about Shays' Rebellion in your textbook or another source. What were the results? Would you say that it was a successful revolt?

2. Mattoon thought he had a right to take the farmers' oxen and plows. What was his argument? Do you agree with him?

3. Why were the people of Pelham and the other towns upset with the General Court? Why couldn't they have any influence on the court?

Wolf by the Ears   Ann Rinaldi
New York: Scholastic, 1991. 248p. (1, 2)

It is December of 1819. Harriet Hemings, teenage daughter of the housekeeper on a great Virginia plantation, seeks to find out if the master is her father before she decides whether or not to leave her family when she turns twenty-one. In order to be safe from recapture, she discovers that papers supporting her status as a free Negro will not be sufficient: she will have to pass as white. Can she live a lie for the rest of her life? How can she disown her mother and brothers? How can she help her people if she must pretend not to be one of them? Harriet learns a lot about herself and other family members before she makes her decision.

Comment

This story is based on research into the private life of Thomas Jefferson that suggests that he had several children with Sally Hemings, one of his slaves. Exploring the theme of alienation, the author illuminates the confusion that comes from knowing or acknowledging only part of one's heritage. Readers who have ever felt that they did not "belong" may identify with the dilemma of Harriet Hemings.

Suggestions for Reports or Activities

1. Locate a biography of Thomas Jefferson. Look for information about his attitude toward slavery and his own slaves in particular. Can you find anything to support the author's contention that

Jefferson was good to his slaves but torn regarding the morality of owning them?

2. When Harriet says goodbye to Thomas Jefferson, she addresses him for the first time as "Mister Jefferson" instead of "Master." Explain the significance of that change.

3. Examine earlier versions of the Declaration of Independence, which was drafted by Thomas Jefferson. What statements regarding slavery and the slave trade were removed before the Declaration was adopted?

MORE CHALLENGING BOOKS
FOR ADVANCED READERS

Arundel   Kenneth Roberts
Garden City, N.Y.: Doubleday, 1933. 486p.

A young innkeeper in Maine tells of the terrible journey made by Colonel Benedict Arnold and his soldiers through the wilderness to Quebec, many months before the Declaration of Independence, in a vain attempt to dislodge the British. The role of the Abenaki Indians in facilitating the journey is described.

Burr   Gore Vidal
New York: Random House, 1975. 430p.

Aaron Burr, a hero of the American Revolution and vice-president under Thomas Jefferson, also killed Alexander Hamilton in a duel and was tried for treason. In this tale Burr has the chance to offer his own explanations of the apparent contradictions in his behavior.

Drums   James Boyd
New York: Scribner, 1925. 409p.

The characters in this novel include Tories as well as rebels, townsfolk as well as country dwellers, women as well as men. The hero's mother's family is loyal to the king, while his father's is not, so he delays his own decision regarding which side to support. In the end circumstances permit no one to remain on the sidelines.

Oliver Wiswell   Kenneth Roberts
Garden City, N.Y.: Doubleday, 1952. 836p.

Told entirely from the point of view of the American Loyalists, this story makes a strong case for viewing the conflict as a civil war pitting friend against friend and dividing families. While Oliver Wiswell travels far from his hometown of Boston and his sweetheart, Sally, during the eight years of war, the two young people maintain their faith and plan one day to be reunited.

Rabble in Arms   Kenneth Roberts
New York: Doubleday, 1933. 586p.

As scouts for the American general Benedict Arnold, sea captain Peter Merrill and his brother Nathaniel take part in the campaigns of the Northern army, culminating in the battle of Saratoga which leads to the defeat and capture of General Burgoyne. As a result, the British have to give up their plan to cut off New England from the rest of the colonies.

The Tree of Liberty   Elizabeth Page
New York: Literary Guild, 1939. 973p.

The hero's lifetime parallels the years of the beginnings of the United States, stretching from the period just before the American Revolution through the return of the Lewis and Clark expedition from the Pacific Northwest. Matt and his wife live through the Constitutional Convention and the first three presidential administrations, learning much about democratic processes and politics along the way.

III *The Civil War and Reconstruction*

Across Five Aprils Irene Hunt
Chicago: Follett, 1964. 223p. (2, 3)

Jethro learns early that the seeming glamor and thrill of war turn to pain as war comes close to home. His favorite brother, deploring slavery but detesting even more what many saw as Northern exploitation of the South, joins the Confederates. Despite the fact that two other brothers are fighting on the Union side, local ne'er-do-wells burn the family barn and poison their well. Although Jethro is only a young adolescent, he inevitably becomes part of the conflict, taking over the major farming chores after his father's heart attack, confronting his brother Tom's death in battle, struggling with his own conscience as he conceals his cousin Eb who is wanted as a deserter, and bravely daring to write of his concerns to President Lincoln. The family reaches that fifth April scarred but strong.

Comment

Against a background including descriptions of some battle details and discussions of war strategy, and showing how good people could have opposing opinions, the author has woven a story of feelings. Jethro, his siblings, and his parents emerge as real human beings, suffering under circumstances they cannot change. Readers will gain an understanding of the complexities of the Civil War and of the powerlessness of ordinary people.

Suggestions for Reports or Activities

1. Jethro was, of course, too young to fight in the Civil War, but nonetheless he was significantly involved. Describe how the war affected Jethro and forced him to mature.

2. Why has the author chosen the title *Across Five Aprils*? Explain the significance of April to understanding the story.

3. The Civil War was well reported in the newspapers. Research one of the campaigns mentioned in the story by checking the *New York Times* (or another paper) for its account of the event.

4. In past times young men have been excited by the idea of war. But some hired substitutes to fight for them, and others felt impelled to desert. What information can you find about desertion or about hiring substitutes?

The Autobiography of Miss Jane Pittman   Ernest J. Gaines
New York: Dial, 1971. 245p. (1, 2)

This saga is so convincing that it has been mistaken for a true story. The indomitable Miss Jane Pittman was freed from slavery at the end of the Civil War and lived to take a stand during the civil rights protests of the 1960s. Starting out naive but determined, she becomes a powerful figure, living out her long years, stalwartly facing grief and trouble, always proud. Her husband, Joe Pittman, is killed demonstrating his manhood while attempting to break a horse; her "son" Ned is ordered killed by whites for his supposedly radical teachings at his school for young blacks; and young Jimmy, the leader, perhaps the "One" the people have been waiting for, is sacrificed on the altar of black liberty during the civil rights demonstrations of the 1960s. Miss Jane Pittman, age 108 years or so, joins in the protest at the water fountain, as Jimmy had requested.

Comment

The book portrays life in the South as experienced from a black point of view, from the turmoil following emancipation all the way up to the civil rights era of the 1960s. Miss Jane Pittman typifies generations of solid, long-suffering black women, the ordinary unsung heroines of a century of slow change.

Suggestions for Reports or Activities

1. What was the message in Ned's sermon at the river (pp. 106–112)? Compare his ideas with those of Martin Luther King, Jr., as expressed many years later in his speech during the March on Washington in 1963.

2. What did Miss Jane Pittman mean when she said, "Freedom here is able to make a little living and hear the white folks say you good" (p. 234)? How does this differ from what Jimmy believed freedom to be?

3. Write a paper on the civil rights demonstrations in the South. Why was the time ripe?

4. If possible, conduct an interview with someone who participated in a protest march or demonstration for civil rights in the 1960s. Plan your interview to include your interviewee's impressions of progress in civil rights since that time.

Be Ever Hopeful, Hannalee   Patricia Beatty
New York: Morrow Junior Books, 1988. 207p. (2, 3)

After Atlanta was destroyed by General Sherman and the Union Army, the city was occupied for a number of years by Yankee soldiers. In 1865, with the war finally over and the farmland in ruins, poor Georgians, white and black, headed for the city to look for work. Hannalee Reed and her family are directed to the camp for white refugees, north of town; black migrants have a similar camp to the south, which is ravaged by smallpox. Prices are high and adequate shelter is scarce, so even small children have to work. Hannalee's older brother Davy, a Confederate Army veteran who had part of his left arm amputated in a Yankee hospital, fails to find a job as a carpenter because of his disability. A wealthy local man whom he admires urges him to join the Regulators, a forerunner of the Ku Klux Klan. But then Davy is arrested for killing a Yankee officer, and Hannalee has to try to save him from being hanged.

Comment

A sequel to *Turn Homeward, Hannalee,* below, this novel tells the story of the poor Southerners who aided in the rebuilding of Atlanta after the Civil War. Martial law ruled the city, and most job opportunities depended on the needs of the Yankees who had moved South and were the only ones with money to spend on goods or services. Mutual suspicion impeded the formation of friendships between Yankees and local whites, and between the latter and the newly freed black people. Yet, as this book shows, there were times when members of all these groups came together and helped each other out, changing lives and attitudes in the process.

Suggestions for Reports or Activities

1. Hannalee mentions several times that her mother was part Cherokee. Read about the Cherokees in Georgia. What happened to most of them in the early part of the nineteenth century?

2. Plantation owners like the Bracketts tried to resume farming and cotton-growing when the war ended. Did they succeed? Read about the changes in the Georgia economy, contrasting the periods just before the Civil War and just after.

3. At the end of the book Davy is heading for Indiana to reclaim Rosellen Sanders. Write the scene when he goes to the house where she is living and she comes downstairs to see who is at the door.

4. Look up Atlanta in an encyclopedia. Concentrating on the inhabitants, see if you can find out how the racial and ethnic composition of the city has changed over the years. When did it first elect a black mayor? What makes it special now as compared to other cities of its size?

Brady   Jean Fritz
New York: Coward, 1960. 223p. (2, 3)

Brady Minton gets himself in trouble by talking when he should be quiet. He falls out of favor with his father when he mentions suspicious activity around hermit Drover Hull's cabin. Talk is in the air about runaway slaves. What Brady gradually comes to realize is that his own father, a minister, is helping to run a station on the Underground Railroad. When his father preaches a forthright sermon condemning slavery as an evil, opposition mounts in the congregation. Threatening notes appear. One night the barn is burned, and Reverend Minton is injured. In a daring secret effort to transport a young escaped slave boy to safety, Brady shows that he can be trusted.

Comment

For younger readers this story is an exciting introduction to the turmoil resulting from proslavery and antislavery sentiments existing in small-town America in the years before the Civil War. Brady's mother is from Virginia, and her feelings are different from those of his father; his brother is an abolitionist. People could agree that slavery was wrong and disagree on how to eradicate it. There is reference to John Quincy Adams and his antislavery stand in Congress. The incident giving an example of the operation of the Underground Railroad is real drama. The book shows how young people can be caught up in the everyday events of history taking place around them.

Suggestions for Reports or Activities

1. This book is largely a story of the Underground Railroad. Read about the Underground Railroad in an encyclopedia. Write a short paper about it.

2. Who were the abolitionists? Why does Brady ask Matt if he is an abolitionist?

3. Why was Bill Williams upset by Mr. McKain's Fourth of July speech? How do you think Tar Adams felt about that speech?

4. In the beginning Brady says that he doesn't know how he feels about slavery. How does he come to have strong opinions on this subject?

Bring Home the Ghost   K. Follis Cheatham
New York: Harcourt, 1980. 288p. (1, 2)

When they return from fighting in the Seminole war to find their home destroyed in an Indian raid, Jason and Tolin continue to share their lives under new circumstances. Tolin (white son of a slaveholding family) and Jason (Tolin's personal slave since both were children) travel west to a new life on the frontier, to excitement and danger. They vainly hope that they will be outside the range of the slave hunters. Tolin often expresses his belief that he and Jason are partners and equals; but since he is anxious for their partnership to continue, he delays showing Jason the freedom papers which he has already signed. When Jason begins to understand what freedom really means, he knows he must strike out on his own.

Comment

This book offers a perspective on the relationships of blacks and whites in the pre–Civil War period. It points out the precariousness of life for free blacks who were subject to capture and sale. Antislavery activities are highlighted, including the operation of a station on the Underground Railroad. Considerable attention is given to the Creek Indians and their relationships with blacks. The difference between being treated as a free man and actually being free is discussed.

Suggestions for Reports or Activities

1. How would you describe Jason's friendship with Tolin? How did this relationship change after the destruction of the Cobb estate? After Jason found out that he was free?

2. The book refers to some specific journals engaged in anti-slavery activity. What were some of the important abolitionist journals? Write a short paper on antislavery newspapers. Or, write about black newspapers before the Civil War such as the *Freedom Journal* mentioned in the book.

3. Indians of different tribes play a role in this story. Checking a reference source, what can you find out about the Seminole war? About the relationships of Creek Indians and blacks?

Bull Run   Paul Fleischman
New York: HarperCollins, 1993. 102p. (2, 3)

Sixteen voices are heard in this novel, eight from the South and eight from the North. Written in short segments from the points of view of the characters, only one of whom really lived, the story of the first battle of the Civil War, fought on July 21, 1861, is revealed in all its complexity. The fictional characters include a boy determined to go to war, a disillusioned doctor, a black man deciding to deny his own identity in order to be able to fight for the Union, a slave woman, a courier, an artist, generals on both sides, the women left behind, and others.

Comment

The book includes maps of the course of the battle during the morning and the afternoon, as well as one of the general terrain, not far from Washington, D.C. Readers easily absorb a sense of the confusion marking the day, as the advantage shifts from one side to the other. The mixed motives of the participants are also made clear. At the end of the book a list of the characters in terms of their affiliations helps keep them straight in readers' minds while they reflect on what they have read.

Suggestions for Reports or Activities

1. Make a list of the characters and their reasons for involvement in the Battle of Bull Run. Select two from each side and explain in detail what they were fighting for.

2. Choose one character, read the three to five entries under his or her name, and write a summary of that character's thoughts and actions related to Bull Run.

3. Read a factual account of the Battle of Bull Run and compare it to what you learned from reading this book. Did the author leave out anything important? Which was more interesting? Which was more balanced? If you could read only one, which would you choose, and why?

4. General Irvin McDowell was a real person. Find out about what kind of life he led before he fought at Bull Run and what happened to him after he was dismissed.

Cezanne Pinto: A Memoir   Mary Stolz
New York: Knopf, 1994. 279p. (1, 2)

The very old black man who writes this memoir begins just before the Civil War, when he is ten or twelve years old. He describes his life under slavery in Virginia, his escape with the plantation cook via the Underground Railroad, his stay in Canada, and his experiences as a cowboy after the war. He tells how he learned to read and write, speak correctly, ride and rope horses, and appreciate good men and women regardless of the color of their skin. At one point he even tries to enlist in the Union army, where he finds that the old prejudices and hatreds remain strong despite Emancipation. During his entire life he continues to mourn his mother, sold away to Texas when he was about seven, and his father, who had run away when he was too little to remember.

Comment

Some little known facts about Pennsylvania, long considered a "free" state, may be learned from this book. Readers may well be surprised to find that, regardless of the weather, black people in Philadelphia at the time were required to ride out of doors behind the horses pulling the streetcars, even while paying the same fare as those who rode inside, protected from the rain and snow. They may also gain new insights into the famed Longhorn cattle roundups, in which many black cowboys are now known to have participated. Finally, this story is a tribute to pluralism and diversity.

Suggestions for Reports or Activities

1. Many U.S. "westerns" and cowboy songs portray the round-ups of cattle, including the branding, as an exciting and even romantic event. After reading Cezanne's version, what do you think? Describe the parts that sound like fun, and the ones that don't. On balance, would you have liked being a cowboy?

2. Read about the Underground Railroad. Were many Quakers involved? What happened to them if they were caught with a fugitive in their homes? What role did Harriet Tubman play?

3. What was the policy of the Union army toward former slaves who wanted to enlist? Find out how this policy evolved during the war years.

Charlie Skedaddle   Patricia Beatty
New York: Morrow Junior Books, 1987. 186p. (2, 3)

In 1864, twelve-year-old New Yorker Charlie Quinn belongs to a gang called the Bowery Boys. Angry at his sister because she plans to marry a man who frowns on his constant fighting, and longing to follow in the footsteps of his brother Johnny, who was killed at Gettysburg, Charlie runs off to join the Union army. Once he is trained as a drummer boy, he can't wait for a battle to prove his bravery. In the heat of combat, however, he runs away again. Given shelter by an old mountain woman who needs a boy to help her plant corn and gather herbs, Charlie learns a lot about himself and the true meaning of courage before he is forced to move on once more.

Comment

This story offers insights into the attitudes of the Southern mountain dwellers who held no slaves and remained more committed to their homes and farms than to the cause of the Confederacy. The horrors of war, regardless of the side on which one is fighting, are made manifest: Charlie worries as much about the soldier he believes he has killed as about the wounded comrades he ran past without stopping to help them.

Suggestions for Reports or Activities

1. Get an outline map of Virginia and, with the aid of an atlas, mark on it the places mentioned in this book: Alexandria, Culpeper,

Chancellorsville, the Rapidan River, the Wilderness, Stevensburg, the Blue Ridge Mountains, Spottsylvania Courthouse, Petersburg, Richmond. Number each location. On a separate piece of paper write down next to each number what happened at that place and how it figured in the story.

2. Charlie did not stop to help when his wounded friend Silas Gorman called to him. Compose a letter to Silas from Charlie, explaining why he continued to run.

3. In the city, the Bowery Boys and the Dead Rabbits had to fight each other; in the mountains, it was the MacRaes against the Bents. Early on, Charlie had no problem with this constant fighting; later, he changed his mind. Why? What made him stop wanting to fight?

4. Why was Granny Bent sometimes called a witch? What did she do with her "yarbs"? Look up "witches" in an encyclopedia and write down any of the descriptions which, in your opinion, apply to Granny Bent.

Cowslip   Betsy Haynes
Nashville: Nelson, 1973. 139p. (3)

When thirteen-year-old Cowslip is sold to Colonel Sprague, her life begins to change. Mistress Sprague is going on a trip and Cowslip is needed to look after the children. Working in the Sprague house, she meets Job, one of the older slaves, who has an air of mystery. Hearing talk about freedom for the first time, Cowslip begins to realize that she too is a person with dignity. Job astonishes her when he says she should learn to read and write. Whispers about running away are in the air. Reba does try to get away, with her man Percy, but they are caught and shot as an example to the others. Cowslip is sure now: she's going to live up to her name and be like the flower, the cowslip, that blooms wild and free.

Comment

This book gives young readers some solid information about conditions under slavery. Through various actions the slaves cleverly tricked their white masters. Barbarously cruel treatment is portrayed (the auction block and the whip). Readers will learn that this was a time of great contradictions, as it became constantly more difficult to keep the system working.

Suggestions for Reports or Activities

1. Look up the Underground Railroad in an encyclopedia. How did it work? Where were some of the stations located? See if you can find a map giving the locations of these "stations." Draw a copy of this map.

2. Who was Harriet Tubman? Write a short paper describing why she was important.

3. Cowslip is surprised to find out that she can learn to read and write. What were some of the means used by slaveholders to keep their slaves under control? What were some of the means used by the slaves to resist their oppressors?

A Dangerous Promise   Joan Lowery Nixon
The Orphan Train Adventures
New York: Delacorte, 1994. 148p. (2, 3)

In Kansas in 1861, two orphan boys—Mike Kelly, age twelve, and his friend Todd Blakely, two years older—decide to join the Union army. Too young to enlist, they learn the military drum calls and run away to join a company in need of musicians. As the days of walking and waiting drag on, they become impatient to participate in a battle; when the time comes, however, Todd asks Mike to promise to send his pocket watch to his sister Emily if he is killed. It is this promise that becomes dangerous, when a Confederate soldier takes the watch from the dead Todd's pocket while Mike, wounded and powerless, vows to get it back. Foster son of a Union army officer, Mike has many adventures behind enemy lines before he has a chance to try to keep his word.

Comment

This is an even-handed narrative that finds good and bad on both sides and horrors aplenty for all. Mike is befriended by Southerners and harassed by Northerners, as well as the reverse. The nature of this war as one in which family members were pitted against one another is epitomized in Mike's being witness to a young Confederate soldier shooting a Union opponent, only to exclaim, "I shot my pa! God help me, I shot my pa!," before himself falling, shot by another of the enemy.

Suggestions for Reports or Activities

1. Mike is wounded at the Battle of Wilson's Creek. Read about this battle in a history of the Civil War: Who were the generals in command? How many soldiers participated? How long did the battle last? What was the count of the dead on both sides?

2. Look up the history of the Children's Aid Society, founded by Charles Loring Brace. How many children did it send from New York City to the West? What was the reasoning behind this project which split families and sent the children to different homes? What was the definition at this time of "orphan"? Is there any record of what happened to children whose foster placements did not work out?

3. Mike writes a lot of letters to his family. Pick one moment in the story when he has time to do this and compose the letter he might have written. Be sure to include the name of the place where he was, the name of the person to whom he was writing, and details of what he had been doing and was about to do.

Eben Tyne, Powdermonkey   Patricia Beatty and Phillip Robbins
New York: Morrow Junior Books, 1990. 227p. (2)
It is 1862, and the age of sailing ships is about over. Around Norfolk Bay in Virginia, the Union blockade is preventing the South from trading its cotton and tobacco for much needed guns, medicines, and machinery. Eben Tyne, thirteen years old and an ardent supporter of states' rights (though not of slavery), is eager to help the Southern cause. He is thrilled to be invited to work on the ironclad *Merrimack* as a powder carrier when the vessel attempts to defeat the blockade. He experiences the glory of the initial victory, and the gloom of the stalemate on the following day, when the *Merrimack* confronts the North's ironclad, the *Monitor.* Then in captivity he meets a Yankee spy who makes him a startling proposition.

Comment

The battle of the *Merrimack* and the *Monitor* comes alive from the point of view of a youngster serving in the midst of the smoke and the noise. The excitement of the first naval battle where the opposing ships depend on steam for movement and metal for protection is conveyed along with the blood, death, and agony that mark any such confrontation. The mistaken belief of the South that courage and sacrifice could overcome the industrial strength of the North is epitomized in this engagement.

Suggestions for Reports or Activities

1. Read about the battle of the *Merrimack* and the *Monitor* in an encyclopedia or history of the Civil War. Tell some details you learned that were not included in this book.

2. Find out about the pirates in the Caribbean at this period of time. What were the names of some of the famous ones? Describe a battle between pirates and a ship of the U.S. Navy.

3. Jack Rawlins served on the *Merrimack* as a Union spy. Speculate about his motivation. Why did he plan to blow up the ship? Did he know people were sleeping on it at the time? Why was he kind to Eben and Kendrick at the end?

Elkhorn Tavern   Douglas C. Jones
New York: Holt, 1980. 311p. (1, 2)

Martin Hasford has gone to fight for the Confederacy. His wife, Ora, and teenage children, Roman and Calpurnia, are diligently struggling to keep up their Arkansas farm. The war comes closer than they expected. They must protect themselves against marauding "bushwhackers" and "jayhawkers," armed men masquerading as soldiers who forage and loot while claiming to support one cause or the other. The little-known and bloody battle of Pea Ridge is fought in the hills around their farm. Ora is tough, a woman of high principles, and her children are imbued with her courage. When a wounded Yankee officer is brought to their doorstep Ora acts quickly to save him. During his slow recovery all of their lives change.

Comment

In this gripping story of courage and survival the strong woman is the true hero. Ora (and Calpurnia, too) exhibit the will to endure and the ability to make the right choices in extreme circumstances. Readers will experience the war from the point of view of people supposedly on the sidelines, yet finding themselves in the crossfire. The ruggedness of farm life in the nineteenth century is graphically depicted, as in the suffering on the battlefield.

Suggestions for Reports or Activities

1. The book makes it clear that the Civil War involved more than generals and battles and that women who were left behind played an important role. Based on what you have learned about the war in this book, write a short paper on the war from Ora's or Calpurnia's point of view.

2. Martin Hasford did not enlist to support the practice of slavery. Check your textbook and an encyclopedia for causes of the Civil War. Then in a short paper give reasons why Martin and many other Southern men joined in the war effort.

3. There are numerous incidents that illuminate the characters of Ora and Calpurnia. Drawing on these incidents, write a short paper on either Calpurnia or Ora as examples of women who can succeed in spite of the problems they face.

Freedom Road   Howard Fast
New York: Duell, Sloan & Pearce, 1944. 263p. (1, 2)

Gideon Jackson, former slave and former Union soldier, returns to South Carolina to find a new world opening for him and his children. At first shamed by his inability to read and write and his lack of experience with the sophisticated world of Charleston, Gideon moves painfully but bravely into his new roles, first as delegate to the Convention aiming to write a new constitution for the state and, much later, as a member of the House of Representatives of the Congress of the United States. When Northern troops are withdrawn from the South in 1877, attacks by the Ku Klux Klan put an end to a temporary idyll created by the willing cooperation of whites and blacks.

Comment

Young people today may imagine that it is only since the civil rights agitation of the 1960s that people of different colored skins have been able to live, study, and work together as friends. Fast's book makes it clear that such a situation indeed existed nearly a hundred years earlier, brought to a tragic end by Northern inattention and a Southern white desire to restore prewar power relationships insofar as possible.

Suggestions for Reports or Activities

1. Fast blames President Grant for much of what happened in the South after his successor, Rutherford B. Hayes, took office. What do you know about the Hayes-Tilden election and what happened afterwards? Could Grant have acted differently from the way he did? Explain your answer.

2. Compare the activities and philosophy of the Ku Klux Klan in the 1870s and 1880s with those of the Klan today. How are they different or alike?

3. The character of Gideon Jackson was based on those of several black congressional representatives of the time. Find out all you can about two or three of these first black legislators.

The Glory Field   Walter Dean Myers
New York: Scholastic, 1994. 375p. (1, 2)

It is July 1753: Eleven-year-old Muhammad Bilal is kidnapped from Sierra Leone, West Africa, and transported to the United States. Four generations later, in March 1864, Lizzy runs away to the North with a new colored regiment of Union soldiers. It is April 1900: On Curry Island, South Carolina, Lizzy's son Elijah Lewis rescues a blind boy, stands up to a white sheriff, and then has to run away to escape a whipping for his courage. In Chicago, Illinois, in May 1930, Elijah's daughter Luvenia learns about integrity and determines to start her own business. It is January 1964: In Johnson City, South Carolina, Tommy Lewis, seven generations removed from Muhammad Bilal, has to decide between being one of the first blacks to attend a white college and standing up for what he believes. Finally, in Harlem in 1994, Elijah's great-grandsons Malcolm and Sheppard are supposed to be on their way to South Carolina, but Shep has spent the money intended for his plane ticket on crack, and Malcolm has to figure out how to get his cousin and himself to the family reunion.

Comment

Covering incidents in the lives of a black family going back nine generations to the kidnapped African ancestor, this novel illuminates many of the struggles in which American blacks have participated in the past 250 years. Slavery, segregation, the exodus to the North, integration, stereotyping, ignorance, as well as the networks of support and encouragement within the black community, all are explored in this fast-paced story of life in the United States from a minority viewpoint. A genealogical chart helps readers keep track of the characters and the generations.

Suggestions for Reports or Activities

1. Lizzy went north with the Union Army near the end of the Civil War. Later she returned to South Carolina and married Richard Lewis. What happened to her in between? Imagine that the author wrote one more part of Lizzy's story, and summarize what happened to her up North and how she got back to the South.

2. When Luvenia helped Florenz Deets play a trick on her father, Mr. Deets fired her. Do you think he was justified? Write a letter that Luvenia might have sent to Mr. Deets after she calmed down: Would she have apologized for her role in the deception? What might she have said?

3. For a while, Tommy Lewis thought seriously about attending a white college. What happened when James Meredith enrolled at the University of Mississippi in 1962? See if you can find out what became of Meredith in later life.

4. What might have happened to Shep after he got back to Harlem? Write two accounts, one explaining how Shep turned his life around and one showing how he slipped back into his old ways. Which seems to you more likely?

Hew Against the Grain   Betty Sue Cummings
New York: Atheneum, 1977. 174p. (2)

In this book an adolescent girl is confronted with important, vital problems as her life revolves around the events of the Civil War. Mattilda realizes that her best friend, Dorcia, who is a slave, is considered to be property. Although her Virginia family chooses not to believe in slavery, her brothers find themselves divided by their loyalties. Their conflict stems from disagreement not over slavery so much as the question of each state's right to self-government. As the war devastates the community, Mattilda becomes a source of strength and courage. Neighbors once considered harmless turn into enemies, even fanatics, who hate her, especially for her friendship with Dorcia. These feelings end only when Mattilda kills her rapist neighbor.

Comment

The brutality of war brings grief and self-examination to this family. Mattilda sees the destruction of her land and life as she has known it, as well as the defeated spirit of the people around her. The war plays a powerful role in the lives of everyone, black and white, as their relationships with each other are changed forever. Here is a moving portrayal of a girl who becomes a woman of substance through necessity.

Suggestions for Reports or Activities

1. Examine the issue of states' rights from Mattilda's and Dorcia's points of view. How and why do they differ?

2. How would living on the border of Virginia and West Virginia affect a person's attitudes during the Civil War? Write an editorial for a newspaper in a border town in favor of siding with either the North or the South.

3. How did the relationship of Mattilda and Dorcia change during the war? What common events happened to them? How did they become "equal" at last?

In My Father's House   Ann Rinaldi
New York: Scholastic, 1993. 312p. (1, 2)

Oscie Mason is perfectly happy with her life in northern Virginia in 1852. Then her widowed mother marries a man who wants her to call him "Daddy Will," a strange slave woman comes to take care of her little sister Sarah, and a Yankee tutor arrives to teach her and her older sister Maria. Nothing feels right any more, thus beginning a tale covering nearly fifteen years and the course of the entire Civil War. Along the way Oscie grows up, falls in love, and learns to appreciate her stepfather Will McLean in whose home in Appomattox Court House the opposing generals sign the surrender ending the war.

Comment

The author notes that the major part of her story is firmly grounded in historical fact, from the first battle of Manassas on the property of Wilmer McLean to the plunder of the furniture in the McLean parlor by Northern soldiers intent on bringing home souvenirs of the surrender. Readers may be especially struck by the little-known incident in which Union and Confederate officers met at the Court House before the signing and revived old friendships from their West Point days as though they had not just participated on opposite sides in the bloodiest war in U.S. history.

Suggestions for Reports or Activities

1. Oscie's friend Thomas Tibbs joined Mosby's Rangers. Find out who Colonel Mosby and the Rangers were, where and when they fought, what made them famous, what happened to them after the war, etc.

2. Analyze the character of the slave woman Mary Ann. What motivated her? Why did she and Oscie get along so poorly in the beginning, and why did they eventually make up?

3. Will McLean was able to provide for his family by "speculating." What does that mean? Look up the progression of prices in the Confederacy between 1860 and 1865. Make a chart comparing the prices for staples (sugar, salt, flour, molasses, cloth, etc.) in those two years.

An Island Far from Home   John Donahue
Minneapolis: Carolrhoda, 1995. 178p. (2, 3)

Twelve-year-old Joshua Loring, living in Massachusetts at the time of the Civil War, cannot wait to be old enough to fight for the Union in order to avenge the death of his father at the hands of the Confederates. His Uncle Robert, deputy commander of a fort on George's Island in the middle of Boston Harbor, distracts him with the suggestion that he write to one of the Rebel prisoners of war held at the fort—a scared, lonely fourteen-year-old private from Alabama named John Meadows. Joshua is appalled: Wouldn't he be a traitor to the cause if he wrote to a Reb? That's what his friend Hogan thinks, and most of his classmates agree. Joshua writes to John anyway, and his later attempt to meet him face-to-face almost leads to disaster for both of them.

Comment

What kinds of circumstances make people enemies? Is it ever possible for enemies to become friends? What happens when you stand up for what you think is right? These questions are addressed in this novel of a developing friendship between boys on opposite sides of the Civil War. Its further depiction of the warmth and compassion that people may show even in combat situations sheds unfamiliar light on this war that pitted brother against brother and friend against friend.

Suggestions for Reports or Activities

1. At the end of the book, John heads for home to look for his family. Write the letter that he might have sent to Joshua after a month or so. Tell whether he found his folks and how people were living in Alabama after the destruction caused by the war.

2. Find out more about the battle at Fort Morgan, Alabama, where John was captured. Look for information in a history of the Civil War or in an encyclopedia. Tell what happened.

3. Joshua says that John became his enemy only because of where he lived. Apply this view to the situation in some of our cities today where people belong to certain gangs and have to fight other gangs because they live in particular neighborhoods. Do you think members of opposing gangs can ever be friends? Why or why not?

Jayhawker Patricia Beatty
New York: Morrow Junior Books, 1991. 214p. (2, 3)
Under the influence of the fiery evangelist John Brown, Lije Tulley, a Kansas farm boy in the late 1850s, becomes a Jayhawk, an abolitionist bent on putting an end to slavery. Though only in his mid-teens, Lije agrees to serve as a spy for the Union. His secret messages to the abolitionists are picked up by a mysterious youth riding Lije's horse, stolen from him during an earlier raid. His situation in slave-holding Missouri becomes increasingly dangerous as the Confederate band around him comes to include a ruthless former schoolteacher named Charley Quantrill, a secretive sharpshooter called Jim Hickok, and the menacing James brothers, Frank and Jesse.

Comment

Kansas and Missouri between 1854 and 1865 were troubled by a brutal climate, featuring severe droughts and terrible heat, in addition to raids in both directions across their common border. Lije Tulley's story, while sympathetic to the abolitionist cause, notes the terrible damage wrought by both sides. In fact, Lije's ability to see that his own friends are not blameless serves him well when he comes face-to-face with the man who killed his father. Incidents of the Civil War in the Midwest such as the bloody August 1863 raid by proslavery forces on Lawrence, Kansas, are made vivid in this account.

Suggestions for Reports or Activities

1. Find out more about some of the historical characters in this novel: John Brown, "Wild Bill" Hickok, Frank and Jesse James, James Montgomery, Dr. Charles Jennison, William (Charley) Quantrill, the Younger brothers, William Anderson. What happened to them in later life?

2. If it had been possible for Lije to send a letter to his mother, perhaps when he felt so lonely on Christmas Day, what might he have said? Write such a letter in your own words.

3. When Mr. Prentiss corners Lije in the cellar, neither of them shoots. What if one (or both) of them had? Write your own account of this scene with a different ending. Should Lije, for instance, have told his mother what Mr. Prentiss had done?

4. Read a historical account of the raid on Lawrence, Kansas. Does it differ from that in the book? If so, how? What additional information does it give you that the book did not?

The Last Silk Dress   Ann Rinaldi
New York: Holiday House, 1988. 344p. (1, 2)

During the Civil War, the North used balloons to examine Rebel positions from points safely out of the range of Confederate guns. The title of this book refers to the decision of women in Richmond, Virginia, to donate their last silk dresses to the Confederacy to make a great patchwork balloon for use in a campaign in the summer of 1862. The story is told largely from the point of view of fourteen-year-old Susan Dobson Chilmark, whose father is away at war and whose mother is emotionally unstable. In the course of the plot, numerous colorful characters represent various attitudes toward the war and the Southern lifestyle which the Rebels were endeavoring to protect.

Comment

Basing her story on a letter (reprinted as prologue) from Confederate General James Longstreet, the author weaves her fictional account against a factual background. Many of the historical details are carefully researched, though there is disagreement among scholars as to the actual existence of a balloon created from silk dresses. The internal conflicts of the Southern way of life are vividly conveyed as Susan matures and discovers hitherto hidden family secrets. From being an ardent supporter of "the Cause," partly in order to please her difficult mother, she moves to the realization that her heart is with the Union despite her unbreakable connections to the South and the people whom she has loved.

Suggestions for Reports or Activities

1. According to the novel, hospitals sprang up on every corner in Richmond to care for wounded soldiers. Read about medical care during the Civil War, especially in the South, and summarize what you learned.

2. What is "martial law"? When is it usually applied? What does it mean for the civilian population and local government? Does the U.S. Constitution provide for it?

3. Do you think Susan's mother, Charlotte, was really "crazy"? List the difficulties and disappointments she encountered after leaving South Carolina, along with her reactions to them. How else might she have reacted? Write a one-page character sketch of Charlotte, being sure to cover her good points as well as her bad.

4. What do you think Susan found up North? Write a letter from her to her mother telling about her life with Tim's family.

A Month of Seven Days   Shirley Climo
New York: Crowell, 1987. 152p. (2, 3)

In 1864, when Zoe Snyder is twelve years old, the Yankees come to her town in northern Georgia looking for places to stay until the next battle. Several of them camp in a nearby field, but the captain and his two aides take over the house itself. Zoe, her little brother, and her mother move to a cabin belonging to a friendly Indian, since the Yankees are sleeping in their bedrooms. While Zoe and her mother wait on the intruders, Zoe tries to figure out how to get them to withdraw before her father, a soldier in the Confederate army, comes home on leave. In the process, she discovers that the Yankees are as different from one another as they seem to be from herself.

Comments

Readers may gain a number of insights from this story of a plucky Southern girl during the Civil War. The impact of war on civilians is made clear by the Yankee invasion of a peaceful Southern farmhouse. The roles that apparently innocent young people may play in such circumstances are also revealed through the actions of subsidiary characters. The contrasting attitudes of local people toward Indians come through in their treatment of Hodge, owner of the cabin and hired man at the farm. Finally, the breakdown of stereotypes that may come from actually getting to know somebody "different" is nicely brought out in the account of the captain's aide.

Suggestions for Reports or Activities

1. How long did the Yankees actually stay at Zoe's house? For each day, list both the good things and the bad things that happened because of their intrusion. Then write a paragraph explaining how Zoe changed during that period.

2. Look up the Battle of Kennesaw Mountain. What did General Sherman claim was his worst mistake? How was it that the South won?

3. What role did Indians play during the Civil War? How many worked or fought for each side? What was Hodge afraid of, and where do you think he was during his absence from the farm?

4. Finish the letter that Joshua Boone was writing to his little sister Emily. What do you think he told her about Zoe and her brother Jim Henry?

Nightjohn   Gary Paulsen
New York: Delacorte, 1993. 92p. (3)

This story, based on events that actually happened, is written in the voice and from the point of view of a twelve-year-old slave girl named Sarny. It tells how she learned to read and write at a time when it was against the law for slaves to do either, and when the penalty for teaching a slave to read or write was dismemberment. Nightjohn, a slave who had escaped to the North, returns south to teach youngsters their letters so that, some day, they will be able to write down what slavery was like. In the course of this book, he is found out and punished and runs away again. But Sarny will never be the same.

Comment

Contemporary readers will marvel at the ignorance of the world in which slave children were deliberately reared. Equally startling will be the heroine's delight at first learning the meaning of letters and how to put them together to make words. Also depicted are the circumstances under which slaves often lived: eating out of troughs, being taken from their mothers so that the women could be readily bred again, not being allowed to sit to eat or to relieve themselves while working in the fields, being whipped for trying to run away, and so on. The conditions described are all the more vivid because presented from the viewpoint of a child who cannot know what is "normal" and what is not.

Suggestions for Reports or Activities

1. Find out when laws were passed to make it illegal for slaves to learn to read, write, and count. Did they appear first in one particular state? Were all the laws the same? What were the punishments prescribed? What were the reasons given for passing these laws?

2. We do not know if Sarny ever told her mammy about the school in the brush. Assume that she did, and tell how Sarny might have described it. Write in her voice if you can, or in your own if you prefer.

3. Try to imagine the point of view of "Master" Waller. Why was he so cruel? What was he afraid of? Have him explain to his wife what he did when he suspected Sarny could write and punished her mammy: How would he justify what he did?

Out from This Place   Joyce Hansen
New York: Avon Camelot, 1988. 135p. (2, 3)

Fourteen-year-old Easter and her friend Obi have run away from the Jennings plantation, unable to take little Jason with them. But Easter comes back for him, only to find that he has become the Mistress's pet and is reluctant to leave. Not knowing what has happened to Obi, Easter persuades Jason to join her and others in making a new home as free citizens on one of the islands off the coast of South Carolina. Although they are not used to working as field hands, the group of friends perseveres for the sake of weekly wages and the promise of their own land. Easter is glad to be free, but torn between wanting to go north to school so that she can become a teacher and wanting to stay to search for Obi. Then the war ends, and instead of jubilation there comes the news that the former owners of the plantation have been promised the return of their land. Only armed resistance can protect them now. (For the story of Obi's adventures, see *Which Way Freedom?* below.)

Comment

Early in 1865 General William Tecumseh Sherman ordered that newly freed slaves should be settled on some of the islands off the Carolina coast. After forty thousand people were relocated there, President Andrew Johnson, in May of that same year, changed the policy of giving temporary title to the land to the ex-slaves and decreed that it be returned to its former owners. While the characters and specific incidents in this story are fictional, there was a real all-black community in South Carolina that developed after the Civil War.

Suggestions for Reports or Activities

1. What was the Northern Missionary Society? Find out how many schoolteachers were sent south to teach the ex-slaves to read and where they went.

2. The end of the book implies that Obi and Easter will find each other. How do you think this came about? Explain how it happened and speculate as to how long it took. Did Easter go north to school? Did Obi go along or did he wait for her in the South?

3. Easter mentions "men in hoods" who tried to burn down the schoolhouse. Find out when and where the Ku Klux Klan was founded and how it has developed over the years. Is it still in existence now? How do you know?

Red Cap   G. Clifton Wisler
New York: Dutton, Lodestar, 1991. 160p. (1, 2, 3)

In 1862 young Ransom J. Powell leaves his home and family in Maryland to join the Union army fighting the South in the Civil War. Too short and slight to be a soldier, the thirteen-year-old becomes a drummer boy with the Tenth Virginia Regiment. When he is captured two years later, he is taken to the notorious stockade at Andersonville, Georgia. Nicknamed "Red Cap" because of the hat given to him by a sympathetic Southern woman, the youngster endures cold, starvation, lice, and all-round misery inside the stockade. A young Confederate guard saves his life as the Yankee soldiers fall dead around him by the thousands.

Comment

Based on a true story, *Red Cap* is a testament to the triumph of the human spirit over unimaginable hardship. While the horrors of

Andersonville are well known, less common are tales of friendship between guards and prisoners, indications of the food smuggled in by slaves, and recognition of the generosity of those who had almost nothing toward those who had even less. An actual letter written by Powell thirty years after his release is reprinted at the end of the book.

Suggestions for Reports or Activities

1. General Ulysses S. Grant is blamed by many for halting the exchange of prisoners of war. Examine a history of the Civil War or a biography of General Grant to uncover his reasoning behind this decision. Is there any evidence that he ever regretted it?

2. After the war an attempt was made to hold Captain Henry Wirz, commandant of the prison, accountable for conditions there. He was tried, sentenced, and hanged. From what you know of him, to what degree was he truly responsible for the evils of Andersonville? What could he have done differently?

3. The author tells us that Powell never saw his Alabama friend again. Write the letter that Powell might have sent to Lewis Jones telling what happened to Powell in later life and thanking him for his kindness and support.

Rifles for Watie   Harold Keith
New York: Crowell, 1957. 332p. (1, 2)

Jeff Bussey knew he was doing the right thing when he left his family's Kansas farm to join the Union forces. The Union was fighting to ensure the freedom of all men; hence they had the best cause on their side. Besides, the war would not last long, and he would have a chance for glory. At least, that was what Jeff thought. Once enlisted, however, he finds that being in the army is mostly dull routine drills. Then when he finally participates in a real battle, Jeff quickly discovers that war is not at all glorious. Eventually he is sent behind enemy lines as a spy. His perspective of war is further enlightened when he realizes that the men of the South share the same concerns for family and farm as he and his Union comrades.

Comment

The author's use of primary sources to research the setting results in a very convincing tale. The action is centered around the far western theater of the war. Readers will read about the conflict between Missouri and Kansas, the issue of states' rights, the gun trafficking between North and South, and the role played by the Cherokee nation. The hardships of life at the front and the involvement of civilians living near the scene of battle are vividly described.

Suggestions for Reports or Activities

1. Stand Watie was an actual person. Using a reference source, find out about his role in the Civil War. How accurate is the information in the novel?

2. In this book, various opinions are expressed by different characters on the most important issues of the war, and on why they are involved. (For example, Jeff wants to fight the bushwhackers; Lucy Washbourne feels that the United States government has betrayed her people.) Compare and contrast two additional Union views with two additional Confederate views.

3. Assume that Jeff kept a journal of his war years. Write an entry as though you were Jeff describing a day on which an important event took place.

4. Find out more about the Cherokee nation and its role in the Civil War.

The Sacred Moon Tree   Laura Jan Shore
New York: Bradbury, 1986. 209p. (2, 3)

Phoebe Sands has a tendency to imagine, to jump to conclusions, and to fabricate (perhaps due to an inherited gift for blarney and seeing fairies and sacred moon trees), but she has no problem convincing others to go along with her impetuous, seemingly hairbrained schemes. Observing what she thinks are suspicious actions, she concludes that her Richmond-bred mother is a Confederate spy. Later her father, taunted by her mother for being a coward, joins the Union army, and her mother takes off to Richmond, presumably to care for her sick grandfather. Phoebe is determined to go to Richmond also. Learning that her friend Jotham's brother Nate is in a Confederate prison there, Phoebe dresses as a boy and masterminds a plan to get herself and Joth to Richmond to try to rescue Nate. Unexpected help makes the venture a success.

Comment

This informative and exciting adventure story depicts how the Civil War was experienced by two lively and inventive young people. The tensions between family members with opposing views on the war are dramatically conveyed. The children suffer hunger, witness fighting, and see the desperate plight of the wounded. The imagined glamor of war fades as danger, devastation, and death become real.

Suggestions for Reports or Activities

1. What was the importance of Richmond during the Civil War?
2. Can you find any information about the role of spies during the Civil War?
3. What is the significance of the title?

Shades of Gray   Carolyn Reeder
New York: Macmillan, 1989. 152p. (2, 3)

At the end of the Civil War, twelve-year-old Virginian Will Page finds himself an orphan, forced to live with his mother's sister and her family, whom he had never met. A city boy unused to hard work, Will has to make many adjustments in his new life. The hardest is to come to terms with his uncle Jed's refusal to fight the Yankees. Since Will's father died as a soldier in the Confederate army, Will resists the idea that a decision not to fight could have any validity. Believing that his uncle must have been a coward, Will goes through many changes before he realizes that good people may sincerely hold opposing views.

Comment

Set at the war's end, this novel confronts the different attitudes toward the war that were held by Southerners at the time. Some had fought for their way of life; others for the right to continue to hold slaves; others to protect their homes from the invading Yankees. And some had refused to fight at all. The reader learns that human dilemmas often have no easy answers, and that all people, on all sides, suffer during a war.

Suggestions for Reports or Activities

1. Write the letter that Will was planning to send to Doc Martin. Explain his decision to stay with his uncle and his family.
2. Read about the Civil War in Virginia. Compare what happened in the Shenandoah Valley (where Will came from) and the Piedmont (where he ended up). Show on a map where the two sections of Virginia are located.

3. Suppose your country went to war: Would you fight? Would the reasons given for needing to fight influence your decision? Would the identity of the enemy matter? Explain your reasoning.

The Slopes of War: A Novel of Gettysburg   N. A. Perez
Boston: Houghton Mifflin, 1984. 202p. (2, 3)

The battle of Gettysburg is encountered from a number of viewpoints in this moving story. In the background are the deliberations and decisions of generals and officers from both armies, all portrayed as human beings grappling with destiny. Against this fact-based setting is woven the story of sixteen-year-old Bekah Summerhill and her family, who live in Gettysburg and are unwitting actors in the drama around the battle. Bekah's story includes that of her brother Buck, enlisted with a Pennsylvania regiment, and that of Custis, her favorite cousin, fighting for the Confederacy. The three days in July change all of their lives. President Lincoln's address several months later helps the events make sense to Buck.

Comment

What was happening at Gettysburg? The author describes the battle maneuvers and evokes the confusion felt by the generals, but brings the event dramatically to life through focusing on the experiences of young boy soldiers who are newly aware that there is little glamor in actual combat. Most vivid is the picture of how the townspeople, particularly Bekah—all merely interested bystanders at first—rise heroically to the fact of the battle around them: they provide food and clothing to stragglers from both sides, dodge flying shells, care for the wounded, and come to terms with death. The concluding chapter on Lincoln's visit to dedicate the cemetery provides a poignant comment on this episode in our history.

Suggestions for Reports or Activities

1. What actually happened at Gettysburg? Why was it such a pivotal event? Why was President Lincoln upset by the results?

2. Suppose that General Meade had followed through on Lincoln's orders. How might the course of the war have gone? Check this in your textbook and in some reference sources.

3. How do you think Bekah changed during the days of the battle? Discuss the effect of the war being fought on their doorstep on the lives of ordinary people in the town.

Something Upstairs: A Tale of Ghosts   Avi
New York: Orchard, 1988. 120p. (2, 3)

After Kenny Huldorf and his family move to Providence, Rhode Island, Kenny develops a relationship with the ghost of a black boy murdered in 1800 in the attic of Kenny's new home. On several occasions he finds himself in the Providence of that period, when the river was crowded with sailing ships and men were arguing about the evils of slavery. Charged by Caleb, the slave boy, with finding his murderer, Kenny runs the risk of having to stay in old Providence, cut off forever from his own time, unless he is willing to commit murder himself.

Comment

Read a good ghost story and learn a little history! Aimed perhaps at the reluctant reader, this slim tale offers insights into the history of a state which was among the most liberal with regard to slavery—and yet allowed its white citizens to make great sums of money bringing black people from Africa and selling them in the South long after the prohibition of the slave trade in 1774. Kenny's uncertainty about how to help Caleb without doing harm to himself appears realistic, despite the fantastical elements of the story.

Suggestions for Reports or Activities

1. Read about Moses Brown in an encyclopedia of American biography. Who was he and what did he do? How is he remembered today?

2. Read about the slave trade in New England. How did the traders manage to keep the practice going after the law said they could not?

3. Write what you think happened to Caleb. Did he make it to Canada and freedom? If so, how did he get there? (An article about the Underground Railroad should give you some ideas.)

Sound the Jubilee   Sandra Forrester
New York: Dutton, Lodestar, 1995. 184p. (2)

When Master and Mistress decide in 1862 that the Northern Bluecoats are getting too close, Mistress heads for her summer home on Nags Head, one of the string of islands off the North Carolina coast. She takes with her only her personal maid Nancy and the cook Ella, along with Ella's family: her husband Titus, her daughters Angeline and Maddie, and her small son Pride. Twelve-year-old Maddie tells the story of their flight to Roanoke Island, where a Union garrison is hiring runaway slaves to build a fort. Titus and Angeline's young man, Royall, eventually join the Union army, while Ella cares for the house and farm animals and Maddie begins a class for the other children on the island. But not all the Union soldiers are friendly, and as the war draws to a close, rumors fly that the land given to the blacks is going to be returned to its original owners.

Comment

Not much is known about the three thousand blacks who settled on Roanoke Island after February 1862. There is no marker today to show where the settlement stood. But for the following three years, the residents of this community, because of its relative isolation from the war raging in the rest of the South, were able to build houses, plant gardens, and begin to become educated for life in a free society. This book is a testament to their courage and perseverance.

Suggestions for Reports or Activities

1. How do you explain the hatred and contempt toward the former slaves expressed by some of the Union soldiers? Is there anything the community could have done to diminish these feelings?

2. When did the Union army begin enlisting blacks? How many served with the Union forces and in what capacity? Can you pinpoint the battle in Tennessee in July of 1864 in which Titus was killed?

3. Find out about the women who went to Roanoke Island during the war to teach the black children. Where did they come from? Did any of them continue their work on the mainland after the war ended?

4. Tell what you think happened to the characters in this book after they left the island. Did Maddie go north? If so, what did she do there? Did she ever come back?

The Tamarack Tree:
A Novel of the Siege of Vicksburg   Patricia Clapp
New York: Lothrop, Lee & Shepard, 1986. 214p. (2, 3)

Arriving from England to live with her brother in Vicksburg, Rosemary finds that she has a lot to get used to. Outraged by the idea of slavery, she finds it difficult to follow her brother's advice and keep her opinions to herself while trying to settle into her new community. But she soon grows to love the gracious life shared with her Southern belle friend, Mary Byrd, the dancing parties, the charming young men. Then comes the war, the blockade, and the disappearance of accustomed luxuries and necessities. Now the worst has happened. The Union ships are bombarding Vicksburg. Life is changing for everyone and maybe, says Rosemary, for the better.

Comment

The author has portrayed the pride, the fear, and the determination of the people of Vicksburg as they tried to fortify their hills to repulse the Union advance. Conversations for and against slavery show how conflicting ideas tried friendships. The author indicates how visitors from another country might have reacted to the institution of slavery. There is a description of the operation of one station on the Underground Railroad. The positive pictures of Amanda and Hector, and particularly of Hector's role in the struggle for freedom, provide an example of the role of the free black in Civil War society.

Suggestions for Reports or Activities

1. Rosemary and Jeff quarrel over the reasons for the conflict between North and South. Mary Byrd and Derek also have a bitter disagreement. Compare the points these characters make with the reasons given in your textbook or another source.

2. Locate Vicksburg on a map. Why was the city an important target for the Union army? Research the effect that the war had on shipping on the Mississippi River.

3. Amanda and Hector were free blacks living in the South during the Civil War. What can you find out about the life of free blacks at that time?

Tancy Belinda Hurmence
New York: Clarion, 1984. 203p. (2)

Tancy's life as a house slave is suddenly changing. Master Gaither has just died; Miss Pudding is in charge now. With her son Billy forced to join the Confederate army, Miss Pudding depends so much on Tancy. But the war is almost over, and the slaves are free. What does that mean for Tancy? Her hope is to find her mother, sold away from

Gaithers when Tancy was only a baby. At first Tancy hesitates to leave Miss Pudding with no one to count on, Billy dead from the war, all the folks going off. But times are different now. Tancy is determined to find her own way. It's scary out there away from the plantation, but Tancy discovers she has strength and sense.

Comment

Told from the point of view of sixteen-year-old slave girl Tancy, this is a moving account of the plight and the resilience of blacks during the dying days of slavery and the upheaval following the Emancipation Proclamation. It is also the story of the plight of whites who had learned from birth their superiority and were ill prepared to cope with the new age brought on by the South's collapse. Billy's thwarted attempts to rape Tancy before he is dragged off to war are symbolic. With background drawn from the collection of slave narratives at the Library of Congress, this account looks realistically at the chaos of the Freedmen's Bureau and the early attempts to provide education for newly freed blacks.

Suggestions for Reports or Activities

1. The Gaithers lived in an area of North Carolina that had been opposed to secession. Check in your textook or a reference source for information on pockets of resistance to the Confederacy. What were some reasons for this resistance?

2. What was the purpose of the Freedmen's Bureau? Was it successful? Write a short paper describing its activities and results.

3. Write an outline for another chapter describing Tancy's life after the end of the book. Do you suppose she continued to work at the bank? Did she decide to become a teacher after all? Why?

This Strange New Feeling   Julius Lester
New York: Dial, 1982. 149p. (1, 2, 3)

Three short stories adapted from slave narratives describe daring escapes. In the first, "This Strange New Feeling," Ras (who has run off once and has been brought back to the plantation) cleverly tricks his master and helps other slaves run away. As he and Sally attempt their own escape, Master blocks their path, but Sally moves quickly. In "Where the Sun Lives," Maria is about to be freed according to her husband's will, but his unpaid debts doom her hopes. "A

Christmas Love Story" chronicles the brave adventure of William and Ellen Craft, who plan an ingenious masquerade to win their freedom. A pallid young "man," obviously a frail invalid, accompanied by "his" manservant, boards the train for Philadelphia. Freedom! But the passage of the Fugitive Slave Law makes their new life a nightmare.

Comment

These stories by the author of *To Be a Slave* reveal the often forgotten ingenuity of the black slave in the United States. Readers will be reminded of how slaves often pretended to be dumb or foolish, and were skillful in saying what they knew their masters wanted to hear. The stories describe the feelings of blacks in bondage, the humiliation of the auction block, the cruel suffering of corporal punishment, their ability to accommodate, and their unflagging zeal for freedom. The activities of some of the Northern abolitionists and reactions to the Fugitive Slave Law are depicted.

Suggestions for Reports or Activities

1. The third story mentions the Fugitive Slave Law signed by President Fillmore. Other fugitive slave laws were enacted earlier. What were the provisions of these laws? How did Northern states respond to the 1850 law?

2. Check in a biographical source for information about Thomas Parker. Who were some of the other well-known abolitionists? Write an account of the activities of another abolitionist.

3. Research some other accounts of attempts by slaves to secure their freedom.

4. The Underground Railroad had many conductors, black and white, and stations in many parts of the North. Write a short paper on the Underground Railroad in a specific part of the country. Include a map.

Three Days   Paxton Davis
New York: Atheneum, 1980. 102p. (2, 3)

General Robert E. Lee is planning a decisive strike against the Union army forces when they are least expecting it, deep in Yankee territory. Through this maneuver he hopes to end the war with less destruction to the South. Therefore, he has the Army of Northern Virginia moving through Pennsylvania. But all the audacity and cunning of Lee and his generals cannot withstand General Meade and the strength and numbers of the Army of the Potomac. The story is well known. This book recounts the events of the days of Gettysburg from Lee's anguished viewpoint. Along with Lee's story are the brief and poignant musings of a young Confederate soldier.

Comment

Three Days is a step-by-step account of Lee's failed strategy at Gettysburg and of the devotion of his generals. The picture of a great man suffering with his decision is moving. The wasteful carnage of the battle is graphically depicted in this three-day memoir.

Suggestions for Reports or Activities

1. Check in your textbook and in another source for information on Lee's plans for overcoming the Union army in Northern territory. According to the novel, why did Lee fail? Does this account seem accurate, based on information from other sources?

2. Aside from Lee, several other important Confederate generals are mentioned in the book, including Stuart, Longstreet, Hill, Pickett, and Stonewall Jackson. In an encyclopedia or biographical source find information about the life of one of these men. (You may compare his background with that of General Lee.)

3. The author states, "History often hinges on trivia" (p. 17). To what is he referring? Is this a true incident? How might the battle of Gettysburg have been different if this "trivial" incident had not occurred?

Turn Homeward, Hannalee   Patricia Beatty
New York: Morrow, 1984. 193p. (2, 3)

Twelve-year-old Hannalee has promised her mother that she will find her way back home. Yankee soldiers from Sherman's army have descended upon her hometown of Roswell, Georgia, burned the mill, and rounded up all the mill hands, transporting them north to replace much needed workers in Kentucky and Indiana. Caught in this tumultuous scheme are Hannalee, her younger brother Jem, and Rosellen Sanders, who is her older brother's sweetheart. The three vow to stay together, but this plan soon is shown to be impossible. Hannalee decides to look for Rosellen; but when it is clear that Rosellen is changing her mind about trying to return home, Hannalee knows she must depend on herself. She locates her brother

Jem, disguises herself as a boy, and together, after some frightening adventures, they find their way back to Roswell. (For the story of what happened after their return, see *Be Ever Hopeful, Hannalee,* above.)

Comment

Readers will learn of a little-known incident of the Civil War, the capture of Southern mill workers in order to force them to toil in Northern factories, or to serve in Northern homes. Using this actual happening as background, the author focuses on how the Civil War touched ordinary people. As she states in an author's note, too much of our impression of the war is based on stories of the aristocracy, such as *Gone with the Wind.* The senseless destruction of property as well as of human beings is movingly depicted through Hannalee's eyes. This spunky heroine shows the resilience of people in times of necessity.

Suggestions for Reports or Activities

1. Read the author's note on the mill workers. Then check into some reference sources to locate additional information on this topic.

2. Sherman's march through Georgia was an important part of the campaign in the South. Read about Sherman's activities in your textbook and in some other sources. Write a short paper on the outcome and effects of Sherman's march.

3. Hannalee states that her family never had slaves. Yet they were loyal Southerners. Can you find information on what percentage of Southern families were slaveholders? Write a short paper on this subject.

The 290 Scott O'Dell
Boston: Houghton Mifflin, 1976. 118p. (3)

The 290 chronicles the adventures of sixteen-year-old Jim Lynn from New Orleans, who at the start of the Civil War is working as a shipbuilder's apprentice in Liverpool, England. During the war he signs on as a sailor on the *Alabama,* a ship he helped to build. Its mission is to seek out and destroy the Union navy. The story vividly describes the battles in which the *Alabama* engaged and recounts an attempted mutiny. It also describes Jim's efforts to free hundreds of slaves held prisoner in Haiti by his father and his father's partner, pending shipment to Cuba.

Comment

The *Alabama* was one of the most famous Confederate ships. The fact that it was built and fitted in England was considered by the United States government to be a violation of neutrality agreements. Because of heavy damage done to the Union navy by the *Alabama* and other British-built ships, claims were filed by the United States against Britain. The book also points out that, although the Confederate constitution forbade foreign slave trade, international slave trade still existed within the Americas and was no doubt still profitable to some American traders.

Suggestions for Reports or Activities

1. Read about the *Alabama* claims in an encyclopedia or other source. What effect did they have on Anglo-American relations?

2. Read about the slave trade in the Americas. What is Jim Lynn's attitude toward slavery? Why do you suppose he feels as he does?

3. Imagine that you are a sailor on a warship during the Civil War. What might your day-to-day existence be like?

4. What was the British attitude toward the American Civil War? Try researching the *Times* of London for editorial opinions.

Which Way Freedom?   Joyce Hansen
New York: Walker, 1986. 120p. (2, 3)

It is April 1864, and Obi, a former slave, is a private serving in the Union army with the Sixth U.S. Artillery of Colored Troops, Thirteenth Tennessee Battalion. Thinking back to the early days of the war, he reminisces about how he got where he is now. He remembers the time when he was a slave on the Jennings farm, with Easter and little Jason; then he and Easter were sent to the Phillips plantation. He remembers their escape, with Easter dressed like a boy, and Obi carrying the old man, Buka, on his back. Obi hoped to find his mother, Lorena, but this has not been possible. And now, after emancipation, he is a soldier, and earning wages. But is this freedom? After surviving the bloody battle of Fort Pillow, Obi is determined to find Easter and Jason, and perhaps to go North with his new friend Thomas. Perhaps someday he will know what freedom really means. (For Easter's story, see *Out from This Place,* above.)

Comment

In this tale of the aspirations and adventures of one young slave who finds his way to freedom, there is a good deal of information about life and times during the Civil War. For example, students will learn that some Southern farms were small, with very few slaves (there were only three on the Jennings farm, in contrast to the large Phillips plantation). The Confederate soldiers at times forced owners to send their slaves to work for the army; other slaves saw action when they had to accompany their soldier masters. Like Obi, there were many black soldiers who fought in the Civil War (more than 200,000, according to an author's note).

Suggestions for Reports or Activities

1. Find information about blacks in the Civil War. Where did they serve? Were there blacks with the Confederate forces as well as in the Union army? In the story, Daniel is asked to spy for the Union. Can you find any information about blacks as spies?

2. What did Buka mean when he told Obi that freedom was "in your own mind"?

3. What do you suppose happened to Obi after the end of the story? Create an additional last chapter. Did he find Easter and Jason? Did he ever find Lorena? Did he go north or stay in the South? What possibilities for work did he have?

Who Comes with Cannons?   Patricia Beatty
New York: Morrow Junior Books, 1992. 186p. (2, 3)

Early in 1861 twelve-year-old Truth Hopkins moves from Indiana to North Carolina to live with her uncle and his family. As she adjusts to her new surroundings, the Quaker girl becomes involved in the antislavery movement and the Underground Railroad. Her cousins Robert and Todd are forced to join the Confederate Army despite their refusal to take up arms for either side; later one of them is captured by the Union forces and imprisoned in New York state. Truth meets with the abolitionist Frederick Douglass and catches a glimpse of President Lincoln when she heads north to rescue her cousin.

Comment

While the role of Quakers as "conductors" on the Underground Railroad is well known, young readers may be surprised to learn the extent of the risks run by these people as members of a diverse community including values very different from their own. Northerners were no more friendly than Southerners to men who would not fight for their cause. Troops on both sides had no compunction about taking away anything they could carry from Quaker farms. The insight that heroes come in many forms can be applied to situations today as easily as to those of a hundred or more years ago.

Suggestions for Reports or Activities

1. Read about Frederick Douglass, either in *The Narrative of the Life of Frederick Douglass* (his autobiography, first published in 1845) or in a more recent biography, to find out how Quakers helped him when he was a youth.

2. Compare the dilemma of Quakers in the South during the Civil War with that of young people in our cities today who choose not to join a local gang. How are they treated by their neighbors? What is likely to happen when they get caught in the cross fire?

3. Read about the conditions in Southern hospitals during the Civil War. Then write a letter from the schoolteacher, Michael Hartling, to Lydia's family telling them what it was like to be a nurse in one of these hospitals.

4. What do you think happened to Squire and his family when they reached Liberia? Read about the flight of American slaves to that African country and describe the kind of life they might have made for themselves.

With Every Drop of Blood: A Novel of the Civil War
James Lincoln Collier and Christopher Collier
New York: Delacorte, 1994. 234p. (2)

In the Shenandoah Valley in Virginia in 1864, the farmers are tired of war and eager to return to their families and their plows. When Johnny's father comes home, however, he suspects that his wounds are fatal. Although fourteen-year-old Johnny promises that he will take care of his mother and younger brother and sister, he cannot resist the adventure offered by joining a wagon train taking supplies to the Rebel troops in Richmond. Hitching up his three mules, he starts off bravely enough, only to be captured by a young Yankee soldier who turns out to be a runaway slave named Cush. Reluctant to take orders from a black, heading for a Yankee prison camp, and remorseful about having broken his promise to his father, Johnny has a lot of decisions to make as the unit moves slowly toward Appomattox Court House and General Lee's surrender.

Comment

The young Confederate is a likeable boy faced with problems of reason and conscience with which contemporary youths can identify. Johnny tries to convince himself that he is keeping his word to his father, even as he plays down the risk when asking permission of his mother to join the wagon train. Presented as a normal adolescent, confused and insecure, Johnny matures through his adventures. The development of a sense of loyalty and friendship between the two boys is slow and far from smooth, but perfectly plausible. Various answers are offered to the question of why the war was being fought, thus highlighting the diversity of motives.

Suggestions for Reports or Activities

1. Mosby's Rangers are assigned to guard the wagon train heading for Richmond. Find out who Colonel Mosby and the Rangers were, where and when they fought, what made them famous, what happened to them after the war, etc.

2. At the end of the book, Johnny and Cush are heading back to Johnny's farm. What do you think his mother will do when they arrive, and why? How will Johnny respond? Write a couple of pages summarizing what might have been a different, final chapter.

3. After spending some time together and helping each other out, Johnny and Cush stop thinking of each other as "the enemy." Has something like that ever happened to you? Write about a time when you and another person started out as enemies and ended up friends. Explain why you think that happened.

4. In your own opinion, what was the major cause of the Civil War? Tell why your position is correct and alternative explanations are not.

A Woman Called Moses   Marcy Heidish
Boston: Houghton Mifflin, 1976. 306p. (1, 2)

Although this book contains some objectionable language and suggestive scenes, the subject matter—the life of Harriet Tubman—is important and interesting. Born into slavery, Harriet knew at an early age that she had to be free. Her many years of hard work as a slave to cruel owners and overseers included a blow to the head from which she almost died. Harriet finally escaped from slavery. Soon she began working as a guide on the Underground Railroad, a secret route followed by slaves running away to the North. Heidish describes several of Harriet's trips, making them a composite of people and experiences.

Comment

The reader gains from this narrative a genuine sense of the ordeal which the escaping slaves had to endure. The trips were difficult, food scarce, and capture always imminent. Historical events such as John Brown's rebellion and defeat are described with feeling and confusion from Harriet's point of view. The risks experienced by Quakers and other sympathizers are noted, along with the death and destruction justified by the promise of freedom.

Suggestions for Reports or Activities

1. Why was Harriet Tubman called "Moses"? What aspects of her life and work reminded people of the biblical story of Moses?

2. Write a description of a day in the life of a runaway slave. How does that person feel? What hopes and plans does the person have? What fears does the person experience?

3. Research Harriet Tubman's life. What details can you add to the story as presented in this book? What part, for instance, did she play in the Civil War? What did she have to do before she received a pension? Why?

MORE CHALLENGING BOOKS
FOR ADVANCED READERS

Andersonville   MacKinlay Kantor
New York: Crowell, 1955. 760p.

Intended to serve as a prison for up to 10,000 captured Yankee soldiers, the Georgia stockade eventually houses more than 30,000 at one time. The author relives the horror of the details of prison life with sketches of individual Yankees and references to the fortunes of nearby families who had themselves lost sons during the Civil War.

The Chaneysville Incident   David Bradley
New York: Avon, 1981. 450p.

Focusing on events in the black section of a small Pennsylvania town, this book conveys the deep resentments felt by blacks as a consequence of slavery, resentments that lingered on for generations. In the retelling of these stories, the hero works through the possibility of a positive interracial relationship for himself.

Gone with the Wind   Margaret Mitchell
New York: Macmillan, 1929. 1037p.

Familiar to many readers as a film, this novel nonetheless paints as vivid a picture through words as the movie does through photographic images of a world destroyed by war. The impact of Sherman's march to Atlanta and the subsequent destruction of one of the South's most beautiful cities is shattering. The reader learns about the period from the viewpoint of the white Southern aristocrat.

High Hearts   Rita Mae Brown
New York: Bantam, 1986. 424p.

The special focus of this novel is the sacrifices made by women and slaves on behalf of the Confederacy. Described especially graphically are the primitive medical care and supplies available to the wounded and dying of both armies.

Jubilee   Margaret Walker
Boston: Houghton Mifflin, 1966. 497p.

The Civil War years, including the horrors of the persecution of blacks both before and after the war itself, are recounted from the imagined point of view of a slave woman. The book is rich in details of life in the Old South from that perspective.

Roots: The Saga of an American Family   Alex Haley
Garden City, N.Y.: Doubleday, 1974. 688p.

Drawing on the oral traditions handed down in his family for generations, the author traces his origins back to the seventeen-year-old Kunta Kinte, who was abducted from his home in Gambia and transported as a slave to colonial America. In this account Haley provides an imaginative rendering of the lives of seven generations of black men and women.

Unto This Hour   Tom Wicker
New York: Viking, 1984. 642p.

The background of this novel is the battle of August 28–30, 1862, known as Second Manassas or Second Bull Run. A counterpoint to the bloody, confused fighting is provided by brief glimpses of life on a rich plantation in South Carolina and the fortunes of a poor white family in northern Virginia close to the battle site.

IV   *Westward Expansion and the Native American Response*

Arrest Sitting Bull   Douglas C. Jones
New York: Scribner, 1977. 249p. (1)
    Willa Mae Favory has lived on the frontier all her life. She has always felt at home in the wilderness settlements, even in the farthest outposts, but teaching at the Standing Rock Agency makes her uneasy. Sitting Bull is here, and his role in perpetuating the ghost dance makes him a key figure in a volatile situation. To the Sioux, ghost dancing is the final hope for a return to the lifestyle of their ancestors. To the whites, it is a dangerous precursor to Indian uprisings. The order to arrest Sitting Bull forces a confrontation of the opposing factions, and Willa Mae finds herself caught up in the struggle of two widely diverse societies.

Comment

    Although it is impossible to rewrite history to create a happier ending, this novel reveals the complexity of the situation. The perspectives of the whites and the Indians are artfully interwoven, and the far-reaching impact of the event of Sitting Bull's arrest is vividly reflected through its effect on the individuals cast in this drama. This fictionalized account is an accurate retelling of fact and a powerful statement about the lives of the people who made up the societies involved.

Suggestions for Reports or Activities

    1. Write a letter from Willa Mae Favory to the family she is returning to, explaining why she has spent the years working with Indians and why she has suddenly decided to return home.

2. Write a history of the ghost dance. Include the effect that Sitting Bull's death had on it.

3. Describe the last years of Sitting Bull's life and the role of his life and death on Indian-white relationships.

Beyond the Divide   Kathryn Lasky
New York: Macmillan, 1983. 154p. (1, 2)

When her father decides that he can no longer endure the shunning inflicted on him by the Amish community for a seemingly minor infraction, Meribah goes away with him. They join a wagon train heading for California, not looking for gold, says Meribah, but for something else. The cheer and optimism of the beginning of the journey deteriorate as personalities clash, supplies run out, and illness and violence develop. Meribah discovers that life outside the secure Amish bounds is not as free as she had thought. When her fashionable new friend Serena is raped by a ne'er-do-well, Meribah is horrified by community reaction. Then when she and her father are left behind by the party because of her father's severe illness, Meribah realizes that she must be able to depend on herself not only to survive but also to make a life for herself.

Comment

In addition to introducing some of the ideals of the Amish, this story affords an experience of the life of people on their way west during the Gold Rush days. Readers will learn of the preparations, the supplies needed, and the importance of skills such as wainwrighting and knowledge of herbal medicine. Good humor and patience often ran out, along with other essential supplies, giving way to selfishness and violence. Meribah's determination to find her own life is an example of the fortitude of pioneer women.

Suggestions for Reports or Activities

1. Find out about the Amish in America. Where did the original Amish people come from? Why do they continue to live apart? What values have continued since Meribah's day? What lessons can our larger society learn from the Amish?

2. Read about the Gold Rush. Was it a dream come true or a sad disappointment to most seekers?

3. What chances would Meribah have for finding her way back to the Valley of the Fontenelle? Write a paper describing the hardships she might encounter and how she might deal with them. Why did she choose this place?

Bold Journey: West with Lewis and Clark   Charles Bohner
Boston: Houghton Mifflin, 1985. 171p. (2, 3)

Hugh McNeal, bored with his army assignment to Fort Massac on the Ohio River, is delighted to join the Corps of Discovery, under the leadership of Captains Meriwether Lewis and William Clark. Their goal is to discover a northwest passage to the Pacific Ocean. Skilled as a boatbuilder and familiar with the ways of rivers, Hugh is an asset to the team. Contending with the harshness of nature, figuring out ways to deal with Indians, and learning to adjust to the personalities both of the leaders and of the other group members—all of this is part of a great adventure capped by the first sight of the "vast, blue glittering Pacific Ocean spread out before us in the morning sunshine."

Comment

Hugh McNeal was the youngest member of the Lewis and Clark expedition. The author has described what life might have been like for a recruit. Readers will gain a feeling for the jealousies, petty quarrels, close comradeship, and exaltation in times of triumph—all part of life for this small band of unlikely companions, including raw soldiers, French adventurers, and the Shoshone Indian woman, Sacagawea.

Suggestions for Reports or Activities

1. Most accounts of the story of Lewis and Clark assign a larger role to Sacagawea. How does this version vary from what you have read in your textbook or in other sources?

2. Hugh suffered considerable remorse for not taking up for Jack at the time of his court-martial. What other course of action might Hugh have pursued? What might the consequences have been?

3. Why was it important to find a northwest passage to the Pacific Ocean? How did the explorations of Lewis and Clark help to influence the course of U.S. history during the first half of the nineteenth century?

Brothers of the Heart:
A Story of the Old Northwest, 1837–1838   Joan Blos
New York: Scribner, 1985. 162p. (2, 3)

This story covers one year, a turning point in the life of Shem, who was born with a lame foot but grew up proud. A brief and unknowing involvement in a shady banking deal causes a bitter quarrel with his father. Feeling unable to prove himself worthy, Shem runs away. He finds employment as a clerk in Detroit and then travels north to keep the books for a fur trading company. Left behind at the company's cabin by his three companions, who fear that his crippled foot will impede their need to travel farther for furs, Shem prepares to spend the winter alone in the wilderness. Through the unexpected assistance of Mary Goodhue, an ailing and elderly Ottawa Indian woman, he survives.

Comment

The story presents a picture of the hardships and successes of pioneers making their way west. The essential survival values of courage, honesty, trust, and dependability are shown in the attitudes and actions of both the pioneer families and the Indian woman who befriends Shem. The book portrays a mutually supportive relationship between a young white man and an Indian woman. Something of the culture of the Ottawa Indians is discussed. The author's use of language based on letters written at the time adds to the authenticity.

Suggestions for Reports or Activities

1. Why were Shem's parents upset about the lot which they had purchased? Can you discover whether this kind of misrepresentation of property was a common occurrence?

2. What can you learn about the traditions or values of the Ottawa Indians from Mary Goodhue? How did her friendship affect Shem's attitudes toward Indians?

3. Can you discover any diaries or letters written by people on their way west? What are the hopes and concerns that these writings reflect?

Call Me Francis Tucket   Gary Paulsen
New York: Delacorte, 1995. 97p. (3)

Continuing the story begun in the same author's *Mr. Tucket* (see below), this short book shows Francis alone on the prairie with his

Indian pony trying to find the way west to rejoin his parents. When a couple of desperadoes, probably thrown off a wagon train, take his pony, his rifle, and all his equipment, fourteen-year-old Francis is left, lost, with the robbers' dying mule and a sense of panic. He manages to retrieve his property and even to rescue two small children whose father has died of cholera. But what will he do with them as he renews his struggle toward the West?

Comment

The simple immensity of the Great Plains is brought home in the image of a boy standing alone on the top of a bluff, looking down at a prairie stretching as far as the eye could see. The bravery (or the ignorance) of the pioneers who set out to cross it in covered wagons is suddenly clear. They could only have imagined the dangers of disease, hostile Indians, lack of water, unscrupulous traders, and stampeding buffalo—all of which the boy experiences in less than a hundred pages!

Suggestions for Reports or Activities

1. Lottie and Billy's father dies of cholera. What sort of disease is that? What causes it, how is it spread, and what treatment is used today? List the countries or regions of the world where outbreaks of cholera are still common. If you were traveling to one of those areas, how could you protect yourself from catching this disease?

2. Find out more about the buffalo on the Great Plains. When were they there in the greatest numbers? What happened to them, and when? How many are out there today? Are any of them roaming free, or are contemporary buffalo herds privately owned?

3. Look into the history of the covered wagons going west. What was the usual size of the wagon train? Where were the travelers heading? What proportion of them died on the way?

The Court-Martial of George Armstrong Custer
Douglas C. Jones
New York: Scribner, 1976. 291p. (1, 2)

Jones bases this fascinating book on the supposition that Custer might not have died at the battle of the Little Bighorn, that he might in fact have been the sole survivor of the massacre by thousands of Plains Indians. In that case, surely he would have been brought to trial for disobeying the orders of his superior officer and causing the death of his entire cavalry regiment. Both prosecution and defense witnesses present their testimony, as the court—along with the reader—tries to reach the right conclusion.

Comment

Was Custer a military genius who had terrible luck? Or was he a glory seeker with political ambitions? The famous battle comes to life as it is relived in the imaginary courtroom. References to problems of communication between military officers, lack of support in money and materiel from civilian leaders, and limited training of recruits and horses illustrate the historical context of this incident. Glimpses of life in New York, of intrigue in Washington, and of the mixture of noble and petty impulses in all the characters flesh out the portrayal of an event and a period which to this day retain many unanswered questions.

Suggestions for Reports or Activities

1. Construct in your own words a chronology of the events at the Little Bighorn, based on the accounts in this book. Compare your narrative with a historical report of the battle. Are there any points of difference?

2. Imagine that you were one of the military officers of the court, charged with deciding Custer's guilt or innocence. How would you have voted? Why?

3. Research the lives and careers of the officers named in the story (for example, Pope, Terry, Sherman, Sheridan, Reno, Schofield). Find out what they did before and after 1876 when the battle of the Little Bighorn took place.

Crazy Weather   Charles McNichols
New York: Macmillan, 1944. 195p. (1, 2)

South Boy has grown up on his father's ranch, learning the Mojave Indian ways and tolerating his mother's Christian and cultural instruction. This summer his mother is away, recuperating from an operation, but South Boy knows that when she returns he will be sent to a boarding school where he will have to be with white people all the time. Then he has a dream—about two hawks. Havek, his Mojave friend, thinks that it may mean something important. It's a time of "crazy weather," a spell of intense heat. Havek and South Boy set off to find the meaning of the dream, to go name traveling. Maybe South Boy will become as one of the Mojaves. But after four days of deep immersion into Mojave life, when the "crazy weather" is over, South Boy realizes he and Havek must separate. South Boy cannot be an Indian, nor can he be what his mother expects. But he is fortunate. There is another choice.

Comment

This story is a tapestry of Mojave legends and practices, rich in Indian lore and also showing rivalries among Indian tribes. South Boy is an example of someone who has come to appreciate another culture and would like to be part of it, but realizes the pull of his own beginnings.

Suggestions for Reports or Activities

1. What is meant by "name traveling"? What was the importance of finding one's new name?

2. South Boy's hair had grown long. What did the Mojaves mean when they wore their hair "half long"? Why does South Boy decide to cut his hair at the end of the book?

3. If South Boy were going to write a letter to his mother telling her that he would not be going away to school, what could he say to try to convince her to see things his way?

4. Check in a reference source for information on the Cherokee removal. Compare the discussion in the historical source with the presentation in this novel.

Devil Storm Theresa Nelson
New York: Orchard, 1987. 212p. (2)

On the Bolivar Peninsula, across the water from Galveston, Texas, Richard Carroll has built a house that has held firm for years through wind and weather. When Richard goes to Galveston on business one bright September day in 1900, he leaves thirteen-year-old Walter in charge of his mother and younger sisters, none of whom have any thought of abandoning the house even when the waves come up so high that their home looks like a boat. A scary black tramp named Tom comes to the door to beg them to leave before it's too late, but Walter's mother refuses to go. Walter has to decide whether Tom can be trusted and, if so, whether he dares defy his mother.

Comment

The hurricane that hit Galveston on September 8, 1900, killed 6,000 Texans. This fictional recreation of the inhabitants of the area, along with their prides and prejudices, brings to life the values and conflicts of a hundred years ago. The resolution of differences of outlook between parents and children, members of different races and classes, and brothers and sisters should strike familiar chords with today's young readers.

Suggestions for Reports or Activities

1. The Carrolls named their animals for Texas heroes: Dick Dowling, Davy Crockett, Sam Houston, and Jane Long. Find out who these people were and why Texans remember them.

2. Tell the story of Tom in your own words as a chronological narrative. Who were his parents? What happened to him and his family? Why did he come to Bolivar?

3. Look up the history of Galveston, Texas. What happened to the town after the hurricane of 1900? Did it ever regain its regional importance? What is it known for now?

4. Imagine the rest of the story about the two little girls and their canary. Did their father ever come back for them? If so, what happened next?

Eyes of Darkness   Jamake Highwater
New York: Lothrop, Lee & Shepard, 1985. 191p. (1, 2)

It is 1890 on an Indian reservation in South Dakota. Dr. Alexander East, an Indian who has been trained in the white man's medicine, is mistrusted both by his tribespeople and by the white agents who are in charge. He himself is torn: How did he get to this place, and how had it happened that he seemed to belong nowhere? He thinks back on his life as Yesa ("Winner") with the People of the Plains before his father, Many Lightnings, returned from ten years away transformed into Jacob East, farmer and Christian. Where had it all gone wrong? And what was he to do now?

Comment

The theme of alienation pervades this touching novel, told from the point of view of the young Indian. Yesa's determination to make the best of his fate and use the medicine he is learning to bridge the distance between the whites and the Indians fails in face of the inability of the two peoples truly to communicate with each other. The way of the native American, who lives off the land without harming it, is contrasted with that of the intruder, who destroys the land and its habitat in order to conquer it.

Suggestions for Reports or Activities

1. Alexander East is confronted with the outcome of the Battle of Wounded Knee. Check a history book or encyclopedia to find out what happened there in December of 1890.

2. When Yesa comes of age his grandmother insists that he sacrifice his dearest possession to the Great Mystery, or Spirit. Imagine that he refused: What might have happened then?

3. Part of this story takes place in Canada. Find out what provisions Canada has made for its native population. Do they also live on reservations? Were they forcibly moved from the east to the west of the country as Indians were in the U.S.? If so, when was this and what happened?

Gently Touch the Milkweed   Lynn Hall
Chicago: Follett, 1970. 160p. (2, 3)

Janny works hard and without complaint, but she feels taken for granted by her parents. Janny's father and mother run an inn, just where the wagon trains stop for a rest on their way west across Kansas. Her father has named the budding settlement Willard's Ford, for himself; Willard feels confident that there will be a real town there someday. He persuades Mel, who aims to start a newspaper, and Mary Pat, his wife, to put down roots here. Janny is delighted. She likes Mary Pat. But even more she is drawn toward Mel, who seems to recognize that underneath Janny's awkward and stolid appearance there is something special. During that next year Janny sees herself changing, becoming a woman and a thinking person, warmed by what she sees as Mel's interest in her. But when the discovery of gold a few hundred miles to the west casts doubt upon the rosy future of Willard's Ford, and Mel and Mary Pat decide that they must move on, Janny realizes that she has grown up enough to appreciate herself.

Comment

Readers will experience a sense of the expectancy that infused the small settlements as people began to build towns on the prairie. Many people hoped to "get rich quick," as the opportunism of the town planner indicates. The precariousness of these new towns is illustrated by the reaction of townsfolk to the news of a gold strike to the west. The description of Willard's Ford with its new and empty buildings shows the reality of the term "ghost town."

Suggestions for Reports or Activities

1. What are some of the famous ghost towns in the history of the West? Write a paper telling the story of one of these towns.

2. Lupin, the town planner, had a clear idea of what was needed at Willard's Ford. Based on his ideas for Eden City, draw a plan for a prairie town. Why was this location considered ideal? What resources would be essential?

3. What is the meaning of the book's title? How does the title help to explain Janny's feelings about herself?

Hannah Herself   Ruth Franchere
New York: Crowell, 1964. 176p. (2, 3)

Sixteen-year-old Hannah finds Ellen and Jonathan's way of life primitive and restrictive. She has traveled from New Haven to visit her sister and her family in a little Illinois prairie village, where Jonathan is attempting to run a school for the grown-up sons of homesteaders, young men who have been working on farms, with no chance for education. There are problems with discipline, with too little money, with too much to do, and Jonathan is impatient. Hannah is unhappy and plans to leave as soon as possible. But then Tim Boone and Marcus Drake begin making her life interesting. And there is the mysterious cabin that must be kept secret. Hannah gradually comes to realize that she is not merely Ellen's little sister or Jonathan's responsibility, but that she is Hannah, herself!

Comment

This glimpse of prairie life shows the hardships that determined people faced in accomplishing their goals. The author has had a special interest in the teachers who traveled west to provide education for children on the frontier. The story also describes the Underground Railroad and conflicting views on slavery.

Suggestions for Reports or Activities

1. What were rural schools like in the mid-nineteenth century? How were the teachers prepared? Write a paper about such a school.

Can you find any information about schools for older children like the one at Brookville? What about education for girls?

2. At the end of the book Hannah says that she is "herself." What does she mean? What experiences contributed to her coming to this new opinion of herself?

3. Hannah's mother is waiting for a letter that really explains what is going on. Compose a letter such as Hannah might write after she decides to stay in Illinois.

4. Start a diary for Hannah. Include at least three entries from different periods of Hannah's time in Illinois.

In the Shadow of the Wind   Luke Wallin
Scarsdale, N.Y.: Bradbury, 1984. 203p. (2, 3)

The conflict of cultures and values tore apart the lives of white settlers and Creek Indians living in Alabama in the 1830s. With the Creek traditions already being threatened by white teachings and ways of living, and with the sheer numbers of whites driving away the deer and making Indian livelihood more and more difficult, the Creeks are no longer strong enough to resist. Brown Hawk wishes to accept this and does not want more fighting. Others of his tribe disagree. Caleb McElroy and his grandfather are considered friends by the Creeks until Caleb is forced to kill Least Coyote, who is about to scalp his mother. Yet when Six Deer lies half-frozen and starved in the woods, Caleb rescues him. Caleb finds himself on both sides of the issue and can resolve it finally only by becoming Creek.

Comment

This story probes into the thoughts and motivations of the Creeks as they lost their trust in the promises of the "White Father" in Washington. The author depicts the tensions between settlers and Indians that led to bitter skirmishes and retaliatory strikes, each against the other. The removal of the Creeks to Oklahoma is the story of the fate of many other Indian tribes. Readers will gain more understanding of the Indians caught in the inexorable march of European settlers to the West.

Suggestions for Reports or Activities

1. What did the Creeks lose in their move to Oklahoma? What did they gain? Can you find out any information about the Creeks today?

2. As you read the book did you find that you sided with the whites or with the Indians? Do you think that Caleb and his grandfather were unique in their attitude toward the Indians? Why?

3. How did the "White Father" in Washington justify the removal of the Creeks to Oklahoma?

4. Compare some of the values and traditions of the Creeks as described in the book with those of the settlers. What might settlers (such as the McElroys) have learned from the Indians?

Killdeer Mountain   Dee Brown
New York: Holt, 1983. 279p. (1, 2)

Sam Morrison, reporter for the *Saint Louis Herald,* is in Dakota country looking for stories. He decides to join a group of passengers on a steamboat going up the Missouri River for the dedication of a new fort named in honor of one Charles Rawley. On the way he talks to a number of different people about Rawley, including a mysterious stranger who might even be Rawley himself, though Sam has been given at least two eyewitness accounts of Rawley's death. The stranger, who calls himself Alex Selkirk (the true name of Robinson Crusoe, though this is never mentioned), might, however, be a former Rebel named Drew Hardesty—also reportedly dead. Is Rawley a hero or a fraud? Is he alive or dead? Morrison is determined to find out.

Comment

In this book, the Old West comes to life as many vivid characters tell their own stories: a surgeon and a steamboat captain; Hardesty's beautiful widow, Kathleen; an Indian girl named Towanjila, or Blue Sky Woman; soldiers and sailors; Indians and settlers; colonels and Canadians. The result is a picture of the West at a time of transition, when relationships shifted and changed, and life from one day to the next was predictably unpredictable.

Suggestions for Reports or Activities

1. Who was Alex Selkirk? Present the evidence from the book to support your conclusion. Explain the evidence to the contrary.

2. The Indian called Spotted Horse complains that the Americans have forced the Sioux into Canada and yet still pursue them there. Is his complaint justified? Check the history of Indian wars along the Canadian frontier.

3. Early in the story Nettie Steever and her husband appear as prospective settlers. What were some of the motives for heading West in that period?

A Lantern in Her Hand   Bess S. Aldrich
New York: Grosset & Dunlap, 1928. 307p. (1, 2)

Abbie Mackenzie Deal becomes a pioneer, first in Iowa, then as a young wife and mother in Nebraska. Her promising career as a singer is placed last in her priorities, as she experiences life in a sod house on the prairie. She bears and rears her children; lives through drought, hard times, and the plague of grasshoppers; and survives the loss of her idealistic husband. Through it all, she carries the lantern of love for her family and her country. Abbie is a remarkable woman, epitomizing the ideal pioneer strength of spirit. Living to the age of eighty, she sees her dreams fulfilled by her children and grandchildren.

Comment

Realism is the key to this novel. The daily struggles of life in a new land are richly described. Two major wars, the Civil War and World War I, touch Abbie by taking first her betrothed and then her sons away from her. The droughts and plague of grasshoppers that beset the Midwest are reflected in Abbie's struggles to survive and to feed her children. The book in general is a portrait of the strong people who built our country.

Suggestions for Reports or Activities

1. Research the beginnings of the state of Nebraska. What kind of people settled there? From where? What kinds of problems did they encounter?

2. What are sod houses? How and why were they built? Are there any examples left today? If so, where are they located?

3. Although Abbie's granddaughter Katherine does not seem to understand her, she tries to find the missing portrait of their ancestor. Write a letter from Katherine to Abbie telling her why she feels the portrait is important. Then write a letter from Abbie to Katherine explaining why the strand of pearls is also important.

Laughing Boy   Oliver LaFarge
Cambridge, Mass.: Houghton Mifflin, 1929. 302p. (1, 2)

Laughing Boy knows that Slim Girl is watching him. She is different, bold; he is entranced. There is some talk about her; Laughing Boy's uncle warns him. Slim Girl has been with the Americans, and some say she is more American than Navaho. Her reputation is not good. But Slim Girl wants to return to the Navahos, to "go back to the blanket." She wants to teach Laughing Boy what she has learned from the Americans, and Laughing Boy will bring her back to the Navaho way. Together they will make a perfect life in the northern desert. Laughing Boy agrees to go with Slim Girl; it's official. Slim Girl wants to settle a score with the Americans, but she cannot explain to Laughing Boy her subtle plan for revenge.

Comment

This book is considered a classic for its sympathetic and informative presentation of Navaho life and attitudes, and for its poetic language. Writing from a Navaho viewpoint, the author describes Slim Girl and Laughing Boy living in a traditional way, pursuing their crafts, silver and weaving. Readers find out about ceremonial dances, the night chant, gambling and games, wedding songs, the concept of "hozoji." Gentle fun is made of "Americans," notably in a bargaining scene as an American haggles to buy Laughing Boy's silver belt. Throughout the book the depth of Slim Girl's anti-American sentiment is poignantly expressed. Her unwitting earlier involvement, leading to present tragedy, is a commentary on U.S.-Navaho relations.

Suggestions for Reports or Activities

1. Why does Slim Girl feel such resentment toward the "Americans"? What does she hope to gain by her relationship with Laughing Boy?

2. How are Laughing Boy and Slim Girl alike? How are they different? How does Slim Girl surprise him? How is he able to explain or excuse her behavior?

3. Several Navaho traditions are described in this book. Check in another source to find more information on one of these Navaho customs. Is the author accurate in his portrayal? What can you add to his description?

4. Read in an encyclopedia or other source about the United States policy toward the Navahos. Write a paper in which you comment on this policy and relate it to sentiments revealed by characters in the book regarding Americans.

Legend Days   Jamake Highwater
New York: Harper & Row, 1984. 147p. (2, 3)

The girl-child Amana draws her strength from foxes who have helped her escape from the owl of death. The foxes have given her the soul of a brave warrior on top of her natural qualities of sympathy and nurturing. Despite the hostility of the tribe that takes her in after the death of her parents, again and again Amana uses her holy powers to help her people. She agrees to marry her sister's elderly husband in order to be under his protection, but refuses to restrict herself to the traditional role of a wife. One person, however, cannot defeat an entire tribe, and she cannot save her friend Yellow Bird Woman from mutilation and madness.

Comment

Using a mystical approach to the demise of the Indians on the northern Plains, this story focuses on a time when Native Americans believed that people gained their power from the spirits of animals. As the forest is torn down, as the buffalo disappear and the old ways are lost forever, the "legend days" come to an end. The young reader learns of a way of life that relied on harmony with nature and all living beings, permanently interrupted by the coming of white civilization.

Suggestions for Reports or Activities

1. Amana's people are virtually wiped out by "the sickness." What sickness was this? Using as clues the symptoms described in the book, read about the white men's illnesses that killed many Indians in this country and figure out which one it was. Justify your conclusion.

2. Many of Amana's people starve because the buffalo fail to come to the winter hunting grounds as in the past. What happened to the buffalo? Find out how many buffalo were on the Great Plains at various times in the eighteenth and nineteenth centuries.

3. At the end of the book, many of the tribes swear allegiance to the "Great White Mother" of England. What was English policy toward the Indians of the Plains?

4. What do you think happened to Amana? Did she survive with the help of the foxes? Did she find another group with whom she could live? Write an epilogue to this story in which you speculate on Amana's fate.

The Massacre at Fall Creek   Jessamyn West
New York: Harcourt, 1975. 314p. (1, 2)

In the year 1824, not far from what is now Indianapolis, Indiana, five white men killed a group of nine innocent, peaceful Indians who were camped nearby. Fall Creek, a settlement about 100 miles northwest of Cincinnati, Ohio, was on the frontier of white civilization. The people who lived there had pushed westward to find their own land, enduring hardships, including Indian raids, before reaching their goal. For many years whites had been killing Indians who were in their way; seldom had they been punished by their communities for their deeds. This time, however, was different.

Comment

Threatened by reprisals from Seneca warriors, the United States government agreed to try the men for murder. If found guilty, they would hang. This book presents a fictionalized account of the crime itself, the trial, and the verdict. The Indians, the settlers, the lawyers for both sides, the accused and their families, all are made vivid and memorable in this moving tale. The lesson regarding what can happen to otherwise moral people who dehumanize those of other cultures or races has its applications today.

Suggestions for Reports or Activities

1. One of the reasons offered for holding the trial was that in the future whites would understand that Indians were not to be killed just because they were "in the way." Was this understanding in fact learned? Why or why not?

2. What happened to the Senecas, the Osage, the Mingos, and the other tribes mentioned as the white settlers moved West? Where are members of these tribes living now? What kind of lives are they leading?

3. Select one of the fictional characters in the story and write another chapter about what happened to him or her. Possibilities are Hannah and Charlie Fort, Johnny Wood, Ben or Caleb Cape, Ora Bemis, or others.

Mr. Tucket   Gary Paulsen
New York: Delacorte, 1994. 166p. (2, 3)

Francis Alphonse Tucket celebrates his fourteenth birthday in 1848 on a wagon train heading west on the Oregon Trail. His father encourages him to stay a little way behind the others in order to practice shooting his brand-new rifle. But Francis dallies too long and is captured by a band of Pawnee Indians. Rescued from the Pawnees by a mountain man named Mr. Grimes, the youngster learns to ride bareback, fight an Indian youth for a pony and a buckskin suit, trap beavers, and shoot straight. Then Francis has to decide if he wants to live by the rules of the plains or head farther west to try to find his folks.

Comment

In the mid-nineteenth century many settlers from the East were heading west along the Oregon Trail to make new lives for themselves. Indian raids were one of the hazards they had to face as they passed through Indian territory. This is a fast-paced story of one young pioneer's transformation from a Missouri farm boy into a hardened rider of the plains.

Suggestions for Reports or Activities

1. What was the Oregon Trail? When was it first traveled, and by whom? On an outline map of the United States trace the path of the Oregon Trail and attach a descriptive or explanatory paragraph.

2. Three Indian tribes are mentioned in this book: the Pawnee, the Crow, and the Sioux. In the mid-nineteen hundreds, what territories did they claim? Were they at peace with one another, or were there frequent fights among them?

3. Francis decides at the end to leave Mr. Grimes to his life and to try to return to his family. List the reasons he gives in favor of going and those in favor of staying with his friend. Do you think he made the right decision? Why or why not?

My Daniel   Pam Conrad
New York: Harper & Row, 1989. 137p. (2, 3)

It's 1885, and Julia Creath and her brother Daniel are living with their parents on a lonely Nebraska farm. Daniel, who has always been interested in fossils, is inspired by the tales of a pair of dinosaur prospectors to search for his very own cache of dinosaur bones. Once he has found them, his next challenge is to preserve them for an honorable paleontologist by keeping away the thief and possible murderer Hump Hinton, who is also looking for them. Near the end of her life, Julia tells her grandchildren this story of ambition, mystery, suspense, and ultimate tragedy.

Comment

Told from the point of view of a twelve-year-old girl, this fictionalized account of the discovery of dinosaur bones in the Midwest illuminates the heartaches and delights of prairie life near the turn of the last century. The loneliness, the babies who died soon after birth, the fear and superstition are balanced by independence, self-sufficiency, and a closeness to nature that has disappeared with the transition to city living.

Suggestions for Reports and Activities

1. What do we know about the "dinosaur prospectors"? Find out when they existed, who they were, what they found, what they did with their finds. Did anybody locate dinosaur bones in the midwestern U.S.? If so, when was this, what kind of dinosaurs were they, and what happened to them?

2. Learn more about Nebraska at this period. What was its population, what kind of climate did it have, and what did its people do? Were they all farmers? When was Nebraska settled, and when did it become a state? Were there any Native Americans living there? What became of them?

3. Speculate as to what might have happened to Amba. If she had written her own story, what might she have said? Include information about how she came to be with Hump Hinton and where she went after his death.

The No-Return Trail   Sonia Levitin
New York: Harcourt, 1978. 154p. (2, 3)
Toward the end of the book, Ben Kelsey reflects, "I reckon I'll remember it for always. And everything we've seen. Even the bad parts, like the stampede and the river crossings and the freezing rain. I'll remember it when I'm old. . . ." For Ben and for Nancy, his wife, the trip by wagon to California along the "no-return trail" is a time

of profound growth and a test of their love. This is especially Nancy's story. Seventeen years old, timid, even terrified, dependent, fearful for their baby, aiming only to please Ben, Nancy discovers that she has immense resources as well as physical endurance and plain common sense. In the end it is Nancy who forces the remnant of the group to hold together and makes the joyous conclusion possible.

Comment

This book is based on the true story of the Bidwell-Bartelson expedition in 1841, the first wagon train to make the trip from Missouri to California. After half of the group decided to take the easier trail for Oregon instead, Nancy found herself the only woman in the party. The hardships encountered by pioneers—hunger, cold, heat, Indians, buffalo stampedes, illness, death, personality clashes and disputes—and the will to persevere to the end provide young readers an inspiring tribute to the indefatigable human spirit.

Suggestions for Reports or Activities

1. This expedition set out for California before the great Gold Rush. They were not in a hurry to get rich. Why did they go? Check in an encyclopedia for information about the earliest settlements in California. Write a short paper on the settling of California.

2. Read about the Gold Rush. Can you find out about some of the fortunate people who actually became rich?

3. One of the reasons for moving West was the lure of new frontiers to cross. What frontiers are there today? Do you feel that it is important for human beings to look for new frontiers? Explain.

Only Earth and Sky Last Forever   Nathaniel Benchley
New York: Harper, 1972. 189p. (2, 3)

Dark Elk has grown up in a U.S. government Indian agency, away from opportunities to take part in traditional tribal feats of bravery. How will he be able to impress Lashuka's grandmother with his worthiness and win Lashuka's love? In the sacred Black Hills he will ask for a vision. Perhaps if he can capture an eagle . . . ? But soon Dark Elk realizes that the real cause—for himself, for Lashuka, and for all of the Indian people—is the fight against the ever-encroaching whites and their broken promises. The Black Hills were to be forever Indian lands. Now the whites wish to dig there for gold. Dark Elk decides to join Crazy Horse and "go with the hostiles."

Comment

Written from an Indian point of view, this book describes the frustrations and disappointments brought about by broken treaties and the desecration of sacred lands. The book gives insights into the relationships between tribes caught in the turmoil of the white advance. Included are a description of the meetings between Indian leaders and white representatives from Washington shortly before the battle of the Little Bighorn and an account of the battle. Customs and traditions are described, such as the importance for a young man to demonstrate his bravery, the respect accorded older people, counting coup, and dressing for battle.

Suggestions for Reports or Activities

1. This story ends with a description of the battle of the Little Bighorn. Read another account of this battle in your textbook or in an encyclopedia. How do the two accounts differ?

2. Basing your discussion on events described in the story, what was the meaning of the phrase attributed to Crazy Horse, "One does not go to a hilltop for water nor to the white man for truth"?

3. What were the terms of the Treaty of 1868 mentioned on page 18? Chapter 6 of the novel gives information on how the U.S. government wanted to change these terms. Discuss.

4. Check in another source (textbook or encyclopedia) for information on Crazy Horse. How does the account in Benchley's book supplement it?

Orphan Train   James Magnuson and Dorothea G. Petrie
New York: Dial, 1978. 307p. (1, 2)

Emma Symns has her hands full. When her clergyman uncle falls ill in Albany and has to stay behind, Emma vows to be responsible for completing their mission: to travel by train escorting twenty-seven New York City street children to hoped-for new homes in the Midwest. A minister from Illinois has written that several children from his church died in the winter, and his congregation will welcome new children to replace those lost. Here is truly a motley collection of irrepressible young people who have had to live by their wits, who have learned to be suspicious of adults, but who have been persuaded to join in the adventure in the hope of belonging somewhere. J. P. has been dancing in the streets for coins; Sara has been a prostitute;

Bruce and Tom can't resist a chance to fight. Some wonder, "will anyone really pick us?" At their first scheduled stop ten children are selected for homes. But it's a long, long way to Illinois; Emma's worries are far from over.

Comment

This story is drawn from accounts of the Children's Aid Society, which between 1854 and 1904 was responsible for relocating 100,000 homeless children from New York City to farms in the West. The plight of orphaned or abandoned young people who lived an Oliver Twist–type of life is vividly described. Readers will be interested in the depiction of an early train, which by present standards meanders slowly and lacks basic safety measures. The incident involving the fugitive slave shows the conflicting opinions regarding law and justice.

Suggestions for Reports or Activities

1. The development of railroads in the United States is a fascinating study. What can you find out about railroad routes in the 1850s? Note that the children did not board a train until they reached Albany. Ideas of safety were quite different. Research the progress of laws for the safe operation of railroads during the past hundred years.

2. There was some opposition to the Children's Aid Society's method of relocating homeless children. Who was opposed? What reasons lay behind this thinking? Would such a plan be feasible today?

3. There was a fugitive slave hidden in the baggage car. What was the law regarding fugitive slaves? Check in your textbook and in reference sources. Do you feel that the engineer acted correctly?

The Ox-Bow Incident   Walter van Tilburg Clark
London: Gollancz, 1940. 238p. (1)

Cattle rustling and murder—these two crimes are sure to arouse passions in Nevada frontier society. Cattle are missing, and Kinkaid is reported shot. The only answer is to raise a posse, find the criminals, and avenge Kinkaid's death. Not everyone agrees: Oxford tries to argue, Davies ardently pleads for patience. The Judge warns, "no lynching!" Nonetheless, led by the determined Major Tetley, the twenty-eight men set out on their quest. They find three men asleep in the Ox-Bow Valley and force them to an impromptu trial, with disastrous consequences. Too late they find out the truth.

Comment

This gripping story of frontier justice explores concepts of good and evil. It depicts the simple system of order that existed in the West toward the end of the past century. The book describes the rough life of men isolated from family, lonely for women, amusing themselves through drink or gambling, and quick to band together in a matter that concerns them. Questions raised about guilt and responsibility and the effects of mob hysteria are applicable to issues today.

Suggestions for Reports or Activities

1. What can you find out about Nevada in the 1880s? How important was cattle raising? What cities had been established?

2. The movies often depict the Old West as a society where men took the law into their own hands. *The Ox-Bow Incident,* a highly rated film, certainly gives this impression. How accurate is the picture of frontier justice?

3. Do you think that Davies was too hard on himself in feeling guilty for what happened? Explain his reasoning.

4. Compose a letter Martin might have written to his wife.

Piper's Ferry   G. Clifton Wisler
New York: Dutton, Lodestar, 1990. 130p. (2, 3)

Texas in the 1830s is still under Mexican rule, so when Tim Piper decides to head out there from New Orleans to take a job with a distant cousin, he's not at all sure what he will find. He finds a good friend in Zach Merkins, who then leaves for the fort called the Alamo. The leader of the defenders of the fort, Lt. Colonel Travis, has called for reinforcements and Zach can't resist. Too few others join him, however, and the fort falls to the Mexicans. Shortly thereafter the territory declares its independence from Mexico, and Tim enlists as a private soldier in the Army of Texas in time for the Battle of San Jacinto. The fate of Texas and its inhabitants will be settled before Tim's fifteenth birthday.

Comment

Readers of this book are introduced to such historical figures as Sam Houston, Stephen Austin, Davy Crockett, and Santa Anna. They also experience the different levels of civilization of settlements in the

Old South (Natchez, Mississippi, and New Orleans, Louisiana) and the West. Hostility toward the Mexican government is not universal, making the desirability of Texan independence far from obvious.

Suggestions for Reports or Activities

1. Find out more about one of the historical figures mentioned in the book. Where did he come from and what happened to him (if he survived) after the incidents discussed here?

2. Read an account of the battle at the Alamo or the one in San Jacinto. Summarize the course of the fighting, the casualties on both sides, and the final outcome. In what year did Texas become a republic?

3. Tim discovers that several of his letters to his mother never reached her. Write two of those letters, one telling of his adventures before he got to his cousin's and another telling some of what happened afterward. Make your letters exciting, but not alarming!

Prairie Songs   Pam Conrad
New York: Harper & Row, 1985. 167p. (2, 3)

Louisa is a child of the Nebraska prairie, loves its vast, lonely beauty, and is eager to welcome the new doctor and his wife who are coming from New York City to settle nearby. Emmeline is beautiful, though fragile as a flower. Best of all, she has brought a trunk full of books, and Louisa is ecstatic. At first it seems that everything will work out, especially when Emmeline agrees to have a school in her sod house for Louisa and her shy brother Lester. And even though she is apprehensive in her unpreparedness for prairie life, and fearful of possible dangers—Indians, snakes, who knows?—Emmeline does look forward to her baby. But the prairie that Louisa loves proves too much for Emmeline.

Comment

The lonely life of settlers in the vast expanses of the West could not be foreseen by all who came there from populated civilization in Eastern cities. This book describes facets of daily life on the prairie, including building houses and making them livable, planting, cooking and heating methods, education of children, scarcity of medical care, need for preparedness. It also depicts the feelings of loneliness and fear that drove some people to escape or to despair.

Suggestions for Reports or Activities

1. Consider the lives of the three families in the book. What qualities seem important for families to endure life as settlers in Nebraska at that time? Write a short paper explaining your answer and using examples from the text.

2. Basing your reply on what you have read in the book, how might you describe Nebraska? If you were going to write to Emmeline before she arrived, how would you prepare her for life on the prairie?

The Raid   G. Clifton Wisler
New York: Puffin, 1985. 120p. (2, 3)

Lige Andrews doesn't seem to be able to please his father, no matter how hard he tries. So he's disappointed, but not surprised, when his father sends him and his little brother Charlie to their uncle's ranch on the northwest Texas frontier for a visit, instead of allowing him to help take the family's horses to market. Then a joint Comanche-Kiowa raiding party captures several of the settlers, including Charlie. Stricken by guilt because he hasn't protected his brother, Lige decides to accompany Zeke Jackson, a former slave, as he searches for the raiders in order to negotiate the captives' release. When it looks as though their mission will succeed, Lige turns back to check on Zeke and finds him tied to a tree. Is there anything he can do to help him escape?

Comment

Set against a background of hostility among blacks, whites, and Indians, this adventure story illuminates the clashes of values and interests that marked the various frontiers of the American push westward. A teenage white boy is the protagonist, but the character who evokes the greatest sympathy is the ex-slave. He is portrayed as a mediator between the settlers and the local Indians, forced to leave their ancestral lands for inhospitable territory far to the north.

Suggestions for Reports or Activities

1. Read about the Kiowa and the Comanche. Where did they first live? What was their way of life? When the United States Army forced them to move, where did they go? How did their new home differ from their old one?

2. Imagine the conversation between Lige and Charlie and their father, after the book ends. How would the boys tell Papa about their adventure? First compose Charlie's account, in which he gives Lige all the credit for his rescue, and then write Lige's tale of how it really happened.

3. Zeke compares the Indian raids on white settlements with the white raids on African villages. In your opinion, how were these actions alike, and how were they different? Base your conclusions on other information you know besides what is in this book.

Season of Yellow Leaf   Douglas C. Jones
New York: Holt, 1983. 323p. (1, 2)

Morfydd Annon Parry is only ten years old when Comanches and Kiowas attack the homestead, murder her parents, and kidnap her and her mentally handicapped four-year-old brother. The Kiowas go off in a different direction with him. Morfydd, renamed Chosen, begins the long and complicated task of learning to think of herself as a Comanche maiden and later a squaw. Despite her origins, Chosen is valued as a female who can help repopulate the tribe, whose numbers have decreased alarmingly from exposure to the diseases and firearms of the white people.

Comment

Told from the points of view of both the kidnapped white girl and the Comanches with whom she lives and identifies, this story shows how people adapt—or do not adapt—to changes in their environment and circumstances. The author offers insights into the reasons for conflict between the various ethnic groups in Texas at the time. Much of the dissension and mistrust between different Indian tribes is attributed to their enforced proximity as the white people pushed west.

Suggestions for Reports or Activities

1. Investigate the historical relationships among the Mexicans, the Texans, and the Native Americans. Which group of whites appears to be most responsible for pushing the Indians off their traditional lands? Did the tribes respond differently to the different whites? How? When?

2. Explore the role of the whites who became Indian traders. How were they treated by the Indians? How did their treatment change over time?

3. When Chosen ultimately returns to the whites who had known her as a child, her son goes off with his Indian aunt. What do you think happened to him? Did he ever see his mother again? Write another chapter for the book.

Shane   Jack Schaefer
Boston: Houghton Mifflin, 1949. 214p. (1, 2)

A mysterious stranger comes into the lives of homesteading Jim Starrett and his wife and son, affecting them all in different ways and leaving behind a challenge. Young Bob Starrett tells the story of how Shane appears from nowhere, wins his family's confidence, and agrees to move in to help with the work of the farm. Shane finds himself in the center of a bitter dispute between Fletcher, the unscrupulous cattle rancher, and the unprotected farmers. Fletcher has a government contract to supply beef to the Indian agent and is determined to appropriate the homesteaders' land to expand his grazing territory. There are some exciting encounters between the good guys and the bad guys. But who is Shane?

Comment

Some of the quality of yesterday's best western films comes through in this novel. It portrays the struggle to hold on to one's property at a time and place where law and order were in the hands of whoever could make other people do what he wanted. The values of standing up for what you think is right, of acting with courage in the face of danger, and of finishing something you have started are presented in an exciting story. Readers will experience the flavor of the raw days in the West.

Suggestions for Reports or Activities

1. The Starretts were being forced to give up their land. What can you find out about the legal rights of homesteaders? What was guaranteed by the government?

2. Where do you think Shane came from? Write an imaginary autobiography of his life before his time with the Starretts. Where was he going when he arrived at their place? What do you think happened to him after he rode away?

3. When did Wyoming become a state? What towns had been settled by the time of this story? Can you locate settlements on an outline map of Wyoming? Where might the Starretts' homestead have been located?

Sing Down the Moon   Scott O'Dell
Boston: Houghton Mifflin, 1970. 137p. (3)

When the Long Knives (U.S. soldiers) begin systematically and ruthlessly to force the Navahos to leave their beloved canyon, the people of Bright Morning's village refuse to obey, even when their homes have been burned to the ground. However, after their crops have been destroyed, they give in and begin the "Long Walk" to Fort Sumner and captivity. It is a time of suffering and sadness. But Bright Morning, determined to return to the canyon, convinces Tall Boy, her husband, that they can live in freedom. Through some risky maneuvers they make their way back despite the tremendous odds against them.

Comment

U.S. government policies toward Native Americans that seemed justified at the time but are difficult to accept today are described, along with the picture of the unquenchable spirit of the Navahos, who maintain their traditions and celebrate life despite privation and cruel treatment.

Suggestions for Reports or Activities

1. At the time of the story, why did the U.S. government force the Navahos to leave their homes? What effect has this had on the history of the Navahos since that time?

2. From the descriptions in the book, what can you learn about the Navaho attitude toward nature and the environment?

3. Bright Morning participated in a "womanhood ceremony." Describe the tasks she had to perform. Why do you think the author included this ceremony in the story?

The Snowbird   Patricia Calvert
New York: Scribner, 1980. 146p. (2, 3)

Willie Bannerman admits she's out of step, "marching left when everyone else is marching right." Maybe that's because she has inherited her parents' gift for dreaming and telling. Spunky, high-spirited, and clever with words, she plans to be a writer. Orphaned after fire destroys their parents' newspaper plant, Willie and her young brother, T. J., are sent by train from Tennessee to the Dakota Territory to live with their father's brother, Uncle Randall, and his flamboyant redheaded wife, Belle. Belle, too, is a dreamer, making the best of her life on the prairie, dreaming of a mansion to replace their sod house. The birth of a silvery foal the night that Willie and T. J. arrive seems to be a good omen. Willie names the foal Snowbird, sensing that there is something different about this foal, just as she knows she is different too, "caught between being and becoming." The story is her journal.

Comment

Prairie life is portrayed as harsh but manageable, and the people as tough, persistent, and full of hope despite disappointments. Readers will experience some facets of everyday existence, such as the sod house, the one-room school, the itinerant preacher, the loss of a new-born baby, and the appreciation of small joys. There is also an aware-ness of new immigrants arriving, confident in the promise of the new life. Even though the Snowbird vanishes, and Belle also leaves, the reader knows that here in the Dakota Territory things will work out for Willie.

Suggestions for Reports or Activities

1. Imagine that you are Willie, writing a letter about the Dakota Territory, trying to impress your friend Beth Ellen back in Tennessee. What would you include? What would you omit?

2. Check in an encyclopedia or other source for information on the settling of the Dakota Territory. What were its boundaries? When did whites move into the area? Where did they come from?

3. Select one facet of life in the territory, such as the sod house or the school or the farm. Write a short paper.

4. What do you think is the significance of the Snowbird? How is the foal related to Willie? To Belle?

The Sodbuster Venture   Charlene Joy Talbot
New York: Atheneum, 1982. 194p. (2, 3)

Glad to be out of her sister's house, thirteen-year-old Maud has been taking care of gravely ill Mr. Nelson. At the point of death, Mr.

Nelson asks Maud to persuade his fiancée, Belle Warren (at that very moment on her way from the East for their wedding), to stay and try to make a go of his claim. He wants her to farm the land for one year. Belle arrives just in time for Mr. Nelson's funeral. Bravely she decides that she will try to carry out his wishes, and Maud is happy to stay on and help her. Certain that a woman cannot possibly manage, the Coddington brothers, drunken ne'er-do-wells, plot to claim the land for themselves. Maud helps Belle get to the land office first and officially register her right to her fiancé's claim. Belle and Maud together endure despite the grasshopper infestation, cattle disease, endless dust, the long winter, and harassment by the Coddington brothers. There is some unexpected help as Maud makes a new friend.

Comment

Maud and Belle demonstrate the brave spirit, determination, and physical endurance of hardy pioneer women. A good picture of early life in Kansas, this book provides readers a sense of the mushrooming growth of the state as Civil War veterans thronged in to claim their promised 160 acres.

Suggestions for Reports or Activities

1. Check an encyclopedia for information on the early history of Kansas. Where did the settlers come from? What can you find out about the government promise of land? When did Kansas become a state? How many people had to live in an area before it could achieve statehood?

2. Belle Warren came from Maine to live on the prairie. In what ways was her life different from what she had known before?

3. Maud at thirteen had some very adult responsibilities. Compare her life with that of a teenager in the United States today. Some teenagers have more responsibilities than others. Write a short paper on how Maud's life is different from yours.

4. List ten adjectives to describe Maud. Write a character sketch of Maud using these adjectives and pointing out sections of the book in which she demonstrates these character traits.

Streams to the River, River to the Sea   Scott O'Dell
Boston: Houghton Mifflin, 1986. 191p. (2)

Sacagawea, the young Indian woman who aided the expedition of Lewis and Clark, tells her story. Kidnapped from her own Shoshone village by neighboring enemy tribesmen and betrothed to the son of their chief, she is given away in a game of chance to become a second wife to Charbonneau, a half-Sioux, half-French trader. The Shoshone thought his friendship was important for the sake of trade. Sacagawea's life changes when Captains Lewis and Clark, leading a U.S. government search for a northwest passage to the Pacific, hire Charbonneau for his knowledge of the rivers and Sacagawea for her familiarity with the ways of Indians whose lands the group must traverse. This story shows the expedition as Sacagawea experiences it, a young wife treated hardly better than a slave, caring for her baby, and finding herself falling in love with Captain Clark.

Comment

The author states that he has relied on the journals of Lewis and Clark. He has chosen to emphasize the role of Sacagawea, positing a possible romantic link between Clark and his Indian interpreter. The inclusion of the black member of the group, Ben York (actually Clark's slave), helps to document the generally unknown role black people played in important historical events. The study of flora and fauna on the route was part of the trip's purpose. The importance of good relations with the Indians in order to accomplish the goals of the young United States is indicated.

Suggestions for Reports or Activities

1. How does this description of Sacagawea's role in the Lewis and Clark expedition correspond with the information in your textbook? What additional information can you discover in an encyclopedia or other source?

2. Why did Captain Lewis want to gather specimens of plant and animal life? What other purposes did the expedition have besides locating a route to the Pacific?

3. Trace on an outline map the route of Lewis and Clark. Include the areas where different Indians mentioned in the book lived.

4. Can you find data to document the role of French fur traders in exploring the West? Write a short paper on your findings.

Wait for Me, Watch for Me, Eula Bee   Patricia Beatty
New York: Morrow, 1978. 221p. (2, 3)

Only Lewallen and his four-year-old sister, Eula Bee, survive the Comanche attack on the Collier family's west Texas farm. Carried off to the Indian camp, Lewallen becomes the property of Many Horses, leader of the war party. Eula Bee is given to another chief and kept separated from her brother. But Lewallen is determined to find a way for both to be freed. When he instinctively saves Many Horses from a buffalo stampede, he is rewarded by being allowed to lead the horses to pasture. Lewallen seizes this chance to escape, but when he returns a year later to rescue Eula Bee he is dismayed by her response.

Comment

The author explains in a note that the Comanches and Kiowas pillaged Texas villages and carried off white captives who were sometimes traded for goods and sometimes bought back by their families. But many remained with their captors, becoming members of the tribe. The book allows readers to see several facets of life in Texas during the Civil War, from different points of view: for example, Confederate and Union soldiers, Indians from two different tribes, Comancheros, and settlers. Some Indian traditions are described, such as the importance of hair to the Kiowa braves. In cutting off Small Wolf's braid, Lewallen destroyed a prized symbol of manhood.

Suggestions for Reports or Activities

1. Explain why Grass Woman remained loyal to Many Horses. Why would it have been easy for Eula Bee to become part of the tribe? What would be the advantages in being regarded as an Indian?

2. Find information on the relationships between white settlers, Indians, and Mexicans in Texas at the time of the story. What was the reason for the Colliers' feelings against the Cabrals? Who were the Comancheros? How did their activities affect Indian-settler relationships?

3. What customs and traditions of the Comanches are described?

Weasel   Cynthia DeFelice
New York: Macmillan, 1990. 119p. (2, 3)

Ohio in 1839 is part of the frontier. The Shawnee Indians who used to live on the land have been killed or forced to move west to Kansas or Oklahoma, but the law of the cities is not enforced and evil deeds may go unpunished for a long time. One day, the father of eleven-year-old Nathan Fowler and his younger sister Molly fails to return from a hunting trip, and the children worry for days, not knowing what has happened to him. When a mute stranger appears with their dead mother's locket in his hand, Nathan and Molly decide that it must be a sign from their father and agree to follow him. Before they go back to their cabin, Nathan comes face to face with the wicked Indian fighter turned outlaw who is known as Weasel. As time goes on, he has to weigh his desire for revenge against his father's warning that he must not fight evil with evil.

Comment

The story of how the white men pushed the Indians off their land is told here from the point of view of a young settler who initially sees nothing wrong with what happened. As he learns of the cruelty of some whites toward the Indians, and the indifference of others, he comes to understand that people and events are not always what they seem.

Suggestions for Reports or Activities

1. Daniel Boone was captured leading a hunting party onto Shawnee land in 1769. Compare the novel's account of this incident with that in a biography of Boone or in a history of the period.

2. Imagine that Nathan had killed Weasel with his father's gun as he was escaping from the cabin. Would that have made him happy? Write how you think he would have felt and why.

3. Find out what happened to the Shawnee when they went west. Do you think Ezra ever caught up with them?

Young Pioneers   Rose Wilder Lane
New York: McGraw-Hill, 1976 (published in 1933 as *Let the Hurricane Roar*). 152p. (2, 3)

Eighteen-year-old Charles and his young bride, Caroline, set off into the Dakota Territory to seek a homestead. On the lonely prairie they have a dugout to live in, a barn, fifty acres of sod already broken for plowing, and a creek with two wild plum trees. In five years, if they stay and work the land, they will have clear title to their claim. Their baby is born on Caroline's seventeenth birthday, congenial neighbors begin building half a mile away, and Charles' wheat promises a rich harvest—until the grasshoppers come. Forced to seek work back in the East, Charles leaves Caroline and baby Charles John. But no one expects that she will have to face the winter alone.

Comment

This book poignantly describes the sturdy determination and hopeful outlook of young pioneers in the face of severe privation and loneliness. Living by their own ingenuity and hard work, they learned to deal with bitter cold and blizzards, heat and fierce winds, wolves, the threat of claim-jumpers taking over their land, and unexpected disasters such as the grasshopper infestation. Caroline's bravery is a testimony to the survival qualities of women who settled the West.

Suggestions for Reports or Activities

1. Caroline wrote a letter to Charles that she could not mail. She might have kept a diary of that lonely time. Create a diary for Caroline, including at least three entries.

2. Check into the regulations regarding homesteading during the mid-nineteenth century. Can you find information on the growth of population in the Dakota Territory?

3. The Svensons came from Sweden. From what other places did settlers come to the Dakota Territory?

4. Two types of houses are described in the story. Find out about how sod shanties and dugouts were constructed. There are some details given in the book, but you will have to look for additional information in another source.

MORE CHALLENGING BOOKS
FOR ADVANCED READERS

The Camp Grant Massacre   Elliott Arnold
New York: Simon & Schuster, 1976. 447p.

This novel recreates the tragic true story of the massacre of an unarmed Apache tribe in Tucson, Arizona. Contrary to tradition, it is the cruelty, betrayal, and hatefulness of the whites and Mexicans that destroy the efforts of the commander of Camp Grant and the Apaches to forge a new relationship based on trust and compassion.

Cimarron   Edna Ferber
Garden City, N.Y.: Doubleday, 1929. 388p.

After Yancey and Sabra Cravat move to the town of Osage, in Indian Territory (later the state of Oklahoma), Sabra comes to set the style for the community. The author paints a vivid picture of the growing settlement, the accommodation of white and Indian populations, and the transformation of Eastern or Southern lifestyles to suit the ruggedness of the new territory.

Creek Mary's Blood   Dee Brown
New York: Holt, 1980. 401p.

The westward encroachment of European civilization upon the Native American way of life is chronicled through such events as the forced journey of the Cherokee nation to the West. This novel presents a powerful and personalized account of the clash between two opposing cultures.

Giants in the Earth: A Saga of the Prairie   Ole Rolvaag
New York: Harper, 1927. 465p.

Rolvaag's tale, translated from the Norwegian, offers a vivid picture of the hardships faced by the Scandinavian settlers in South Dakota. The land itself figures throughout as a kind of demon or troll with whom the settlers must constantly do battle. Other confrontations are with locusts, snowstorms, rival claimants to the same land, and bouts of homesickness and doubt.

Little Big Man   Thomas Berger
New York: Delacorte, 1964. 440p.

Jack Crabb, adopted into a Cheyenne tribe as a child, describes his adventures, including his survival of the battle of the Little Bighorn, in which all the whites reportedly died. His frequent moves between the white and Indian worlds allow him to participate in the traditional activities of the western frontier: cheating at poker, learning to shoot, visiting a bordello, fighting with and against the Indians, and hunting buffalo. Particularly valuable are those episodes seen from the point of view of the Indians.

My Ántonia   Willa Cather
Boston: Houghton Mifflin, 1918. 372p.

This story of an immigrant family from Bohemia totally unprepared for the demands of frontier life presents a lasting sense of the rhythms of life on the Nebraska prairie at the end of the nineteenth century. The compassion of some of the earlier settlers of English and Irish origins for their new immigrant neighbors is contrasted with the condescension and contempt of others.

No Resting Place   William Humphrey
New York: Delacorte, Seymour Lawrence, 1989. 249p.

The Cherokee Indians of the state of Georgia, including those who have been Christian for generations, are forced to move west along the Trail of Tears. Nothing—not the white man's God nor the Chief Justice of the Supreme Court—can change their fate.

The Predators   F. M. Parker
New York: NAL, 1990. 280p.

In 1859 a group of Mormon converts, mostly young women, pull carts filled with their belongings across the trackless Great Plains and the Rocky Mountains. Their lives are threatened by heat, starvation, lustful Indians, and unscrupulous bandits.

The Way West   A. B. Guthrie
New York: Sloan, 1949. 340p.

Here is a fine picture of the way a wagon train gets started: finding enough of the right people to go; electing a governing council; establishing rules and levying taxes; imposing punishments; setting the amount of provisions per person. The trip to Oregon encompasses boredom and seeming endlessness, problems with weather and Indians, individual fears and concerns, and the necessity of adapting to and caring for one's traveling companions.

V Immigration, Industrialization, Urbanization

After the Dancing Days   Margaret I. Rostkowski
New York: Harper & Row, 1986. 217p. (2)

His face is so horribly burned that Annie is repulsed. But gradually she learns to accept Andrew for himself. Despite her mother's firm objections, Annie spends her summer days assisting at the soldiers' hospital where her father, a doctor, is treating wounded World War I veterans. Annie finds in Andrew a true friend; her caring draws him out of his shell and helps him realize that life is still worthwhile. Andrew helps her find out what actually happened to her favorite Uncle Paul, who did not return from the war. Annie matures over the summer. Her experience at the hospital makes her aware of the reality that, for some people, the war will never end.

Comment

This story, set in a small midwestern town, dramatizes the long-term effect of war on both those who had to fight and those who did not. The townspeople's narrowly patriotic feelings are expressed in the war memorial, the parade, and their reactions to the wounded veterans. Annie's mother's attitudes seem to typify those of many people who would rather look the other way than be involved with either painful memories or present suffering. Descriptions of life in the trenches give a poignant picture of the day-to-day existence of foot soldiers during World War I.

Suggestions for Reports or Activities

1. Look up information on the Purple Heart. Write a short paper on its history and how one earns it.

2. Andrew mentions fighting at Belleau Wood. Look up this battle in your textbook or other source. Where were the important scenes of fighting in France during World War I? Draw a simple map locating these places.

3. What is a hero? Was Annie's uncle less of a hero than Andrew? Explain.

4. What is the significance of the title? How does Andrew show that all is not over "after the dancing days"?

April Harvest   Lillian Budd
New York: Duell, 1959. 309p. (1, 2)

Seventeen-year-old Sigrid, daughter of Swedish immigrants, orphaned and alone after the death of her father, is determined to be self-sufficient. Rejecting help from neighbors, she figures out a plan to keep her family's house; establishes contact with her long-lost grandmother in Sweden; rescues her friends' son Michael in the disastrous boating accident that kills his parents; nurses her pastor's wife during her terminal illness; and bravely breaks off plans for what she is sure will be an unsuccessful marriage. In a stroke of good fortune, through winning a writing contest (based on her father's diaries), Sigrid has enough money to visit her Swedish relatives. There she discovers a surprising fact concerning her treasured blue wool shawl and unravels some family history.

Comment

Of most significance is the picture of immigrants becoming part of American society. The prejudice experienced by the Swedish is described in Sigrid's father's journals. Newcomers established close communities where they could give support to each other, as shown in the way that Sigrid's neighbors rallied around her when her father died. Becoming thoroughly Americanized was important to immigrants; Sigrid had not learned any Swedish and knew little of her heritage, as a result of her parents' desire to become assimilated. In the background of the story are the election of Woodrow Wilson, World War I, and Prohibition, and the way these events affected the lives of Sigrid's community.

Suggestions for Reports or Activities

1. Using an encyclopedia, find out where people from Sweden settled in the United States. When did the Swedish begin to arrive? What was the impetus to leave Sweden?

2. Sigrid's father's name was changed at Ellis Island. Find out about the procedures that took place at Ellis Island as the immigrants arrived. Why were names changed?

3. How might the story have been different if Sigrid's father's name had not been changed?

Call Me Ruth   Marilyn Sachs
Garden City, N.Y.: Doubleday, 1982. 131p. (2, 3)

Eight-year-old Rifka, while sorry to leave her grandparents behind in Russia, is excited about going to the United States, where she will finally meet the father she has never seen. Her twenty-four-year-old mother, apprehensive about the move and her new responsibilities, finds adjustment to life in a New York tenement almost more than she can stand. While Rifka, now known as Ruth, tries to emulate and please her teachers, Faigel (or Fanny) cries from homesickness and frustration. Eventually, Fanny finds identity and recognition as a member of the International Ladies' Garment Workers' Union, even though Ruth continues to be embarrassed by her mother's broken English, work-worn hands, and unstylish clothes.

Comment

Told from the point of view of Rifka, now called Ruth, this story vividly portrays the intergenerational immigrant conflict between the child who is working hard to belong and the parent who strives for dignity and self-esteem by challenging the "establishment." Ruth's insensitivity to Fanny's situation is mitigated only by her affection for her mother and her wistfulness when she thinks back to the time in Russia when all they had was each other.

Suggestions for Reports or Activities

1. Look up the history of the International Ladies' Garment Workers' Union: When did it begin? Who were its first members? What were working conditions like when the union called its first strike? Can you find out any more about the Shirtwaist Makers' Strike of 1909 than you learned from this book?

2. What values does Miss Baxter promote? What kinds of behavior does she find inappropriate? Write a letter from her to Ruth in which she praises her for what she considers Ruth's good qualities and chides her for what she thinks is bad or unmannerly.

3. Suppose Ruth had brought her mother to meet Miss Baxter on Parents' Day: What would they have said to each other? Write the

dialogue for their interview based on what you think they might have said about Ruth.

4. Describe living and working conditions for immigrants on the Lower East Side in the early 1900s. What problems did they have? How long was their work week or day? What did they do, or where did they go, for fun?

Dragon's Gate   Laurence Yep
New York: HarperCollins, 1993. 273p. (1, 2)

Fourteen-year-old Otter, living in Kwangtung Province, China, in 1865, is delighted to join his father and uncle in helping build the great transcontinental railroad across America. Once in California, however, Otter discovers that the Chinese workers are no more than slaves, working long hours in bitter cold and dangerous conditions. The Chinese are whipped when they disobey and are forbidden to leave their jobs chiseling a path for the railroad through the Sierra Nevada. As he copes with disabling accidents and natural disasters, Otter refashions his dreams to conform with reality, even as he volunteers to try to save his fellow workers from an impending avalanche. (Other books featuring some of the same characters are *Dragonwings*, *Mountain Light*, and *The Star Fisher*, below.)

Comment

A gripping account of the experiences of the Chinese working on the transcontinental railroad, this novel challenges the young reader to adopt the viewpoint of the Chinese toward their "western" bosses. The author notes that as many as twelve hundred Chinese, or 10 percent of the Chinese workers, are estimated to have died building the railroad. Ten tons of bones were shipped back to China. The assignment of the workers to teams based on their province of origin may also remind readers of the way in which different ethnic groups have chosen to settle in separate neighborhoods in American cities.

Suggestions for Reports or Activities

1. Find one of the books or newspapers listed by the author in his "Afterword." Write about something you learned from reading it that supported one of the events in the novel.

2. Check a history of China to find out when the Manchus were overthrown and who succeeded them as rulers of China. How old would Otter have been at that time? Speculate on whether what he

learned in the United States might have helped in getting rid of the Manchus.

3. According to the author, more than ten thousand Chinese survived building the railroad. What happened to them? Check a history of immigration into the U.S. to see how many of them stayed on. Where did they go? What did they do? How many Chinese are in the U.S. today?

Dragonwings   Laurence Yep
New York: Harper & Row, 1975. 248p. (1, 2)

Moon Shadow tells his story. When he is eight years old, his father, Windrider, sends for him to come from China to America, the "demon" land, where many Chinese men have gone to work as laborers to save and to send money home. The country of the demons is strange, and the demons do not like the Chinese. But the Chinese stay together in the Tang village and support each other. Windrider, a talented kite maker, is a dreamer. Inspired by news of the Wright brothers' invention, he, too, wants to make a flying machine. Through a lucky chance he gets a job working as a handyman out in the demon community, and he and Moon Shadow move to a former stable owned by Miss Whitlaw, who is different from other demons. A firm friendship is established with Miss Whitlaw and her niece, Robin, that lasts even through the great San Francisco earthquake and fire. Windrider continues to pursue his dream of flying. (Other books featuring some of the same characters are *Dragon's Gate,* above, and *Mountain Light* and *The Star Fisher,* below.)

Comment

This story describes how the Chinese came to America and the difficulties they faced in being accepted. Life in the Chinese section of San Francisco was guided by the old principles as passed down through the generations, but it was also necessary to learn to live in the demon country. This story, written from a Chinese point of view, will give readers the chance to appreciate from that perspective the unfriendliness and prejudice with which the immigrants were confronted. The great San Francisco earthquake and fire are touched on.

Suggestions for Reports or Activities

1. Find out about the beginning of the immigration of the Chinese to the United States. Why did they come? Where did they settle?

What kinds of jobs were they able to find? Why were the women left behind?

2. The United States established quotas limiting the number of Chinese immigrants. Write a short paper explaining this policy. How has the policy changed through the years?

3. Read about the great San Francisco earthquake. Write a paper including information about its effect on the Chinese community.

4. From information in the book and additional information in an encyclopedia or other source, discuss the meaning of dragons in Chinese tradition.

5. Write a letter that Moon Shadow might have sent to his mother describing his life in the land of the demons.

The House of Mirth   Edith Wharton
New York: Scribner, 1905. 329p. (1)

This story depicts New York society and its skewed values and false ideals at the turn of the century. Prominent socialite Lily Bart discovers that beauty and intelligence without money cannot ensure position. Gus Trenor, whose wife has befriended Lily, woos her with money under false pretenses; Sim Rosedale, up-and-coming Jewish financier, pursues her, but she rejects his advances until too late; long-time friend Lawrence Selden cannot resolve his feelings toward her; and social butterfly Bertha Dorset, thinking Lily is pursuing her wealthy husband, spreads false stories about her. With her reputation sullied, albeit unjustly, Lily sinks ever lower in the social scale. She resorts to using her knowledge of society to assist a succession of newcomers to gain entry. Ironically, they succeed while Lily's descent continues. Ultimately, she lands employment in a millinery shop, only to realize that her social upbringing has not equipped her for the life of a working woman. Bereft of hope, she takes her life hours before the priggish Selden decides to propose marriage.

Comment

Having grown up in New York society in the Gilded Age, the author writes with an insider's knowledge. That world was clearly held together by money and the social ambitions of wives. Far from being a closed society, it took in the new millionaires, provided they were willing to spend money on the right things and learn the correct manners. Matchless are the descriptions of the homes of the idle rich, their architecture, and their interior furnishings, lending credence to characterizations of the period as "the brown decades" and "the gingerbread age."

Suggestions for Reports or Activities

1. The author stands as one of this country's foremost novelists of manners. What important manners are dealt with in this story? Do they tell us something meaningful about the times? Have things changed significantly in the years since?

2. *The House of Mirth* is clearly a "woman's novel." Not only is the leading character female, but there is no sympathetic male character. Why is there no such character? Are there ways in which the story might be viewed in terms of women's liberation?

3. Does the author's treatment of Rosedale suggest anti-Semitism? Or should that treatment be seen more in terms of social class than of ethnicity? What was the situation facing wealthy Jews in that period?

I Be Somebody   Hadley Irwin
A Margaret K. McElderry Book. New York: Atheneum, 1984.
170p. (2, 3)

Ten-year-old Anson J. (Rap) Davis lives in Oklahoma in 1910. Founded by black people leaving the South after the Civil War, the town of Clearview is about to come under white folks' law, and its black inhabitants are becoming nervous. Many of them are thinking about moving to Alberta, a province of Canada, where they hope they will be safe. Rap's Aunt Spicy is considering going along, while Rap tries to figure out who or what Jim Crow might be. Then a strange fellow, part black, part Indian, named Jesse Creek starts hanging around, and Rap doesn't know what to make of him. As he struggles also to unravel his own identity, Rap matures and learns to make some important decisions by himself.

Comment

Many of the blacks who moved west after the Civil War did not find the place of refuge they were seeking. Some of them moved on to Canada, despite propaganda indicating that black people could not survive in the cold weather of the far North. This story presents some of the pros and cons faced by people determined to live out their dreams despite obstacles and resistance from others. It also notes the interdependence of blacks and Indians who found themselves in the same spot at the same time.

Suggestions for Reports or Activities

1. Explore the place of black people in Canadian society, particularly in the prairie provinces of Alberta, Saskatchewan, and British Columbia. When did they start coming in substantial numbers; where did they settle; what happened to them?

2. Rap has to figure out who he is and what matters to him. Tell how *you* know who you are and what's important to you. What part of your identity depends on you and your family, and what part depends on how people outside your family or your neighborhood view you?

3. Find out about the relations of blacks and Indians in the Western territories after the Civil War. Did they mostly get along, or did they fight? What factors might have led them to be friends or to become enemies?

The Keeping-Room   Betty Levin
New York: Greenwillow, 1981. 247p. (2)

A social studies project sends Hal into an exploration of the land near his house where a developer is putting up new houses. Interviewing elderly Hattie and her infirm brother Harvey, whose family had settled on the land at the time of the American Revolution, he learns about the Candlewood Curse. Hannah, the great-aunt of Hattie and Harvey, twelve years old at the time, ran away from her job in the Lowell clothing mills and returned home to the farm to protect the family's claim to the land, but she disappeared. Some old magazine stories by Hattie's grandmother provide some clues, and a bulldozer leads to the rest. In counterpoint to this story is the tale of Emily, daughter of Hal's social studies teacher, and her possible connection with Hannah.

Comment

British author Jill Paton Walsh commented on the superb sense of history in this novel provided by the interweaving of the stories of Hannah and Emily. Young readers will derive an awareness of their own connectedness to their family's past, while absorbing specific information about the life of young children in the mills and about survival under primitive conditions.

Suggestions for Reports or Activities

1. Look for information about the clothing mills in New England, particularly in Lowell, Massachusetts. What can you find out about the plight of young children in the mills? When were child labor laws enacted in the United States? How did these laws affect the lives of children?

2. How was Hannah able to survive without being noticed? What did she have to do to make her "keeping-room" habitable and her daily life possible?

3. Hannah felt that she had to live on the land to keep it from slipping out of her family's hands. Was she correct in this belief? Explain how you arrived at your conclusion.

Land of Dreams   Joan Lowery Nixon
Ellis Island series
New York: Delacorte, 1994. 152p. (2, 3)

It is 1902, and Swedish-born Kristin is beginning a new life with her parents in Minnesota. While reluctant to leave her grandmother and friends, the impatient sixteen-year-old is looking forward to having more freedom to be herself in this new country. Her disappointment at the discovery that her parents and their friends are intent on making their lives correspond as much as possible to what they were in Sweden increases with every setback she encounters. She even refuses to marry a boy she likes because he has been chosen by her parents. Her goal is to grow up, move to the city, and make her own decisions.

Comment

Young readers may be startled to learn how shocked the older generation was when younger women began to wear men's clothes because they were more comfortable and practical. While they may agree with Kristin that the pace of change is much too slow, they will perhaps question the adjustments to reality that she decides to make at the end. The conflict between cultures and generations is nicely depicted.

Suggestions for Reports or Activities

1. Kristin is drawn to Fröken Larson, who is working for voting rights for women. When and how did women get the vote in the United States? Who were the heroines of the women's struggle?

2. At the turn of the last century, very few women wore "men's clothes," that is, trousers and loose-fitting shirts. Look into a history or encyclopedia of fashion and find out when wearing such clothes by women and girls became common. What connection did this change have with other changes in lifestyle and life choices for women?

3. The life of a farmer is often hard. What was wheat farming like in Minnesota in the early part of the 1900s? Find out what kinds of machinery were used; what the weather was like; and any other conditions that made it better or worse for the immigrants trying to tame the land.

Land of Hope   Joan Lowery Nixon
Ellis Island series
New York: Delacorte, 1992. 169p. (2, 3)

No longer feeling safe in Russia, Rebekah Levinsky and her Jewish family head for the United States in 1902 at the urging of Uncle Avir. The escape over the Hungarian border into Austria; the interminable and recurrent standing in line for humiliating medical examinations; and the horrible conditions of traveling steerage—these and other trials leave the fifteen-year-old girl uneasy about what awaits her in the new country. Sustained by her hope of freedom and security, she is almost defeated by the discovery that Uncle Avir has greatly exaggerated his circumstances. Instead of being able to go to school to become a teacher, Rebekah, along with her whole family, is expected to work seven days a week, fifteen hours a day, sewing ugly clothes in a sweatshop. How will Rebekah make her dream come true when even her own parents don't understand her?

Comment

During the first ten years of the twentieth century, more than six million immigrants were processed through Ellis Island. The majority of these came from Italy, Russia, and Austria-Hungary. Rebekah's story illuminates the experience shared by many of them, thereby offering young readers a glimpse of the hardships they encountered and the depths of courage and stamina on which they drew to survive and succeed in the new world.

Suggestions for Reports or Activities

1. What sorts of assistance did the Hebrew Immigrant Aid Society offer? Who started it, and why? How long did it function, how many people did it help, and so on?

2. Compare the immigration to the United States in the first decade of the twentieth century with that in the years following World War I: From which countries did people come, how many came, what was their social or economic background? You may present your information in the form of a chart or a narrative.

3. What do you think happened to the young people in this book: Rebekah, Nessin, Jacob, Aaron? Write a paragraph on each telling what they were doing ten years later and why.

4. Rebekah is sad to leave behind her friend Chava when the family departs for the United States. What might have happened to Chava? Find out what went on in Jewish villages in Russia and Ukraine during the first decade of the twentieth century and speculate on Chava's fate.

Land of Promise   Joan Lowery Nixon
Ellis Island series
New York: Bantam, 1992. 167p. (2, 3)

When fifteen-year-old Rose Carney arrives in Chicago in 1902, she immediately sets about transforming herself from an Irish country girl into a sophisticated city shopgirl. Dismayed by her father's drinking problem and her brothers' involvement in a radical group dedicated to freeing Ireland from British control, she nonetheless saves as much money as she can to help bring her mother and little sisters to America. Two family tragedies place more and more responsibility on Rose's shoulders, even as she signs on to Jane Addams' campaign to help the poor and work for world peace.

Comment

This book offers insights into how big city politics in the early part of the twentieth century worked to help the poor and made office holders rich. It also makes clear the role of women in European immigrant families: to cook and clean for their menfolks while holding down a full-time job. There is no disability insurance or unemployment compensation for people injured on the job or laid off from one. That there is a solution for Rose and her family at the end depends on a chance meeting with a wealthy benefactor; in real life there might well have been no solution at all.

Suggestions for Reports or Activities

1. Who was Jane Addams? Find out about her background and life's work. When did she found Hull House and for what purpose? How long was it in existence?

2. If Michael had been injured on the job today, who would have helped him? What roles would the government and his employer have played? For how long? When was unemployment insurance first required in this country?

3. The book indicates that the Irish controlled politics in Chicago. When did this come about? In what other large American cities did the Irish take charge? Speculate as to how this happened. Can you find out how many U.S. presidents are descended from Irish immigrants?

4. Rose's brother Johnny was caught trying to smuggle money to the Irish rebels. What was the rebellion all about? What happened to people like Johnny? Write a letter that Johnny might have sent to Rose from prison explaining why he supported the rebels and what he thought would happen to him at the hands of the English.

Letters from Rifka   Karen Hesse
New York: Holt, 1992. 148p. (2, 3)

For over a year, from September 1919 to October 1920, twelve-year-old Rifka writes to her cousin Tovah about her adventures on the way from Russia to America. Even though Rifka has no way to mail the letters, she uses them to record and reflect on her feelings as she becomes separated from her family, falls ill twice with contagious diseases, watches her beautiful golden hair fall out, survives a storm at sea, and then is detained at Ellis Island and forbidden to rejoin the family she loves. Rifka's experiences are based on a true story from the author's family.

Comment

Many people living in Eastern Europe after World War I found life very difficult. Because of the war, food and other goods were scarce and families suffered also from the changes in national boundaries agreed to by the European powers. In Russia, the government placed agents in the villages to stir up trouble among the peasants, diverting their anger from the government toward the Jews. Many Jews fled their homes in search of a better and more secure life somewhere else. This book epitomizes the great migration toward the United States and Canada in the story of one girl's escape.

Suggestions for Reports or Activities

1. Select one of Rifka's letters. Assume that she was able to send it to her cousin. Compose the reply that Tovah might have written, including comments about Rifka's adventures and some information about what was happening to Tovah and her family back in Russia.

2. Rifka suffered from typhus and then from ringworm. (a) What is typhus? How is it contracted and spread? What treatment is common today? (b) Do people still get ringworm? Why do you think Rifka's hair didn't grow back for such a long time and then started to grow?

3. What can you find out about the Hebrew Immigrant Aid Society? When did it start, how long did it function, how many people did it assist, and so on?

4. Compare the immigration to the United States in the late nineteenth century with that in the years following World War I: From which countries did people come, how many came, what was their social or economic background? You may present your information in the form of a chart or a narrative.

Lyddie   Katherine Paterson
New York: Puffin, 1991. 182p. (1, 2)

Papa has disappeared, and Mama has gone crazy. How can ten-year-old Charlie and thirteen-year-old Lyddie keep the farm going by themselves? Actually, they survive the long Vermont winter of 1843–44 only to learn in the spring that Mama has hired them out in town and turned over the farm to a stranger to pay their debts. Charlie is lucky with his job at the mill, but Lyddie heads south to Lowell, Massachusetts, to work in a weaving factory in the hope of recapturing her beloved farm. Her single-minded determination helps keep her going when the factory owner increases the speed of the machines and the output required of the operators, but then Mama dies and

Lyddie inherits the care of her little sister Rachel. How will she manage now?

Comment

The appeal of factory work to girls right off the farm is made vivid and credible; the reality of the noise, the danger, and the exhaustion from thirteen-hour work days dawns on the reader even as it does on Lyddie. The mutual suspicions of members of different ethnic and religious groups are also embodied in the relationships of the characters in the story. Lyddie's brief encounter with a runaway slave offers insight into why Northerners, despite their antislavery sentiments, sometimes turned the fugitives in.

Suggestions for Reports or Activities

1. Look for a copy of Charles Dickens' *American Notes for General Circulation,* in which he describes factory life in Lowell. How does it compare with what this book describes?

2. Examine a history of higher education in America for information on Oberlin College. When did it open? Were women admitted from the beginning? How many other colleges had women students at that time?

3. Imagine a conversation between Lyddie and Luke over breakfast the morning after the book ends. Does she ask him to wait for her? Does he plead with her not to go? Write at least two pages of dialogue between them.

Mountain Light   Laurence Yep
New York: Harper & Row, 1985. 282p. (1, 2)

Set in 1885, this novel deals with the adventures of teenager Squeaky Lau as he fights the Manchu rulers of China, falls in love with a girl from an enemy village, and sails to America to work in the gold fields alongside other Chinese immigrants. The loyalties and hostilities that united and divided Chinese peasants at the time torment Squeaky as he tries to figure out where he stands. In the process he learns that character is more important than clan. He also suspects that he may never be able to go home again. (Other books featuring some of the same characters are *Dragon's Gate* and *Dragonwings,* above, and *The Star Fisher,* below.)

Comment

The exotic names and locations in this book never stand in the way of the universal experiences of love, fear, death, and hope. Squeaky and Cassia could be Romeo and Juliet, or Tony and Maria from *West Side Story*. At the same time readers can learn much about why so many Chinese fled their country for North America during the last half of the nineteenth century. While life in the New World held its own dangers and uncertainties, it also offered the irresistible possibility of eventual wealth, power, and independence.

Suggestions for Reports or Activities

1. Who, exactly, were the "Strangers"? Also called the Hakka, they played an important role in Chinese history. Consult an account of China in the past or *Strangers at the Gate* by Frederick Wakeman for the story of their persecution.

2. Summarize the conditions on the ship that took Squeaky and Tiny to San Francisco. Then compare them with the conditions on the slave ships from North Africa two hundred years earlier. How were they alike, and how were they different?

3. Read about the Gold Rush in California. What is said about the Chinese who were looking for gold? Explain how Foxfire was able to find gold in "worthless" claims.

Now Ameriky   Betty Sue Cummings
New York: Atheneum, 1979. 179p. (2, 3)

Brigid Ni Cleary sets out on a walk across Ireland, carrying only her grandmother's cooking pot. Like thousands of other poor people whom the potato famine has left desperate and unable to pay their rents, Brigid's family will be evicted from their home. Brigid will make the trip to America, find work, save money, and send for her family and her fiancé to join her. But first she must face injury, insult, starvation, and disease. After surviving her barefoot trek and horrendous shipboard conditions, Brigid is dismayed by the Irish ghetto she discovers in the "golden" city of New York. Swallowing her disappointment, she finds employment, enduring hard work, low pay, discrimination, and loneliness. Eventually she is able to fulfill her dream of replanting her family on land newly purchased in America.

Comment

This novel offers vivid descriptions of wasteland Ireland as well as ghetto New York. Although physical conditions are gruesome, the human element that preys on the weakened victims is more fearsome. These unsavory elements, however, are contrasted with the tenacious will to survive that the immigrants needed to truly win the freedom offered in America. This story illuminates the era of the potato famine and the plight of the brave people driven to this bold venture.

Suggestions for Reports or Activities

1. How did the potato famine start in Ireland? Could it have been avoided?

2. Write a short paper on the anti-Irish discrimination in a major American city (Boston or New York, for example).

3. Who are some of the important people in America today who are of Irish descent? Write a short paper on one of these.

4. If you can, locate someone who came to America as an immigrant from Ireland and find out about his or her experience. Compare this experience with Brigid's.

One-Way to Ansonia   Judie Angell
New York: Bradbury, 1985. 183p. (2, 3)

Moshe Olshansky's five children arrive in New York from Russia in 1893 the day he is to be married for the fourth time. His new wife, a widow with a six-year-old daughter, has been told only about Moshe's youngest, the same age as her own child; confronted with the shock of the four older children, she refuses to consider having them live with her. By the time the wedding festivities are over, Moshe has found homes for the others with four of his "landsmen" from the same village. The rest of the story belongs mostly to Rose, who, in the time it takes to grow from ten years old to sixteen, becomes the one most determined to learn English and make a better life for herself and her child.

Comment

Young readers will be amazed by the way the children are parceled out among strangers for whom they must work to pay for their room and board. The different adjustments and accommodations that they make to their various circumstances provide glimpses into living and working conditions among immigrant families at the end of the nineteenth century. Unions offer some hope, but women remain mostly subject to the whims of their fathers and husbands. The warmth and support which the young people offer to each other are a beacon in the darkness.

Suggestions for Reports or Activities

1. What were conditions like in the garment workers' factories? Read about the beginnings of the ILGWU (International Ladies' Garment Workers' Union) and the conditions it was determined to correct.

2. Of all the children, Yette was the one who was sacrificed to convenience. Summarize what happened to her and why. Could it have turned out differently? What might she have done to escape her fate?

3. The story ends when Rose is on the train heading for Ansonia. What happened next? Write a synopsis of the next chapter. What did Rose find in Connecticut? How long did it take till she could send for Hyman? Did he join her? Why or why not?

The Other Shore   Lucinda Mays
New York: Atheneum, 1979. 223p. (2, 3)

Gabriella is struggling with her Italian identity and trying to be an American. She recalls the painful, poverty-stricken time in Italy as her mother waited and waited for Pietro, Gabriella's father, to send the money so they could join him. Now, almost grown up, she lives within the traditions of New York's Little Italy, but she wants more from her life. Even a high school diploma for girls is almost unheard of. But Pietro's harrowing experiences as an unwitting strikebreaker sentenced to prison and his association with Carlo, a philosopher-union organizer, have broadened his vision: Gabriella's future will be what she can make it.

Comment

This book poignantly portrays the suffering of the poor in an Italian village, their hopes for a new life in America, and the roadblocks of prejudice and tradition which made becoming American so difficult. Working conditions in New York City's garment district were appalling, as the graphic description of the factory fire indicates. The family succeeds in attaining the goal of most new Americans: a house of their own. There are some sexual references.

Suggestions for Reports or Activities

1. Check in a reference work or other source to find out where Italians settled when they came to America in the early twentieth century. What kinds of jobs did they find? Can you find any information about the prejudice they encountered?

2. Several interesting traditions and proverbs or sayings from Italy are mentioned. Write a short paper commenting on how these traditions and sayings are similar to or different from some in your family.

3. Find out about the Triangle Shirtwaist Factory fire. Was this a real event? Write a short paper about factory conditions in the clothing industry.

4. Gabriella's father was forced to become a strikebreaker. Look up the early history of unions in coal mines, railroads, or another industry. Write a short paper on the problems faced by union organizers. How were immigrants involved?

Ragtime   E. L. Doctorow
New York: Random House, 1974. 270p. (1)

The lives and fortunes of three families from different backgrounds and walks of life intertwine in this funny and impressionistic novel of the early twentieth century. Mostly given generic titles (Father, Mother's Younger Brother, the girl, the boy, the old man, the colored girl, the brown baby), the characters are nevertheless highly individualistic, even peculiar. They interact not only with each other but also with numerous real personages, such as J. Pierpont Morgan, Harry Houdini, Evelyn Nesbit, Emma Goldman, Admiral Peary, and others. The end result is a story sometimes satirical, sometimes outrageous, but always entertaining.

Comment

Numerous historical events, both major and minor, play their part in this narrative: the development of motion pictures; Peary's expedition to the North Pole; Freud's first visit to the United States; the invention of ever-more-elaborate fireworks; Morgan's opinion of

Henry Ford; Harry Thaw's shooting of Stanford White over Evelyn Nesbit; the textile workers' strike in Lowell, Massachusetts; and other noted events or situations dot the novel's pages. A special puzzle for students should be the sorting out of fact from fiction, as they are cheerfully mingled throughout.

Suggestions for Reports or Activities

1. Explore further the lives of one or more of the historical characters mentioned. Are Doctorow's characterizations plausible or not?

2. What is "ragtime"? How does it differ from jazz or blues music? Why does Doctorow use the word for the title of his book?

3. At the very end, Doctorow mentions a series of films made about a group of children from different ethnic backgrounds. Read a history of film in the United States to find out what he was talking about.

The Sport of the Gods   Paul Laurence Dunbar
New York: Dodd, Mead, 1902. 255p. (1)

A close-knit black family seeking refuge and opportunity, the Hamiltons (mother Fannie, son Joe, and daughter Kitty) move to New York City from the South in the mid-1890s after father Berry has been unjustly convicted of a crime and sentenced to prison. Over the next few years, the city exacts its toll on the Hamiltons. Joe falls in with a fast, sporting crowd, becomes an alcoholic, and goes to prison for murder. Against her mother's ardent wishes, Kitty becomes a singer-dancer in an all-black musical comedy. Out of loneliness, Fannie marries a gambler who mistreats her. When Berry's innocence is proven, he is freed, rescues Fannie, and with her returns to their home in a small Southern town where these victims of racial intolerance and the temptations of the city are sustained only by a fatalistic faith in God.

Comment

Before the great northward migration during World War I, there were few black people in cities. The author explores certain facets of urban black culture, spotlighting the social club and the theater, with their particular social and aesthetic values, prefiguring the Harlem Renaissance of the 1920s. Especially interesting is the portrayal of whites who frequented these institutions; fascinating, too, is the discussion of the role of "yellow journalism" in race relations.

Suggestions for Reports or Activities

1. This story occurs only a few decades after the abolition of slavery. How does the legacy of slavery manifest itself in the interracial and intraracial relations of the Southern town? Why is Mr. Oakley so quick to accuse Berry of stealing the money? Are the black townspeople justified in ostracizing the Hamiltons?

2. How does the story reflect the small-town bias against the city that was common at the time? Is it a well-rounded account of black life in Northern cities at the turn of the century? What insights does it provide into urban black culture?

3. In 1895 in his famous Atlanta address, Booker T. Washington counselled black people "to cast down your bucket where you are" (in the rural South). Is the author of this story saying the same thing? Or does the story reflect a different perspective? Explain.

The Star Fisher   Laurence Yep
New York: Morrow Junior Books, 1991. 147p. (2, 3)

A Chinese-American family moves in 1927 from Ohio to West Virginia to start a laundry in pursuit of the American dream. But the Lees are the only Asian family in town, and they are greeted with prejudice and scorn. Fifteen-year-old Joan tells this story of their gradual integration into the life of school and town, thanks in large part to the support of their landlady, a retired schoolteacher. Joan's decision to befriend a classmate who is also an outcast ends up opening doors for both families. (Other books featuring some of the same characters are *Dragon's Gate, Dragonwings,* and *Mountain Light,* above.)

Comment

While written from the point of view of a young Chinese-American girl, this novel points out that there are many ways of being alienated besides having an appearance different from anyone else's: the girls who are ostracized because they come from a family of actors suffer no less than the newcomers. The bravery of the immigrant parents as they cope with the demands of a strange culture also becomes evident, even to their children. Ultimately all the battles are resolved on a basis of mutual acceptance and respect.

Suggestions for Reports or Activities

1. When did theater people become "respectable"? Look through a history of the theater to find out (a) why they were first considered *not* respectable and (b) when this attitude changed.

2. What kind of revolution took place in China in 1911? See what you can find out about it and also about how many Chinese emigrated in the following decade.

3. The girl in the legend of the Star Fisher, like Joan Lee, is pulled in two directions by two very different traditions. In what ways are the experiences of the two girls similar, and in what ways are they different? What kind of choices will Joan have to make when she grows up?

The Store That Mama Built   Robert Lehrman
New York: Macmillan, 1992. 126p. (3)

During and after the first World War, many Americans died of influenza. One of these was twelve-year-old Birdie's papa, who was supposed to build the grocery store that would support the family newly arrived in a small Pennsylvania town. Birdie is certain that Mama, who speaks very little English, cannot possibly manage the store and care for six children all by herself. Relying on the advice and good will of Uncle Izzie, Mama opens the store, while Birdie and her older brothers set out to make it a success. Despite warnings from well-meaning friends, the children distribute their flyers in a poor black neighborhood with surprising results.

Comment

The age-old conflict between generations, especially acute in immigrant families, is played out here. Mama, originally pictured by her daughter as lonely, fearful, overwhelmed, and dependent, astonishes her children by her courage in making a series of unpopular decisions. The children acknowledge her competence at the end, even as the United States prepares to join the war in Europe. An important subplot deals with another long-term conflict, that between different minority groups, in this case blacks and Jews.

Suggestions for Reports or Activities

1. In this story there seems to be a lot of tension in school between children from different groups. List some of the possible rea-

sons for this discomfort. Did Birdie make the right decision in be-friending Roxanne? What did she have to give up? What did she gain?

2. How was life in New York City different from life in Steelton? If you were Mama and had to decide where to live, what would be the good things and bad things about each place? Make a list of both and then explain how Mama made her choice.

3. As the family adapted to life in Steelton, they had to give up some of their old customs. Which were they able to keep, and which did they have to forgo? How did they feel about the changes they had to make?

The Streets Are Paved with Gold   Fran Weissenberg
New York: Harbinger House, 1990. 145p. (2, 3)

Debbie Gold's family has been in the United States for eighteen years, but her mother still speaks no English. Now in the eighth grade, Debbie is enjoying the delights of first love while wrestling with such issues as whether she will be chosen to play the lead in the class play, what will happen to her favorite aunt who wants to marry a non-Jew, how she can be friends with a rich girl from a different neighborhood, and the like. A bout of appendicitis and her father's struggle with tuberculosis help her sort out her true values.

Comment

This story of immigrants and their children is marked less by generational conflict than by problems common to many young people of any period: how to see beyond physical attractiveness to the person beneath; how to become friends with classmates from different backgrounds; how to decide between buying something one desperately wants and helping to meet the needs of one's family. At the same time the reader is introduced to the extra burdens imposed by poverty, illness, and distance from the mainstream culture.

Suggestions for Reports or Activities

1. Find out more about tuberculosis, or "consumption." What are its symptoms, how is it spread, and what is the treatment today? After nearly disappearing, "TB" is now making a comeback in many cities: Why is this?

2. Write a letter from Debbie to her cousin Annie, who has just moved to Buffalo. Tell about the move to the new house, the reasons

for the sleeping arrangements, and Debbie's discovery about her feelings for Iz.

3. Aunt Sadie tells about the Triangle Shirtwaist fire on March 25, 1911. What happened on that day, and why? What new laws were passed afterwards to help ensure that such a disaster would never happen again?

Streets of Gold   Karen Branson
New York: Putnam, 1981. 176p. (2, 3)

In this sequel to *The Potato Eaters,* Maureen, her father, and her two brothers make the voyage to America hoping to find a livelihood. Arriving in New York, they soon realize that the streets are not paved with gold, that living conditions are not much better than they were in Ireland, and that jobs are hard to find if you're Irish. Hearing that there is work in Pennsylvania, her father leaves Maureen in charge of the two boys. Maureen finds a position as a washerwoman. A chance meeting with the sailor who had been kind to her on the ship is propitious.

Comment

Readers will gain some appreciation of how the dream of a new life enabled people coming to America to endure hardships aboard ship (hunger, stench, sickness, death, unfeeling treatment by the crew). But they were ill-prepared for the prejudice which many encountered once they arrived. Paddy's bitter hatred of the English and his suspicion of anyone not Irish are understandable, as is the need for the Irish to stick together. The qualities of determination, hard work, and thrift are portrayed as necessary attributes for success in the new land.

Suggestions for Reports or Activities

1. The book describes the voyage to America. Is this an accurate portrayal? What can you find out about conditions aboard an immigrant ship? How long did the voyage take? What happened when the ship docked in New York harbor?

2. Why were the other women who worked in the Cabot house so unfriendly to Maureen?

3. Why was it necessary for Da to flee to Canada?

4. How can some experiences of European immigrants be compared with the experiences of blacks in America? Discuss in a short paper.

The Sunita Experiment   Mitali Perkins
New York: Hyperion, 1993. 179p. (2, 3)
   Sunita Sen, the child of parents who immigrated to the U.S. from India, hates being singled out as different from her classmates. But in honor of her grandparents' visit, Sunita's mother has given up her teaching job and is wearing sarees all the time instead of her elegant suits and silk shirts. Sunita's friend Michael Morrison is no longer allowed to come to the house, and she can't figure out how to tell him without sounding dumb. Torn between her family's culture and that of her school and friends, she thinks of herself as an experiment and wonders how she will turn out.

Comment

   Fitting in nowhere exactly, the immigrant youngster has to make many decisions every day regarding conflicting customs and values. Other children may laugh or make cruel remarks, magnifying the immigrant's sense of otherness. The basic questions of identity and belonging should strike a chord in the hearts of adolescents of any ethnic background.

Suggestions for Reports or Activities

   1. There are many Asian immigrants in the U.S. today. Where do they come from, and why are they here? Compare the levels of Asian immigration in 1850, 1900, 1950, and 1995, noting the countries from which the largest number of immigrants came in each period.
   2. Make a list of the customs of Sunita's family that are different from those in a regular "Euro-American" family in the United States today. Next to each one explain the reason behind it as inferred from the comments in this book or anything else you may know.
   3. Sunita and the black girl, Ilana, miss an opportunity to get to know each other when they hear someone whisper "the colored girls stick together," and Sunita then backs out of her suggestion that they sit together at the tennis match. Is there any other way Sunita could have handled the situation and not have hurt Ilana's feelings? Starting with the whisper, rewrite the scene so that the two girls could comfortably implement their original plan.

The Tempering   Gloria Skurzynski
New York: Clarion, 1983. 178p. (2, 3)

This story is about growing up in a small-town neighborhood close to one of the giant steel mills not far from Pittsburgh at the turn of the century. Itching to work in the mill, Karl has pretended to be sixteen. But he loses his job on the first day. His only choice is to return to school and wait for his birthday. Meanwhile, he begins to notice that things are changing, both for himself and around him. His friend Jame Culley next door is secretly courting Karl's sister. But what will happen when his mother, who has borne a long and deep hatred for the Culley family, finds out? At school there is a new teacher, young and pretty Yulyona, who attempts to convince Karl to set his sights higher than the mill. Karl is infatuated with Yulyona and tries hard to impress her. After an incident in which he erroneously believes that he has found Yulyona in a compromising situation, the devastated Karl leaves town, but he returns to decide about his life.

Comment

In portraying the lifestyle of mill families in the early 1900s, this story describes a neighborhood where several ethnic groups live, bound together by the mill, and for most, by the Roman Catholic church. Because they could not imagine another life, young men looked forward to leaving school and working in the mill. Readers will learn about the dangerous work, the long hours, the kind of extortion workers might expect (being told whom to vote for, having to pay to cross the bridge to the mill, kowtowing to the mayor or other politicians). There is also a look at the way people lived in their homes, how they saved their money, how they spent their free time, the closeness and loyalty to family, the ways young people rebelled. The story touches on the rising movement toward unionization.

Suggestions for Reports or Activities

1. Karl's family and their neighbors came from several different countries in Europe to settle in the area around Pittsburgh. Select one of the countries and find out why people left to come to America and in what parts of the United States they settled. Why did many people come to Pittsburgh?

2. Andy decides to go to Gary, Indiana, to try to organize a steelworkers union. What can you find out about the beginning of the steel industry union?

3. Who was Andrew Carnegie? Write a paper on his life as industrialist and philanthropist.

Voyage   Adele Geras
New York: Atheneum, 1983. 193p. (2, 3)

Crowded in the steerage section aboard the *S.S. Danzig,* the diverse community of chiefly Jewish immigrants finds much to bind them together as they share their hopes for a new life in America. Chapters are written from the varied viewpoints of passengers of several ages and backgrounds. Eighteen-year-old Rachel finds the attentions of Yasha pleasing; can she forget the sadness of her fiancé's death? Now her father realizes that the marriage he is planning for her in America may not take place. Mr. Kaminsky wonders if he should be making the voyage at all; at his age, will he not be a burden on his nephews? Golda will join her husband, whom she scarcely knows, but she worries that their baby will not live through the voyage. Mina is concerned about her little brother Eli who seems backward; she fears he may not pass the inspection when they reach land. The trip is trying, personalities clash, there is sickness and death, but there is also joy, and the travelers care for one another.

Comment

The author provides a kaleidoscopic look into the lives of several people in a time between two lifetimes, on the voyage to the promised land of America. Brave thoughts for the future are mixed with poignant remembrances of the past. Preserving the old ways, timeworn traditions, is important to the older passengers; but everyone realizes that life in America will be different. Commentary on the passage to America from several viewpoints affords readers some understanding of the wrenching worry that so many of our ancestors underwent in seeking a better way of life.

Suggestions for Reports or Activities

1. Different characters in the story had different ideas about what would happen when they reached America. What were some of these visions of a new life?

2. Mina is concerned that Eli might not be admitted to the United States. Could there have been any justification for her fears? What regulations existed at the checkpoint at Ellis Island?

3. Interview one or more older relatives or friends who emigrated to America. What were their hopes and concerns? Ask them to describe the journey. How does a real story compare with the accounts in the book?

Wildflower Girl   Marita Conlon-McKenna
New York: Holiday House, 1991. 173p. (2)
Her family torn apart as a result of the Great Famine in Ireland, Peggy O'Driscoll decides to leave her brother, sister, and great-aunt behind and sail alone for America. She is thirteen years old, excited and terrified at the same time. Once in Boston, after a dreadful voyage in steerage, Peggy and her friend Sarah trust their fortunes to an Irish immigrant woman who promises to find them jobs. As she adjusts to life in the new country, Peggy meets good people and bad and has many occasions to regret her decision. Abused by her first employer, accused of stealing a ring by her second, she looks forward in the end to making the most of her opportunities.

Comment

Readers will be struck by the exploitation of the newcomers, from the ship captain's restrictions on soap and water to the American employers' expectations of their maids' continuous availability. Peggy's courage at leaving her older siblings and emigrating in order to find work may strike contemporary youngsters as more strange than admirable, though they may also see their own circumstances as more fortunate than they had previously imagined. The experiences of Peggy and her friends appear to be a fair reflection of what poor immigrants could expect as they fled Europe for what they believed was the Promised Land.

Suggestions for Reports or Activities

1. What was the Great Famine? When did it start and how long did it last? Find out how much of Ireland's population died at the time and how many people emigrated to the United States.

2. Describe the conditions of the men's boarding house where Peggy first worked. Then write a description of the meal Peggy prepared from the point of view of one of the men who had to eat it. Did he find anything good to say about it?

3. What did you think of the way Peggy helped get rid of the housekeeper, Miss Lewis? Were you impressed or dismayed? Can you think of any way she might have gotten the same result without making people sick?

4. Imagine another chapter for the book. After she had saved some money, what did Peggy do and where did she go? Write a summary of what might have happened to her after working for the Rowans for five years or so.

MORE CHALLENGING BOOKS
FOR ADVANCED READERS

The Jungle   Upton Sinclair
New York: Doubleday, 1906. 413p.
This story focuses on many of the evils that led to reforms in the Progressive era: terrible factory conditions; false advertising; child labor; adulterated food; prostitution; and political corruption. With its graphic depiction of vile and unsanitary practices in the packing plants, the book created an international furor, speeding the passage of laws tightening food inspection.

The Late George Appley   John P. Marquand
Boston: Little, Brown, 1936. 354p.
The author portrays the attitude of the old upper-class families who felt that family, tradition, and Boston were foremost. He also shows the inevitability of change as other groups, notably the Irish, begin their ascendancy and the children of the old families start to stray.

The Magnificent Ambersons   Booth Tarkington
New York: Doubleday, 1918. 516p.
As Midland, Indiana, changes from a pleasant town to a grimy industrial city of factories, immigrants, civic boosters, and suburbs, the leading family loses its fortune and, with it, its influence. The rapid social changes brought about by the first great American Industrial Revolution are memorably portrayed in this classic novel.

Main Street   Sinclair Lewis
New York: Harcourt, 1920. 451p.

This famous novel of life in Gopher Prairie, Minnesota—intended to symbolize life in any small town in the United States of the early twentieth century—is not only a portrayal of small-town pettiness, hypocrisy, and complacency. It is also a clear depiction of how not to try to bring about change. The conflict of values is timeless.

The Pit: A Story of Chicago   Frank Norris
Philadelphia: Curtis, 1902. 412p.

This story focuses on the Chicago grain market called "The Pit," where speculating on wheat futures at the turn of the century brought on financial panic across the nation. Insights into the motives of those who gambled with other people's money and played other people's produce up and down in the stock market are also offered. The collapse of the market and subsequent consternation mirror similar financial crises occurring later on.

The Rise of David Levinsky   Abraham Cahan
New York: Harper, 1917. 529p.

Written by a participant in the movement from Eastern Europe to America, the story describes Jewish life in Czarist Russia, the ghetto of New York's Lower East Side in its heyday, and the garment business at a time when Russian Jews began to succeed German Jews in this important industry. The many sides of New York Jewish life—the struggle to survive, the process of Americanization, labor-management conflict, the rise of Jewish socialism, religious conventions—provide the backdrop for this tale.

Sister Carrie   Theodore Dreiser
New York: Doubleday, 1900. 557p.

The position of women in a success-oriented society is epitomized by the story of Caroline Meeber, who leaves her small Midwestern hometown in 1889 to start life anew in Chicago and later in New York. In her quest for riches she becomes a famous actress, only to realize that despite her material acquisitions true happiness remains illusory.

VI The Jazz Age and the Depression

Appointment in Samarra John O'Hara
New York: Duell, 1934. 301p. (1, 2)

Although the book begins and ends with Lute Fliegler, it is really the story of Julian English and the year his life suddenly falls apart. Son of a prominent local physician, head of a General Motors dealership, husband of bright and beautiful Caroline, member of the Lantenengo Country Club, Julian seems to be at the top of his small-town world. When he gives in to an impulse to throw a drink in the face of a fellow club member, however, he sets in motion a chain of events and inferences that leads to his undoing.

Comment

Readers interested in the effects of the Depression and Prohibition on the upper-middle class will find some insights in this novel. The complicated relationships of otherwise law-abiding citizens with the hoodlums who have access to illegal liquor form one thread of the narrative. The entanglements resulting from the need of some of the characters to borrow money from one of their peers form another. A general tone of sexual amorality suffuses the story, despite ardent lip-service to convention.

Suggestions for Reports or Activities

1. What does the title of the book mean? How does it relate to the story?
2. O'Hara details the pairing-off customs of the young people in the country club set. How are these similar to or different from the customs of high school- and college-age people today?

3. Julian English tries to talk to Harry Reilly in his office, but Harry has to leave at once to catch a train. Suppose he had had time to talk. What would Julian have said to him? What would Harry have replied? Write a dialogue for the two men in a style as much like O'Hara's as you can. Then speculate as to how this conversation might or might not have changed the outcome of the story.

The Bread Winner   Arvella Whitmore
Boston: Houghton Mifflin, 1990. 138p. (2, 3)

It's 1932, and the Pucketts have lost their Midwestern farm to debt. Trying to start over, they find that the only house they can afford is a shack in the poorest part of town. Sarah's mother takes in washing from the neighbors and Sarah herself bakes bread and sells it for 15¢ a loaf, but her father looks in vain for work. Finally, he decides that he is just a burden on the rest of the family and heads for California to try to find a steady job. Sarah and her mother have to face the landlord demanding the back rent, and the grocer who refuses to extend any more credit. No matter how hard they all try, there is no running away from the Depression.

Comment

This story offers a good picture of the impact of the Depression on ordinary people. Some of the issues raised—for instance, are certain jobs appropriate only for men or for women?—resonate today as well. Sarah's initiative and resourcefulness in starting a family business, while she copes with the local bullies and even a tornado, are applicable to any time period.

Suggestions for Reports or Activities

1. Sarah's father tells of applying to the county for "relief," only to be told that the funds were all used up. What happens today when someone applies for welfare? If the person is eligible according to the rules, is the money ever "all used up"? If not, where does it come from?

2. Sarah's father heads out West to look for work, even though her mother points out that the Depression "is all over the country." Check the unemployment statistics for 1932: Was the economic situation worse in some parts of the country than in others? Chart the

changes over time from 1930 to 1938 for at least three regions (e.g., East, Midwest, West).

3. Sarah's solution to the problem of bullies at school and in her neighborhood is to fight them. In your opinion, is there anything else she could have done? Explain one or two alternative courses of action that might have had a similar result.

4. Think about how Sarah and her parents used their skills and their brains to keep the family together. Write down in chronological order all the things they did to take care of their needs. Who were the people who helped them at critical times?

Circle of Fire   William H. Hooks
New York: Atheneum, 1982. 147p. (3)

In rural North Carolina during Depression times, blacks and whites share much of their everyday life. Harrison Hawkins, a white boy, and his two black friends, Kitty Fisher and his sister Scrap, swim, gather walnuts, and try to avoid meeting up with their cantankerous and prejudiced neighbor, Mr. Bud Highsmith. The children make a new friend who is part of a band of gypsies, Irish tinkers who have camped in the woods. Shortly afterwards, Harrison overhears Mr. Highsmith and a stranger boasting about the Ku Klux Klan and plotting to "clean out a nest of thieving Catholic gypsies" to give a warning to "uppity" blacks. Harrison knows he must act quickly.

Comment

For younger readers this book provides a glimpse of life in a corner of America during the 1930s. According to a note, the author has tried to use the speech patterns of the time, the grammar, and the terms of address. (Some pejorative terms are used but in appropriate context.) Readers will gain an awareness of activities of the Klan and of the climate of fear that engulfed innocent people, black and white.

Suggestions for Reports or Activities

1. Find out about the Ku Klux Klan. Why was it started? Why does it still exist? Why is it permitted to exist?

2. What is meant by the term "gypsy"? Are gypsies make-believe people found in books? Are they real? Who are the gypsies? What does the word mean? Where are gypsies to be found today?

3. This book describes several interesting beliefs, superstitions, and customs of people from the tidewater country of North Carolina, where the story takes place. Drinking St. John's tea for a cold is one of these customs. List at least six of these practices and write a short paper telling about one or two of them. Then briefly describe any interesting traditions or customs of your own family or community.

The Dark Didn't Catch Me   Crystal Thrasher
New York: Atheneum, 1975. 182p. (2, 3)
Seely's family is moving to a house her dad has bought down in the Indiana hills. Jase Perry says there's a chance to get work there. It's the Depression, and even though Mom doesn't want to move, they have to. And it's tough—not even indoor plumbing and a one-room school. But Seely begins to feel at home and even to like the hills. She makes friends. Even though Seely doesn't feel poor, she's aware of the Depression's effect on those around her. Dad has to go out of town to work and comes home short-tempered and surly. He and Mom argue. There's sadness but there's joy, and Seely does a lot of growing up. When they move on, she leaves something of herself there in the hollows.

Comment

Families coped with the Depression by tightening their belts and doing their best. Seely's family moved to where there was a promise of work. But some people couldn't cope: Jase Perry commits suicide and his wife is sent to an institution. President Roosevelt's program to provide work for young men, the CCC (Civilian Conservation Corps), is described. Seely's family seems strong at the end, despite their personal tragedy.

Suggestions for Reports or Activities

1. Read in your textbook and in an encyclopedia about the Depression. What were some of the programs devised to help people who were out of work? Write a short paper on these programs.
2. What is the meaning of the title, *The Dark Didn't Catch Me*?
3. What do you think happened to Seely after she left Greene County? Write another chapter to conclude the story.

The Elderberry Thicket   Joan T. Zeier
New York: Atheneum, 1990. 154p. (2, 3)

Life in the Wisconsin farm country in the late 1930s is not easy, but Franny is thrilled that Papa has a good job as hired man on the Coppers' farm and Mama is slowly making the old house comfortable. Then the Coppers' no-good nephew comes to take Papa's place, and Papa goes away to look for work. Mama, who has always relied on her husband for everything, has to learn to take charge. Little by little Franny discovers that people are not always what they seem to be at first acquaintance. When her mother figures out how to teach the village nurse's slow-witted son to read, and the nephew saves her little brother's life, Franny finds reasons for hope even in her father's absence.

Comment

Set in Depression-era America, this story stresses how the toughness and resilience of a loving family (like those of the "elderberry thicket" of the title) can keep hope alive under the most trying circumstances. The characters grow and change as they come to understand better their own strengths and weaknesses. The lengths to which people went to find work to support their families, in a time without unemployment insurance or welfare, may startle young readers.

Suggestions for Reports or Activities

1. Papa writes about getting a job working on the Grand Coulee Dam. How far away from Wisconsin is the state of Washington? Describe the dimensions of the dam and explain where it was located and what it was supposed to accomplish.

2. Gil's reading problem seems to be due to what is now called "dyslexia." What are its symptoms and how is it treated today?

3. At the end of the book, Smokey has to decide whether or not to go to agricultural college. What do you think he did? What was the impact of his decision on the Parsons family?

A Girl Named Sooner   Suzanne Clauser
Garden City, N.Y.: Doubleday, 1972. 277p. (2)

Sooner, a sensitive little Southern girl from the backwoods, is being raised by the Bible-quoting Old Mam, who mistreats her. Dr. McHenry (called Mac), a veterinarian, discovers her and takes her to live with him and his wife, Elizabeth. However, Elizabeth resents Sooner; children at school are cruel; and adjustment to town life is not easy. A sad incident with Sooner's pet bird causes Sooner to return to her former life, thereby bringing Elizabeth to the realization of her love for the child.

Comment

The Depression is an integral part of the book, as the programs initiated by President Franklin Roosevelt serve as a catalyst to Old Mam's actions. She loses Sooner, for example, by demanding money from the Works Progress Administration and the county. The presence of the Civilian Conservation Corps makes her greedier still, so she chances selling her bootleg whiskey when the "revenuers" are watching her. The hard times and deprivations are presented with sympathy and realism.

Suggestions for Reports or Activities

1. Research the Works Progress Administration and the Civilian Conservation Corps. Find out what they were, who benefited from them, and how long they existed.

2. Interview several people who lived during the Depression. What was different about their lives then as compared to now? How do their recollections of the Depression affect their lives today?

3. Sooner, Mac, and Elizabeth all react differently to the death of the girl's pet bird. Make three columns on a sheet of paper: in the first column list words that describe Sooner's reaction; in the second, Elizabeth's; in the third, Mac's. How do they differ? Why?

The Great Gatsby   F. Scott Fitzgerald
New York: Scribner, 1925. 182p. (1, 2)

Jay Gatsby, grown rich through bootlegging and racketeering, pursues his five-year-old dream of winning his old love, Daisy Buchanan. Daisy, married to Tom and the mother of a three-year-old, cannot decide what to do. Their story is told by Daisy's poor cousin Nick Carraway, who rents a house next door to Gatsby's mansion on Long Island. Other characters who have major roles are Daisy's friend Jordan Baker, Tom's mistress Myrtle Wilson, and Myrtle's husband, George. Only Nick is aware of the harm that people like them can and do cause for themselves and others.

Comment

The book paints a vivid picture of the careless, sophisticated, and self-centered life led by the idle rich in the post–World War I era. The modern reader will be struck by the characters' lack of attention to anything beyond their immediate pleasure in the form of games, parties, new clothes, and drunken oblivion. Loyalty, fidelity, true caring, and even honest communication seem out of place and alien in this setting.

Suggestions for Reports or Activities

1. Look through a history of the Jazz Age. Were the characters portrayed in *The Great Gatsby* typical of the time? How did the rest of society regard them?

2. Fitzgerald has been described as both a participant in and an observer of the lifestyle depicted here. Is this true? Check a biography of Fitzgerald to see what part of his own life may have furnished the material for this story. Were people like Gatsby and the Buchanans among his friends?

3. Fill in some of the gaps in the past of Jay Gatsby, formerly James Gatz. What did he have to do to become Gatsby? Was any of it legal? What motivated him? How did he get away with his illegal activities?

King of the Hill   A. E. Hotchner
New York: Harper & Row, 1972. 240p. (2, 3)

The struggle to survive during the Great Depression is seen through the eyes of a twelve-year-old boy growing up in St. Louis. Forced by the national economic situation to live in poverty, Aaron is often unsure about where he will get his next meal or whether his family will be locked out of their apartment for not paying their rent. Despite his resourcefulness in earning money and staying cheerful, Aaron nonetheless experiences genuine hopelessness regarding his future. Many adventures and mishaps accompany Aaron's long wait for his family finally to regain a satisfactory lifestyle.

Comment

The effects of the Depression on an average American family are vividly portrayed in this book, with special emphasis on the problems it caused for adolescents already grappling with the uncertainties of their own personal stage in life. The story indicates how decision making can be entirely dictated by economic circumstances regardless of people's intent and desire to consider other factors. Students who have fortunately not known true financial hardship should find intriguing and insightful the thoughts of a twelve-year-old who suffered greatly from economic deprivation.

Suggestions for Reports or Activities

1. According to your textbook, what circumstances brought about the Great Depression? What does the novel tell you about the Depression beyond the information in your textbook?

2. Compare Aaron's lifestyle with that of a modern twelve-year-old. Look for similarities as well as differences.

3. Aaron feels at one point that everyone around him is dying. What events led him to this impression and how does it affect his outlook on the future?

Mississippi Bridge   Mildred D. Taylor
New York: Dial, 1990. 62p. (3)

In a 1930s rural Mississippi town, the inhabitants often gather at the general store. On this particular rainy winter day many of them, black and white, are waiting for the bus to Jackson. Just as it is ready to depart, a white family arrives and prepares to board. In order to make room for them, the bus driver forces the black passengers to get out. Jeremy Simms, the ten-year-old white boy who tells this story, is shocked by the injustice but powerless to do anything but watch. Then tragedy strikes. (For other books about some of the same characters, see *Roll of Thunder, Hear My Cry,* below, and *The Road to Memphis,* Section VII.)

Comment

The daily humiliations and indignities to which black people were subjected at this time are made vivid and disturbing in this short book. The distress and helplessness of the sympathetic white youngster are also memorable. Young readers should come away with a greater understanding of the conditions that inspired the civil rights movement thirty years later.

Suggestions for Reports or Activities

1. How did the problems of the Depression impact the characters in this book? Cite specific examples of the lack of work, food, and material goods to support your position.

2. Most of the white people in this book were mean and hateful to the black people of their town. Why did they behave this way? Why did Jeremy Simms not join them?

3. List the cruelties and kindnesses performed in this story along with the names of the persons responsible for them, the names of those they helped or hurt, and your explanation of the reason they acted as they did.

4. Black people were once required to sit at the back of the bus. Thirty years after the events in this story a woman in Montgomery, Alabama, finally put a stop to this practice. Who was she and how did she do it?

Moonshiner's Son   Carolyn Reeder
New York: Avon, 1993. 202p. (2, 3)

Tom Higgins and his Pa have an illegal still hidden in the woods. As if it weren't hard enough hiding the evidence from the government agents intent on enforcing Prohibition, all of a sudden they also have to worry about the new preacher, who spends a lot of time ranting against the evils of liquor. His daughter Amy is a particular pest, though she seems to like Tom personally. In the Blue Ridge Mountains of Virginia, however, making whiskey is often the family business, and Tom is proud to be a moonshiner's son. Then the preacher persuades Pa to help build a combination schoolhouse and chapel, the gentle widow Brown almost dies in a fire, and Tom makes some serious decisions about his future.

Comment

The author uses the story to raise a lot of questions about value conflicts, such as obeying the law versus earning money for food and other necessities; being willing to take charity versus making do with clothes that are torn and stained; telling the truth versus misleading without actually lying; praising one's children versus taking it for granted that they will behave. Readers should come to understand that people often have to make decisions when the right way is far from clear.

Suggestions for Reports or Activities

1. What was "Prohibition"? When did it exist and how long did it last? Research the reasons given for instituting it and the reasons given for terminating it.

2. Imagine the reasons why Tom's mother ran away. Write the letter to her husband that she might have left if she had been educated enough to write it. What did she say?

3. How did "bootleggers" get their name? Find out how they sold the illegal whiskey once they got it to the cities.

No Promises in the Wind   Irene Hunt
Chicago: Follett, 1970. 249p. (2, 3)

It is 1932. Josh's father has been out of work for eight months. His mother irons in a laundry. There is not enough to eat. Alienated by his father's ill humor and anger, Josh decides that he must strike out on his own. At least that will make one less mouth to feed. His best friend, Howie, eagerly joins him. Unexpectedly, Josh's little brother wants to come along, and Josh reluctantly agrees. Hoping to support themselves with their amateur musical talent, they hop a freight train heading south. Howie is killed in a tragic accident, but Josh and Joey manage to eke out a bare existence, sometimes begging, sometimes picking from garbage cans. A generous truck driver heading toward New Orleans puts them in touch with a carnival, where for a while they are able to make a small living. But this kind of life does not last. When will Josh forgive his father and return home?

Comment

This graphic picture of how the Depression affected millions of Americans effectively portrays the human suffering. Thousands of jobless men rode the rails, creating the unique way of life of the hobo. People are described as beaten and tired, angry, sometimes compassionate toward the suffering of others, sometimes vengeful toward those with more to eat. Readers will learn of the strain on family relationships and of the desperation of people driven to stand in soup lines, forage in garbage cans, or rob someone of a few potatoes. The author describes the hope evoked by the election of Roosevelt.

Suggestions for Reports or Activities

1. Trace Josh and Joey's journey on a map. What do you think of Josh's decision to run away? Would this be a reasonable option in present-day America?

2. Read President Roosevelt's inaugural address of 1933. What plans did he announce for coping with the Depression?

3. Write a short paper on the meaning of Roosevelt's words, "The only thing we have to fear is fear itself."

4. What were the causes of the Depression? How did the United States find the way back to prosperity?

Nothing to Fear   Jackie French Koller
New York: Harcourt Brace, Gulliver, 1991. 279p. (2)

Danny Garvey's father is out of work in Depression-era New York City. The family survives on Mama's laundry business and the few pennies that Danny earns shining shoes. When their neighbors start being evicted because they can't pay the rent, Pa decides to go away to look for work. Then Mama's difficult pregnancy requires her to give up the washing and ironing. Thirteen-year-old Danny tries to keep up the work before and after school, but he can't do it. At this low point, a sick and starving stranger comes to their door. Poor and hungry as they themselves are, the Garveys have to decide if and how they can help him.

Comment

This touching story of an Irish immigrant family in 1932 emphasizes the love, pride, and mutual support of the Garveys and their neighbors. It also points up their helplessness in the face of widespread unemployment and the absence of mitigating social services. Danny is made suddenly aware of the nature of homelessness when he finds his friend Luther and his mother living inside a piano crate in the park, a revelation which comes as a shock to the reader as well as to Danny.

Suggestions for Reports or Activities

1. What was the "Bonus March"? When did it take place, who were the marchers, and what was the outcome?

2. Sometimes it seemed that the only people who had money at this time were the bootleggers. What is the origin of the word itself?

How did they get their cash? Compare the bootleggers of the 1930s with the drug lords of today. Would you be in favor of decriminalizing drug possession? Why or why not?

3. It was hard for Danny to accept charity or to beg for his family. Why do you think this was? Compose a letter from Danny to you explaining his feelings.

The Rock and the Willow   Mildred Lee
New York: Lothrop, Lee & Shepard, 1963. 223p. (2, 3)

A poor Alabama truck farm during the 1930s is the environment with which adolescent Enie Singleton must contend. She aspires to go to college, even though the farm barely meets the family's daily needs. Enie's mother is a soft, understanding woman who works too hard and has too many babies. Her father is hard-working but insensitive to Enie's need for higher education. It is only after her mother dies that life changes for the better for the Singletons. While Enie suffers the sadness of her mother's death, later she is able to begin living her dream of a different sort of life.

Comment

The Depression makes daily survival even harder for the Singleton family. A drought destroys one crop, and food and money are scarce. The family is too proud to accept charity. A drifter (a familiar figure of the time) helps for a while, but he travels on after an involvement with Enie. Through this story, the young reader may come to a fuller understanding of a period in U.S. history still recalled by many who are alive today.

Suggestions for Reports or Activities

1. Enie keeps a journal in which she writes about her feelings, her school, and her surroundings. Write a few pages from the journal after she leaves the farm. Include descriptions of her new surroundings, activities, future plans, and so forth.

2. On a piece of paper make two columns. In the first column list all of the reasons why Enie should go away from the farm; in the second column list her father's reasons why she should not. Which set of reasons makes more sense to you? Why?

3. Research the life of small farmers during the Depression. How accurate is the picture offered by this book?

Roll of Thunder, Hear My Cry   Mildred D. Taylor
New York: Dial, 1976. 276p. (2, 3)

Growing up in rural Mississippi during the Depression, Cassie Logan and her brothers Stacey, Christopher John, and Little Man are more fortunate than many folks, black or white, because the Logans own their land. They are a loving, close-knit family, disciplined and highly principled. Mama teaches in the Negro school. There's not enough money from the cotton crop to pay the taxes, so Papa works on the railroad. They live within the prevailing system of white dominance but resist where possible. For example, Mama organizes a boycott of the Wallaces' store when it is learned that the Wallaces are responsible for setting some black men on fire. But Cassie is beginning to learn that justice for blacks does not exist in this place at this time. (For other books about some of the same characters, see *Mississippi Bridge,* above, and *The Road to Memphis,* Section VII.)

Comment

This story, a Newbery Medal winner, shows that, despite the pain suffered each day of their lives in the South during the Depression, black families strove to teach their children dignity. The book points up the treatment of blacks by poor whites who were also struggling for existence; the faulty criminal justice system; the worn, soiled textbooks given to black schools; the demeaning use of first names for blacks while blacks had to use respectful titles when addressing whites; sly attempts by white landowners to steal land owned by blacks; various methods of making blacks submit to white demands.

Suggestions for Reports or Activities

1. What advantages did the Logans have over T. J. Avery's family? Why did T. J. try to act important? Why did he hang around with Jeremy's brothers?

2. How did the Depression affect the lives of farmers in the South? How did the U.S. government attempt to improve the farmers' lot?

3. The author gives some examples of how blacks tried to resist mistreatment or to "get back at" some of their tormentors. Comment on these efforts. Do you think they helped to bring about changes? Explain.

A Time of Troubles   Pieter van Raven
New York: Scribner, 1990. 180p. (1, 2)

In the midst of the Great Depression, Roy Purdy's father, Harlow, gets out of prison and decides to head west to look for a job. Fourteen-year-old Roy reluctantly abandons his boat-building job by Chesapeake Bay to accompany his father to California. They are befriended by other job-seekers along the way until they reach a camp of would-be fruit harvesters near San Francisco. There, to Roy's dismay, his father signs on as a security guard with the Growers' Association, while Roy and the others are earning less than a dollar a day picking oranges. What will happen if the workers decide to go on strike to improve wages and working conditions?

Comment

Many of the practices of the 1930s are illustrated in this story: people "riding the rails" to California to look for work; the deceptive and greedy practices of the orchard owners; the labeling of the union organizers as "Reds"; the scourge of polio; the lack of government support for the unemployed and the unemployable; the faith of the poor in President Roosevelt. Young readers should come away with a new understanding of the basis for current laws and government policies.

Suggestions for Reports or Activities

1. Mary has to wear a brace on one of her legs because she had polio. What kind of disease is that? Find out how many people had it in the United States in the period from 1930 to 1955. What were the usual effects? How and when was the disease brought under control?

2. Picking fruit and vegetables from California orchards and farms has always been a job for the poor and helpless. In the 1930s the people looking for work were sometimes called "Okies": Why was that? Who does most of the picking today? Read about César Chavez and the United Grapeworkers Union and explain their aims.

3. What kinds of laws were passed under the Roosevelt Administration to assist the poor? What was the "New Deal"? Which of those laws are still operative today?

4. Write what you think happened after the end of this story: Did the strike succeed? Were the men who killed Mr. Landon and

burned his house punished? What happened at the end of the 1930s to boost the economy of California?

Tracks Clayton Bess
Boston: Houghton Mifflin, 1986. 180p. (2, 3)

It is the middle of the Depression. Eleven-year-old Blue, feeling that he no longer fits in at home, manages to scramble aboard a freight car, following after his big brother Monroe. Monroe is already experienced in riding the rails to look for work. It's a rough life, Blue finds out. Although they find a friendly welcome among the hoboes, there are also unpleasant characters like Blade, who is surly and vindictive. Food is scarce, baths are few, and riding the rails is dangerous. Monroe and Blue get work for a while, helping an Italian farm widow whose husband was killed by the Ku Klux Klan as he tried to unionize the sharecroppers. When the boys chance to witness a group of Klansmen butchering a Mexican youth for courting a white girl, the Klansmen spread the rumor that the boys are the murderers. Monroe is seriously hurt in their escape, but help comes through the brotherhood of the "tracks."

Comment

The adventures of Blue and Monroe evoke the life lived by thousands of desperate men during the Depression. The culture of the hoboes is a fascinating part of the American past: the dangers and discomfort of traveling by freight car, the gatherings in "jungles," begging at farmhouses for work or food, friendships made on the road. This book also provides a chilling look at the activities of the Ku Klux Klan, the plight of sharecroppers under federal agricultural policies, and the lives of people in the Dust Bowl. The use of speech patterns and aphorisms of rural Oklahoma adds to the sense of history.

Suggestions for Reports or Activities

1. What was the Dust Bowl? Locate this region on a map. How did the Depression affect the people who lived in the Dust Bowl? Check in a reference source for information on the tree-planting project mentioned in the book.

2. Find out more about the hoboes. Write a short paper on the lifestyle of the hoboes. Were there any unwritten or informal codes of behavior which hoboes followed?

3. This book includes several terms which belong to the slang of the hoboes. What is a "jungle"? A "bull"? Can you locate any other slang terms of the hoboes?

4. Research the attitudes of the Ku Klux Klan toward unions. Discuss these in a short paper. Does your research correspond to the events in the book?

Walk Gently This Good Earth   Margaret Craven
New York: Putnam, 1977. 172p. (1, 2)

The Westcott family is affected by various events in history, starting with the Depression. Close-knit and affectionate, the family weathers all the tragedies and good times that befall them by relying on traditional values. The father, Judge Westcott, is portrayed as a solid and wise anchor who leaves a tremendous gap when he dies. Then World War II separates Cathy from her adopted brother, Angela marries hastily, and Maria becomes a nun. How the family survives as a unit makes for a story of compassion.

Comment

The economic misery of the Depression, the personal and political hardships of World War II, and the social turbulence of the 1960s all take their toll on the family in various ways. At the same time, all are made vivid and meaningful for the modern reader because of their impact on the fictional characters. The Westcotts meet their problems in general with independent yet cooperative spirits.

Suggestions for Reports or Activities

1. Find out what the Spectre of the Brocken is. Write a description of it and of the children's experience with it. How did they feel?

2. Write an article for the People section of the local newspaper about Neal's return from the war.

3. Make a family album for the Westcotts by cutting out or drawing pictures to represent family members. Show their development through the years. Write a paragraph about each phase in history to include with the different sections in the album.

MORE CHALLENGING BOOKS
FOR ADVANCED READERS

All the King's Men   Robert Penn Warren
New York: Harcourt, 1946. 464p.

A classic study of the corrupting effects of power, this book offers vivid characterizations of political figures typical of the era. Believing that the end justifies the means, Willie Stark, governor of an unnamed Southern state, hurts many people on the way to the top. The reader comes away with a greater understanding of the choices people in power may have to make.

The Grapes of Wrath   John Steinbeck
New York: Viking, 1939. 619p.

Uprooted from an Oklahoma farm by drought, tractors, and grasping bankers, the impoverished Joad family goes West, there to become itinerant workers on the large corporate farms of California. The author captures the spirit as well as the trials of the thousands of refugee families who went from being farm owners to toiling as migrant day laborers in a West where there was no more cheap, fertile land.

Let the Circle Be Unbroken   Mildred D. Taylor
New York: Dial, 1981. 445p.

Through the day-to-day experiences of the Logan family in the hostile environment of Depression-burdened Mississippi, young readers are shown the qualities of suffering and resistance, and of determination despite enormous odds, as lived by black people, particularly in the South in the years before the Civil Rights movement. The book also provides a view of the failure of federal farm programs designed to help the rural poor.

Manhattan Transfer   John Dos Passos
Boston: Houghton Mifflin, 1925. 404p.

The characters in this impressionistic novel set in New York City are immigrants and old-line Americans, rich and poor, honest and crooked, lawyers and soldiers, men and women. The story touches on World War I, immigration from Eastern Europe, Prohibition, unemployment, and speculation in stocks as issues directly affecting the lives of the characters.

Native Son   Richard Wright
New York: Harper & Row, 1940. 392p.

Total isolation—physical, geographical, psychological—of blacks and whites from each other appears to mark this period of history. In 1930s Chicago, American Communists are presented as the only whites genuinely interested in twenty-year-old Bigger Thomas as an individual, rather than as a representative black. The capitalists' hostility to the development of labor unions is also emphasized.

VII *The United States and World War II*

Alan and Naomi Myron Levoy
New York: Harper, 1977. 192p. (2, 3)

Alan grumbles about his parents' request that he spend time with a strange girl, the silent and withdrawn Naomi, who with her mother has escaped from war-torn France and moved in with the Liebmans upstairs. Naomi is in shock. She has seen her father killed by the Gestapo. Now she simply sits tearing paper into little pieces. With Alan's help she begins to respond and goes to school with him. But her recovery is not so simple. A distressing incident plunges her back into her shell.

Comment

Since America was spared invasion and bombing, World War II was experienced differently here. This book shows one facet of the impact of the war on the United States: the accommodation of refugees from Hitler's Europe by American society. It shows the psychological effects of war experiences on one young person and touches on the damaging consequences of religious prejudice.

Suggestions for Reports or Activities

1. One important anti-Nazi activity during World War II was the operation of the French Underground, which facilitated the escape of Jews hunted by the Gestapo. Read about the underground movement in France. What was the importance of the Paris sewer system?

2. Check some facts on the coming of persecuted Jewish people to the United States during the Second World War. From what countries did they come? Who were some of the people well known today

who came to America as a result of Hitler's purge? Write a short paper telling of the life and contributions of one such person.

3. Would you have preferred another ending to the book? Since this is a story which points to some of the terrible effects of war, is the ending appropriate? Try writing an alternate conclusion.

Annie's Promise   Sonia Levitin
New York: Atheneum, 1993. 186p. (2, 3)

In this book, the third in Levitin's series about the Platt family, the youngest sister, Annie, takes center stage. Sickly and insecure, she seizes an opportunity to attend summer camp in the mountains as a means of establishing her independence from her parents. Since she is well aware of the prejudice and discrimination suffered by Jews in Germany, from which the family has fled, she is shocked by her parents' hostility to her new black friend, Tally. While at camp, however, she thrives in the diverse community and learns that she has many skills and gifts to offer. It is when she herself deliberately humiliates another girl that she sees how easy it is to make choices that are not only wrong but irrevocable. (For other stories featuring the Platt sisters, see *Journey to America* and *Silver Days,* below.)

Comment

This story may resonate with any youngster who has felt that he or she did not "belong." Generational clashes in values and priorities also ring true: dreams change as people get older, and everyone makes adjustments to reality. Much of Annie's confusion, while typical of young adolescents, is also specific to the post–World War II period in its emphasis on interethnic suspicion and antipathy.

Suggestions for Reports or Activities

1. The war finally ends with the atomic bombing of Hiroshima and Nagasaki. Find out why the U.S. dropped the bombs and what the casualties were. Was there any controversy about the decision to use the bombs? More than fifty years later, are people still suffering the effects?

2. The war with Germany ended in May of 1945. What made the Germans agree to unconditional surrender? How long did it take till the American soldiers could return home? Did some of them stay

with the Army of Occupation, or were new men sent over for that purpose?

3. Think about Nancy Rae, the girl whom Annie mistreated. Explain why, in your opinion, Nancy Rae was so cruel. How might Annie have handled the problem differently?

Between Two Worlds   Joan Lingard
New York: Dutton, Lodestar, 1991. 186p. (2, 3)

The Petersons, a Latvian family left homeless after World War II, migrate to Toronto (Canada) in 1948 to start a new life. Lukas, the father, falls ill immediately, and the family's sponsors move away. The children—eighteen-year-old twins Astra and Hugo, and twelve-year-old Tomas—realize that they will have to find jobs to hold the family together, as Kristina, their mother, is needed to care for their father. Surprisingly, finding work turns out to be easier than making friends or locating an acceptable place to live. Astra and Hugo, in particular, have many adventures before they save enough money to think about buying some land and building their own house.

Comment

Moving from Europe to North America (whether to the United States or to Canada) has often meant a reversal in roles for the youngsters in the family, as they learn more easily to cope with a strange language and customs. Because of the father's illness in this story, it is no exception to that pattern. The loyalty that the children show to their parents and to each other provides a gentle lesson in values and priorities for today's young readers.

Suggestions for Reports or Activities

1. What happened to the three Baltic nations—Estonia, Latvia, and Lithuania—at the end of World War II? Research their history during the first half of the twentieth century, including how long they were independent, what their relations were with each other, and their fate during the War itself. What is their status today?

2. Has your family ever moved to a different neighborhood, city, or country? If so, tell what problems you had that resembled some of those encountered by the children in this story.

3. Write Hugo's letter to Bettina breaking off their engagement. What reasons did he give? How did he try to tell her that it wasn't her fault?

Hang Out the Flag   Katherine McGlade Marko
New York: Macmillan, 1992. 159p. (2, 3)
　　Leslie Jamieson's father has a few days leave from the Navy before being sent overseas in World War II. Leslie wants to do something special for his return, but it is hard to figure out exactly what. She is also coping with wartime shortages, blackouts, a classmate who is sure that a German-born neighbor is a spy for the Nazis, an irritating older cousin, and a little brother for whom she is responsible while her mother works in a war materials factory. Will Buddy and Leslie turn in the neighbor and risk hurting innocent people? And what will Leslie do to welcome her father home?

Comment

World War II was the last U.S. military engagement that had a daily impact on civilians as well as on members of the armed forces. Today's young readers have had no direct experience of blackouts, rationing, urban vegetable gardens, collections of newspapers, cans, and grease, and such other "patriotic" activities as spying on one's immigrant neighbors. This story imparts the flavor of that period through the concerns of a sixth-grade girl with whom contemporary readers should be able to identify.

Suggestions for Reports or Activities

1. Do some research about rationing during World War II. How many gas coupons could a family get per month? How were coupons for shoes and other personal items allocated? What different kinds of shortages was the rationing system supposed to remedy?
2. Leslie took a big chance when she called the police about Mr. Von Desch. If he and his wife had been innocent, they might have been badly hurt. List all the clues that suggested to Leslie that the Von Desches might be dangerous. Do you think she did the right thing by not giving her name to the police?
3. Leslie promised her father that she would write to him after he left. Compose one of Leslie's letters describing what she was doing

and thinking about six months after the time of this story. Did she and Ruthie become friends? What happened to Buddy? Make up some adventures for the children and have Leslie tell her father about them.

Journey Home Yoshiko Uchida
New York: Atheneum, 1978. 131p. (3)

At last Yuki Sakane and her parents are on the outside. They have been released from the concentration camp in Utah and are living in an apartment in Salt Lake City. When will they be able to go home to California, to their own house? After a time they learn that Reverend Wada at a Japanese church in Berkeley has set up a hostel and will sponsor them. But troubles tarnish their new happiness. Jobs for Japanese-Americans are hard to find, vandals ransack the Buddhist temple where many of the evacuees have stored their belongings, and then arsonists attempt to destroy the recently restored Japanese grocery store. Yuki's brother Ken, returning from serving with the American army in France, has a shattered leg and seems strangely withdrawn. Will the Sakanes ever really be at home again?

Comment

In this sequel to *Journey to Topaz* (below), the author shows how hard it was for Japanese-Americans returning from the camps to pick up the pieces of their lives. Anti-Japanese sentiment took different forms, from personal insults to major criminal incidents. The determination of these people to show themselves loyal Americans and to overcome prejudice while upholding Japanese ideals is vividly portrayed. Readers will experience from a Japanese-American point of view the relief that the war was over combined with the pain of losing loved ones in the bombing of Hiroshima.

Suggestions for Reports or Activities

1. What events led to the United States' decision to drop atomic bombs on Hiroshima and Nagasaki? Would you agree that this was the best decision at the time?

2. Uncle Oka does not feel friendly toward Yuki's white friends. Why?

3. One of the important values in Japanese culture is respect for the elderly. Write a short paper on how this value is expressed in the story.

Journey to America   Sonia Levitin
New York: Atheneum, 1972. 150p. (2, 3)

In Berlin in 1938 terrible things are happening. Although it is clear that Jews are no longer safe in Hitler's Germany, the Platt family cannot decide if they should emigrate. Finally, Papa decides to go to America, leaving behind Mama and the three girls. Lisa, the middle daughter, tells this story of their escape to Switzerland and then the long wait for Papa to save enough money to pay for their tickets to join him. The girls spend some time in a camp for refugee children, where they are ill-fed and mistreated; meanwhile, Mama develops pneumonia and is hospitalized. A number of adventures mark their lives until they are at last allowed to sail for America. (For other stories featuring the Platt sisters, see *Silver Days,* below, and *Annie's Promise,* above.)

Comment

Readers will learn what it was like to live in a country and at a time when there was no security, no certainty, and no defense against either insecurity or uncertainty. The obstacles placed in the way of those trying to leave Germany, on the one hand, and those trying to enter the United States, on the other, appear as arbitrary as they are numerous. People met along the way may be kind and generous, or abusive and capricious; this, too, appears to be arbitrary.

Suggestions for Reports or Activities

1. Make a list of all the difficulties faced by the Platts as they prepared to leave Germany and started on their trip. Next to each obstacle write what the family did to overcome it.

2. Lisa and her Swiss friend Erica both wonder if religion has anything to do with goodness. What do you think? What sort of people tend to be cruel and what sort tend to be kind? Write about your own experiences with cruelty and kindness.

3. Find out how many Europeans emigrated between 1935 and 1940. What countries did they go to? List at least ten German emigrants from this period who later became famous in the United States.

Journey to Topaz   Yoshiko Uchida
New York: Scribner, 1971. 149p. (3)

Life changes suddenly for Yuki Sakane and her family on December 7, 1941. After the bombing of Pearl Harbor, all Japanese-Americans living on the West Coast are the objects of suspicion. Because Yuki's father works for a large Japanese business firm, he is immediately taken into custody by the FBI. Yuki's brother Ken leaves the university. Then comes the official order: pack two suitcases and prepare to be evacuated. Mr. Sakane has been sent with other prominent businessmen to a camp in Montana. Yuki, her mother, and Ken are finally sent to Topaz, Utah. Anxious to prove their loyalty to the United States, the Sakanes and other internees make the best of an unfortunate and painful situation. (For another part of the Sakanes' adventures, see *Journey Home,* above.)

Comment

The fact that during World War II there were actual concentration camps in the United States is little known by young people. This book allows readers to experience the incredulity and fear, the disruption and unhappiness, endured by thousands of innocent people in a time of national alarm. The story points up the resourcefulness of the internees, who managed to hold together their lives in spite of difficult living arrangements and material deprivation.

Suggestions for Reports or Activities

1. Read President Roosevelt's order for the evacuation of the Japanese-Americans. What was the reaction in leading newspapers? Compare editorials in a Los Angeles or San Francisco newspaper with commentaries from one or two newspapers from Eastern and Midwestern cities. Can you notice any difference in attitude toward the evacuation?

2. Who were the Nisei? Why were Yuki's parents considered "enemy aliens"? What were the restrictions against Japanese becoming citizens of the United States? When were changes made in these restrictions?

3. Since the end of the war, has there been any attempt to repay the Japanese internees for any financial losses they suffered as a result of the evacuation?

4. Describe the home that Yuki's family made for themselves at Topaz.

The Last Mission   Harry Mazer
New York: Delacorte, 1979. 182p. (2, 3)

Jack Raab is determined to fight Hitler. When the Army turns down his brother Irv because of his rheumatic heart, fifteen-year-old

Jack has his chance. Borrowing Irv's birth certificate, he enlists in the Air Force. Pretending in a note to his parents that he's gone exploring out West, Jack heads for basic training and soon is a gunner on a B-17 bomber. He makes fast friends with the rest of the crew but never reveals his age. They fly twenty-five missions over Germany and narrowly escape after a crash landing in the English Channel; then their luck runs out. Jack is a prisoner of the Germans when the war in Europe ends. Hitler is dead. And now, he just wants to go home.

Comment

Based on the author's own World War II experience, this story is an authentic rendering of the close-knit fellowship aboard a B-17. For young readers it is a look at war from the perspective of a young man who yearns to be in the fray of battle, to be a hero saving the Jews from Hitler. A year later, however, the boyish idea of war is transformed into a grim and painful reality. The occasional use of so-called vulgar terms adds to the reality of conversation among soldiers.

Suggestions for Reports or Activities

1. Read about the Allied bombing of Germany. What major cities were targets? What important historic buildings were destroyed?

2. Jack's actions caused considerable pain for his family. Do you feel that he was justified or unjustified in running away to join the Air Force? Why?

3. What do you think happens to Jack after the story ends? How will he get along with young people his own age who simply stayed at home and went to high school?

Molly Donnelly   Jean Thesman
Boston: Houghton Mifflin, 1993. 186p. (2, 3)

Molly and her two friends, Louise and Emily, do everything together. Then comes December 7, 1941, and the Japanese attack on Pearl Harbor. Emily's family, the Tanakas, suspected of being spies, are forced to leave the house next door, and after a while a new family moves in. Molly writes letters to Emily in the form of entries in her journal, which she plans to have Emily read as soon as she comes home. Four years pass till Molly learns Emily's fate and decides her own.

Comment

Molly is an ordinary person living an ordinary life when the war begins. Then, in a world changing in unexpected ways, she learns to deal with such issues as the news of cousins killed overseas, parents going to work in war-related factories, and a younger brother running wild, as well as the normal anxieties of growing up. The breakdown of communication and fellowship within the family is especially hard to bear.

Suggestions for Reports or Activities

1. Find out more about the internment camps for the Japanese-Americans. Who had to go there? When were they opened and for how long? Did anyone ever try to escape? What happened to the internees when they were allowed to go home? Did anyone publicly (that is, in the newspapers or in Congress) object to the internment?

2. Molly's cousin Maureen was captured by the Japanese in the Philippines. What was the name of the battle in 1942 at which the American Army was defeated? How many prisoners did the Japanese take and what happened to them? Were any of them still alive when the war ended in 1945?

3. Compose the letter that Emily might have sent to Molly if she had written from the hotel where she and her family were first sent. Tell how much space they had for a family of four; what her father and mother might have been saying or doing; what they thought might happen to them; and anything else you can imagine.

4. The book ends when Molly and Andrew are about to meet again after exchanging letters for some years. What did they say to each other? How did they act? Write the journal entry that Molly might have composed when she got home after seeing Andrew.

The Moon Bridge   Marcia Savin
New York: Scholastic, 1992. 231 p. (2, 3)

Despite the bombing of Pearl Harbor in 1941, the group of fifth graders in San Francisco pays little attention to the war. Then their teacher's fiancé is killed, and Ruthie's friend Shirl refuses to play with her anymore if Ruthie insists on befriending a new girl in school, Mitzi Fujimoto. Ruthie can hardly believe that her friend is serious, but she defies Shirl until Mitzi's family is relocated to an internment camp.

Then Ruthie writes letters to her friend which she cannot mail since she has no address for her. Finally, more than three years later, she hears that Mitzi is coming home. Will they still be friends?

Comment

This book tells the story of the national injustice done to Japanese-Americans from the point of view of a child who sees all the horror and unreason of it—particularly when the family in question also has a son fighting in the U.S. military. The gradual understanding of what it means to be a member of a despised and helpless minority dawns on Ruthie even as it may dawn on the young reader.

Suggestions for Reports or Activities

1. Ruthie's parents appear to be opposed to the internment of Japanese-Americans. Look through an index of newspaper articles of the period (1942) and see if you can find anything actually published in opposition. If so, tell what reasons they gave. If not, tell what reasons the articles in favor of internment gave to justify that action.

2. In the minds of the children who were mean to Mitzi, all people of Japanese descent were a threat to other Americans; that is, individuals were reduced to just one aspect of their entire selves. Have you ever seen this happen in your own community? Give some examples of the treatment of people based solely on their religion, race, neighborhood, or social class.

3. Mitzi's brother fought against the Japanese in one of the "Nisei units." Find out how many Japanese-Americans were in these units and what kind of fighters they turned out to be. How did their casualty rate compare with that of other units? What do you conclude from this?

4. Mitzi had missed three years of education. Do you think she ever caught up? Imagine that you left school in the fifth grade and then started again in the eighth: How would you manage? What would be your hardest subject, and why? Tell what you would do to catch up with your classmates.

A Necessary End   Nathaniel Benchley
New York: Harper & Row, 1976. 193p. (1, 2)
Ralph, a new Navy recruit, has received a diary as a seventeenth-birthday gift from his family. Following his English teacher's advice,

he begins recording all the details in case it should be published one day. He is assigned to a PC, or submarine chaser, patrolling the Atlantic coastal waters for German submarines. Ralph thinks it's pretty boring duty. But there are some laughs, and he does take part in some amusing escapades. Although letters from home are eagerly awaited, his family sends advice about keeping his feet dry; letters from his best girl become shorter and fewer. Ralph knows that he is becoming a different person because of his new life. Then suddenly his ship is ordered to the Pacific, and here he finds that the war is very real. Two months after Hiroshima, Ralph's ship is escorting occupation troop ships through mine-infested waters. He sends his diary home to his teacher—just in case.

Comment

The poignant depiction of a young man growing and changing under harsh circumstances shows how the war affected young American enlisted men. As the author states, "The men at the lower levels have no sense of global strategy; they have, very simply, the fervent hope they will survive the twin enemies of man: hostile action and boredom." In the background is the progress of World War II: the end of the Atlantic conflict; the intensified action in the Pacific; President Roosevelt's death; and the bombing of Hiroshima and Nagasaki.

Suggestions for Reports or Activities

1. Ralph's ship is patrolling the Atlantic coast for submarines, which he considers a boring assignment. Find out about the threat to the U.S. mainland from German submarines. Write a short paper on the importance of this duty.

2. In the front of the book, the author quotes a passage from Shakespeare. Did you notice it before you read the book? How does this hint make the conclusion inevitable? Write another ending for the story and suggest another title for the book.

3. Research how World War II was fought on the seas. Discuss your findings in a short paper.

One More Time   Charles Ferry
Boston: Houghton Mifflin, 1985. 171p. (2)

The Gene Markham Orchestra is on its last cross-country tour as Skeets Sinclair, the clarinetist, tells the story. The United States has just been plunged into World War II. Because the bandleader has enlisted, the number-two band in the country will have to break up. The members have grown to depend on each other. This last trip is a time of remembering, of appreciating, and of questioning as they travel by bus and train between one-night stands from college campus to military base to club. The war is beginning to reach into all of their lives. Some band members are finding draft notices in the mail. Gus, the manager, has not heard from his son in the Pacific. What about the combo Skeets hopes to start? And what about Polly, the vocalist? They are all in love with her, but Skeets is seriously smitten. What will happen to everyone?

Comment

World War II in some of its aspects and effects on people in America is effectively evoked through the hopes and fears of the band members. In the background are comments about the draft, rationing, new jobs in defense plants, German U-boats off the New Jersey coast, the bombing of Tokyo. Entertaining the troops was an important role for bands and other entertainers. A racial incident at a hotel in Detroit shows the reality of prejudice in the North in the 1940s. The author has created a historical atmosphere in which the uncertainties caused by the war are mirrored in the concerns of the characters.

Suggestions for Reports or Activities

1. What were the regulations for enlistment in military service during World War II? Why was Skeets 4-F? How did Harry get deferred?

2. The big band was a phenomenon of American life. Write a short paper on the rise of the big band. Or select one of the famous bandleaders (Benny Goodman, Harry James, Count Basie, Glenn Miller, for example) and write a short paper on his wartime activities.

Rain of Fire   Marion Dane Bauer
New York: Clarion, 1983. 153p. (2, 3)

When Steve's brother Matthew comes home in 1946 after serving in the American Army of Occupation in Japan, he seems like a stranger. His inability to share his experiences and feelings with twelve-year-old Steve leads the younger boy to invent his own stories for his friends to explain Matthew's reserve. A rivalry with an older boy, new in the neighborhood, for the allegiance of Steve's childhood friends leads to several dangerous exploits, culminating in unanticipated injuries, both physical and emotional. Matthew at last attempts to explain to Steve what it was like to be in Hiroshima after the dropping of the atomic bomb and to discover that the Japanese were not "Japs" but human beings like himself and his family.

Comment

The complexities of war and life itself come alive in this tale of a young boy's addiction to lying as he attempts to color reality more to his liking. Serious value conflicts come to the fore in the course of Steve's confrontation of issues of competition, loyalty, patriotism, honor, and war itself. Matthew's identification of a dying Japanese boy with his little brother emphasizes the truth of the notion of the human family in a way that young readers can understand and appreciate.

Suggestions for Reports or Activities

1. Steve tries to tell his brother that the atomic bombings saved many American lives. Is there another interpretation of the decision to drop the bombs? Read about the controversy surrounding that decision and draw your own conclusions regarding its necessity.

2. What is shrapnel and how does it harm human beings? In your opinion, will the boys recover without scars? What will they say to each other when they meet again?

3. Compare the stories Ray and Steve told about their relatives (Ray's father, Steve's brother) who were in the war with the truth in both cases. Explain why the boys made up these particular stories. What values were most important to each of them?

4. Imagine the scene where Steve tells his mother what really happened to Ginger and why. What does he say? How does his mother respond? Write out their conversation.

Raspberry One   Charles Ferry
Boston: Houghton Mifflin, 1983. 232p. (2, 3)

For so many young men and women during World War II, life was to be lived for the moment because life was precious. Yet they did not know what war really meant. While awaiting their orders to ship out to the Pacific, Nick and Hildy, two young crewmen on a Navy bomber, strike up a merry friendship with college sophomores Fran and Diane. By the time their orders come, Franny and Nick are engaged and determined to work out an interfaith marriage when the war is over. The story shifts then to the Pacific, to the frightening experience of the Japanese kamikaze offensive and the struggle to control Iwo Jima. Nick and Hildy's plane, *Raspberry One,* is shot down and their beloved senior officer killed. Although Nick and Hildy are both seriously wounded (Nick loses a hand, and Hildy probably will never have full use of one leg), they do return, inevitably wise beyond their years, ready to take adult responsibility for their lives.

Comment

Based partly on the author's own experience, *Raspberry One* shows how the war created intense friendships, wrecked lives, and forced young people to grow. The pain, terror, excitement, and carnage aboard an aircraft carrier in the midst of bombing attacks are described graphically. In addition to experiencing feelings of young men in wartime, such as deep devotion to friend and officer, readers will learn of the actual operation of a Navy bomber and of the magnitude of the Pacific operation. The fate of European Jews and the bombing of Hiroshima and Nagasaki are also discussed.

Suggestions for Reports or Activities

1. Is the author correct in his description of the training of the crew for *Raspberry One*? Research the preparation of bomber crews during World War II.

2. Iwo Jima is discussed in considerable detail. Look up Iwo Jima in an encyclopedia or other source. Where is it located? What was its importance to the Allied forces? Can you locate a copy of the famous photograph of the flag-raising on Iwo Jima?

3. From what you have been studying about World War II, and from the experiences of the war in the Pacific described in this book, do you feel that the United States was justified in dropping atom bombs on Hiroshima and Nagasaki? Discuss.

The Road to Memphis   Mildred D. Taylor
New York: Dial, 1990. 290p. (1, 2)

In Mississippi in 1941 black people had to watch themselves around the local whites. Cassie Logan, her brother, and a number of their friends run into trouble with three brothers whose favorite sport is humiliating and intimidating their black contemporaries. Moe Turner is a decent young man who is in love with Cassie. One day, when he is changing a tire and has a crowbar in his hand, the three turn on him. Unable to bear their teasing in Cassie's presence, he strikes out at his tormentors. In the next few days, even as the nation readies its response to the Japanese attack on Pearl Harbor, the youngsters take on adult responsibilities in order to cope with the aftermath of Moe's resistance. (For other books about some of the same characters, see *Mississippi Bridge* and *Roll of Thunder, Hear My Cry*, Section VI.)

Comment

In the South before the Civil Rights movement, black people learned ways of retaining their dignity along with their lives. Occasionally, they were shown some compassion by whites, but mostly they were on their own. The dilemma posed by the onset of war is very real: Should the young men go off to fight for a country run by whites who mistreat them? Or should they aim to fill the good jobs being left open as the white youths join the Army? Or will they even have a choice?

Suggestions for Reports or Activities

1. What do you suppose happened to Moe in Chicago? Write a letter that he might have sent to Cassie and Stacey telling about his life there. Include information about where he was living, what kind of work he was doing, what was different about life in Chicago as compared to Mississippi, and so on. You will want to read a little about what life in the big Northern cities was like for black people in the early 1940s.

2. Jeremy Simms is an unusual character. Explain the conflicting pulls on his loyalties and how he resolved them. What experiences or traits made him different from his relatives?

3. The black man Solomon Bradley was born, brought up, and educated in the North. Why did he go South to practice law? What did he hope to accomplish by giving up the law and going into another profession?

Silver Days Sonia Levitin
New York: Atheneum, 1989. 186p. (2, 3)
When the Platt family—Mama and the three girls, Ruth, Lisa, and Annie—finally join Papa in America in 1941, they hardly know what to expect. As German Jews who have already waited a whole year in

Switzerland for entry into the United States, all they are certain of is that they are lucky to be out of Europe and far from the trauma of war. Then comes the Japanese attack on Pearl Harbor, and the Platts, by then living in California, feel threatened once again. Told from the point of view of the thirteen-year-old middle sister, "silver days" are not quite golden but hope is strong. (For other stories featuring the Platt sisters, see *Journey to America* and *Annie's Promise,* above.)

Comment

The immense changes in one's life and self-image that come from leaving one's home and emigrating to another country are made clear in this story. Lisa's struggle to be as American as possible while holding on to her dream of becoming a dancer is interposed with the need for her previously pampered mother to do menial work to help support the family while confronting her sense of guilt for leaving her own mother behind in Germany. It takes Mama's brush with death to give the family a new perspective and new sources of courage to face the future.

Suggestions for Reports or Activities

1. Early in 1942 Annie's friend Setsu and her family are forced to leave their homes to go to an internment camp in the desert. Find out what laws were passed regarding Japanese-Americans, how many were interned for how long, and what happened to those who spent the entire war in the camps. What did the U.S. Congress do in the early 1990s to make up for the internment?

2. What do you think Ruth said when she told Peter Ross that she wasn't going to Michigan with him to meet his parents? How did he react? Using the hints in the book, write out the conversation that they might have had on the telephone.

3. The girls' grandmother, Lucille Weiss, was sent to Auschwitz. Read about the concentration camp there and speculate about what happened to Mrs. Weiss. Is there any way she could have survived? How many inmates were found alive at the end of the war?

4. In this book all the young men seem to be ready to go to war, some of them even enlisting when they are under age. But suppose one of them decided not to go, even when drafted: What would have happened to him? Read about provisions for conscientious objectors (people who refused to fight) during World War II and summarize the choices they faced.

Stepping on the Cracks   Mary Downing Hahn
New York: Clarion, 1991. 216p. (1, 2)

Margaret and Elizabeth are affected by World War II mostly because they worry about their big brothers who are fighting the Nazis overseas. Back home, they have their own problems with Gordy, the local bully, and his two sidekicks. As the children get ready to enter sixth grade, the girls discover that Gordy is hiding someone in a hut in the woods, a man who turns out to be an Army deserter and a conscientious objector. Should they help him, or should they turn him in? When the man becomes so ill that they can no longer care for him by themselves, Margaret and Elizabeth have to make a decision.

Comment

This story is a good introduction to the idea of opposition to war even when patriotism calls for joining up. As the two girls come to an understanding of the deserter's feelings against killing, regardless of who does it, so does the reader. Also considered is the issue of a decent citizen's responsibility to interfere on behalf of a family in which the wife and children are being battered.

Suggestions for Reports or Activities

1. U.S. law allows people to refuse to fight on the ground of conscientious objection to war. Find out how many conscientious objectors there were during World War I and World War II; what happened to them? What kinds of alternative service were available?

2. Margaret's mother observes that her son Jimmy had asked her to interfere on behalf of Stuart when he was a child, just as Margaret had asked her to help Gordy and his little sister. Imagine that her mother had reported Mr. Smith to the authorities as Jimmy had asked: What might have happened as a result?

3. What is your opinion about conscientious objection? Would you require every able-bodied male (or female) to fight in case of war? List the arguments in favor of your position and then list the counterarguments.

Summer of My German Soldier   Bette Greene
New York: Dial, 1973. 230p. (2, 3)

Excitement comes to the sleepy town of Jenkinsville, Arkansas, one summer when a camp is set up there for German prisoners of war.

For Patty Bergen it means a small break in the monotony and unhappiness of her life. Bright and outspoken, she seems able only to antagonize her unfeeling parents, proprietors of a small department store. Patty's only real friend is the black housekeeper, until the day she hides an escaped German prisoner in the room over her family garage. Anton appreciates Patty and treats her as "a person of value." He has to move on, and Patty is unable to keep secret the ring he has given her, although she invents a story about its origin. When it is finally revealed that Patty, whose family is Jewish, has sheltered a Nazi soldier, the town is in an uproar and Patty is sent to a reform school. But she knows that she cannot be kept down forever.

Comment

The presence of German prisoners on the outskirts of town added fuel to the already hot anti-German sentiments. Greene shows how suspicion builds in tense times. The latent anti-Semitism of the townspeople is also revealed. Anton, the German prisoner, is depicted as far more compassionate and intelligent than most of the people of Jenkinsville.

Suggestions for Reports or Activities

1. Stereotyping, using the same label to apply to everyone in a group, is especially likely to occur in times of tension, such as during a war. Discuss some of the stereotypes that Americans have used at different periods of this century.

2. Check some newspaper accounts of hysteria in the United States over enemy nationals within U.S. borders. From today's perspective, was this attitude justified? Discuss.

3. If you have not read the sequel to this book, how would you continue Patty's story? How does this memorable summer affect her life?

A Summer on Thirteenth Street   Charlotte Herman
New York: Dutton, 1991. 181p. (2, 3)

In Chicago in 1944 growing up is complicated by the war. Shirley Cohen and her friends look forward to the summer months, even while coping with shortages, blackouts, and casualty lists. They plant a victory garden, although unsure of how that will help the war effort. Of course, if they can show that the German-speaking janitor of

Shirley's apartment building is a spy, that will prove their patriotism once and for all. Meanwhile, the cat has kittens, tomboy Shirley develops a crush on the druggist's son who has joined the Army, and the janitor's true situation is revealed.

Comment

The ways in which war intrudes into everyday civilian life are made clear in this story. At the same time, children grow up, accidents happen, misunderstandings occur, and life continues. While the urban setting of fifty years ago was generally safer and more predictable than it is today, contemporary readers will empathize with youngsters whose judgments and assumptions do not always coincide with the reality they are experiencing.

Suggestions for Reports or Activities

1. The main wartime shortage that affected Shirley was that of bubble gum. What else was missing for American civilians? Find out what kinds of civilian goods were not readily available during World War II.

2. Shirley was hoping that Manny Zelnick would write to her. If he had had time to write from basic training, what might he have said? Write a letter from Manny to Shirley telling about his first few weeks in the Army. Base your letter on further reading about basic training and cite your source.

3. Shirley and her friends formed a Victory Club to help in the war effort. What purpose might such a club have today? Tell how children could join together to make their communities better places in which to live.

A Time Too Swift   Margaret Poynter
New York: Atheneum, 1990. 216p. (2)

The world is at war in mid-1941, so fifteen-year-old Marjorie Ellison cannot concentrate exclusively on her school work and her first crush. Then comes the Japanese attack on Pearl Harbor, which leads her eighteen-year-old brother, Dave, to enlist in the Marines. Marjorie's efforts to befriend a Japanese classmate are interrupted when the family is sent off to an internment camp. Her best friend Ellen mourns the loss of her father on the battleship *Arizona*, while Dave's friend Larry struggles to come to terms with his classification as 4-F due to a heart murmur. All the while Marjorie tries to reconcile her romantic daydreams with the anxieties and uncertainties of real life. It is only when Dave is wounded on Guadalcanal that she finally gives up her fantasies.

Comment

Very much a girl's coming-of-age story, this book makes clear the impact of war on everyday life. Women and teenagers go to work in factories; wounded servicemen fill the local hospital; everyone listens to the radio for news of the fighting and waits for letters from loved ones at the front. That there are many different ways of being brave and of assisting the war effort besides fighting is a concept that is developed throughout the story.

Suggestions for Reports or Activities

1. Kaye Narasaki writes of being housed in a stable near Los Angeles. Find out more about the internment camps for Japanese-Americans: When did they start? Who had to move there? How long did they last? Were these U.S. citizens ever offered any compensation for their ordeal?

2. Research the progress of the war in the Pacific. When did the Japanese start losing, and why? What happened at Guadalcanal?

3. During World War II a lot of women and girls like Beverly, Marjorie, and Marjorie's mother went to work in factories. What happened when the war was over? Did they all go back to being housewives? Draw a graph showing employed women as a percentage of total women in the U.S. population at five-year intervals from 1935 through 1965. Cite your sources.

MORE CHALLENGING BOOKS
FOR ADVANCED READERS

The Dollmaker   Harriette Arnow
New York: Macmillan, 1954. 549p.

The production requirements of the Second World War lured many country people from the South to the big cities of the North, and most of them never went back. In this story, living in a housing project situated near a Detroit factory, a "hillbilly" family from Kentucky faces the alien demands of city life. Unions and strikes, fear of

"Communists," hostility toward new immigrants, and other issues also have their impact.

Rumors of Peace   Ella Leffland
New York: Harper, 1979. 389p.

A young girl in World War II experiences blackouts, air-raid drills, rationing, and the removal of Japanese-Americans to internment camps, while she tries desperately to understand what is happening and why. The book records the feelings of exhilaration at the end of the war in Europe and the tentative jubilation when the atomic bomb brings about the surrender of Japan.

VIII *America in the Modern World*

And One for All Theresa Nelson
New York: Orchard, 1989. 182p. (2, 3)

Geraldine Brennan worries a lot about her older brother Wing, who can't seem to keep out of trouble. Unlike his best friend, Sam, who is good at everything, Wing lives only for sports. When he is taken off the basketball team because his grades are low, Wing acknowledges his eighteenth birthday by enlisting in the Marines. But it is 1967, and Wing is sent to fight in Vietnam. Sam, whose father was killed in an accident in Korea when he was a baby, moves to Washington, D.C., to attend college and protest the war. Geraldine and her family believe that the protesters are prolonging the war by misleading the enemy into thinking that the United States does not support its armed forces. Then the dreaded news arrives, and Geraldine sets out to find Sam to tell him that he is to blame.

Comment

This story brings to life the brutal dissension in the United States during the Vietnam era. It shows how the armed conflict in that far-off Asian country divided families and friends, but also how it provided an opportunity for youngsters uncomfortable with their schooling to run away to war. Once overseas, many of the young soldiers discover the dark side of combat, as Geraldine realizes when she sees a mutilated veteran at a peace march in Washington. In the end, the reader understands, along with Geraldine, that there is more than one way to be patriotic, more than one way to show one's love for one's friends.

Suggestions for Reports or Activities

1. Read about the protests at the time of the Vietnam War. Find some statistics on the percentage of eligible young men who fled to Canada or went to jail rather than fight in Vietnam. Do you think the protests prolonged the war or hastened its end? Explain your conclusion.

2. At the time of the Vietnam War, many young men who didn't like school enlisted in the armed services, even though they knew they would probably go into combat. In time of peace, does the military ordinarily take people who haven't finished high school? Find out what the minimum requirements are. Are they different for the different branches of the armed services?

3. Geraldine probably replied to Wing's letter telling of Hopkins' death. How do you think she tried to comfort her brother? What did she say, besides telling him of the candles she had lit for both of them? Compose the letter you think Geraldine might have written.

The Bridges at Toko-ri   James A. Michener
New York: Random House, 1953. 147p. (1, 2, 3)

Harry Brubaker, Denver lawyer and reluctant Navy pilot, is part of a naval task force flying jet bombers from an aircraft carrier operating off the Korean shore. Their mission is to destroy the heavily guarded bridges at Toko-ri, thereby preventing essential supplies from moving to the Communists' front lines. The complicated task of landing the planes on the pitching decks of the carriers—which are no longer located where they were when the pilots took off—is portrayed with particular vividness.

Comment

Michener, who wrote this short book while the Korean War was in progress, contrasts the tension and high drama of the war with the apathy and ignorance of the folks back home. At the same time, the war is not in any way glorified: disappointment, despair, and death are daily hallmarks of life in combat. Brubaker, who does not want to be there, is portrayed with sympathy, but so are the enthusiastic helicopter pilots, the admiral, and the commander of the air group.

Suggestions for Reports or Activities

1. Brubaker complains that nobody back home cares about the war in Korea. Was this true? If so, why? Check lead articles in national newspapers such as the *New York Times* for supporting evidence.

2. Many American servicemen, like Mike Forney, developed emotional ties with Japanese and other Asian women they met during their rest-and-recreation stops. Some of them married their sweethearts and brought them home, but others did not. Look into the fate of the Amerasian children whose fathers abandoned them following this and other wars in Asia. How have they survived?

3. Write the letter that Admiral Tarrant had to write to Brubaker's family. Then write Nancy Brubaker's reply. Did she understand why Harry died?

Call Me Danica   Winifred Madison
New York: Four Winds, 1977. 203p. (2)

Twelve-year-old Danica (pronounced Dánitsa) is fascinated by the postcards that she receives from relatives living in Vancouver, Canada. While happy enough in her small village in Croatia, she cannot help dreaming about the excitement and glamor of faraway city life. When Danica finally gets her wish, she finds, as do most immigrants, that hardship and confusion await her along with the shining water and tall buildings. It takes a frightening accident to set Danica back on course toward fulfilling her true dream of becoming a doctor.

Comment

While children in any circumstances may conclude that their parents cannot help them understand the world around them, children of immigrants are especially vulnerable to the impression that they are on their own. Readers will identify with Danica's insistence on maintaining her own identity while at the same time longing to become something that she is not (in this case, "Canadian"). Her selection of a troubled older child as an untrustworthy friend is another experience common to many youngsters today.

Suggestions for Reports or Activities

1. When Danica says she wants to be a Canadian, what does she have in mind? List the kinds of things she longs for (particular clothes,

language, music, hairdo, etc.) and compare them with the Croatian equivalents. If she acquires all these things, will she then be a Canadian? If not, what will it take?

2. Write the letter that Mirjana's friend Ana sent to her in which she revealed that she was dating Mirjana's boyfriend, Mirko. Did she try to put it gently, or did she just blurt it out? Then compose the letter that Mirjana wrote back to Ana in which she reacted to the news.

3. What seem to be the criteria for making good in a new country? What kinds of skills or attitudes should one have? Analyze the character of Mama in terms of your list. What factors made her successful?

Caribou   Meg Wolitzer
New York: Greenwillow, 1985. 167p. (2, 3)

Becca's family hovers around the television set as the Vietnam draft lottery begins. The very first date drawn is her brother Stevie's birthday. Stevie is devastated. He does not report for his physical as scheduled; he has decided to go to Canada. Father is angry, Mother is upset, and Becca knows only that she is going to miss Stevie very much. But she is busy with her best friend Kate, and with school, and especially with the My Country 'Tis of Thee art contest for a school mural. If she is the one chosen to paint the school mural, she will win the $100 prize and go to Canada to visit Stevie, despite her father's violent opposition. Becca is the winner, for her proposal to paint a parade with American flags. But while she is painting and thinking about Stevie and Vietnam and her father, she has another idea.

Comment

Conflicting views of the Vietnam War are depicted: Becca's father's conviction that one's first duty is to one's country; her mother's indecisiveness; and Stevie's determination to make his own decisions about his life. Becca is shown maturing, also affected by the war. The book captures the ambience of the early 1970s, with references to Beatles music, smoking pot, and communal living. For young readers *Caribou* is an informative and thoughtful picture of a tense time.

Suggestions for Reports or Activities

1. What was the date of the Vietnam draft lottery on television? What were some of the reactions of people to this event? Read editorials and letters to the editor in your local newspaper. Check also the *New York Times* or another national paper. Write a brief paper on your findings.

2. Find out about the young men who emigrated to Canada to avoid serving in Vietnam. How many went? Where did they go? What did they do? What has happened to them?

3. What do you think about Stevie's decision? Why? Discuss in a short paper.

Fallen Angels   Walter Dean Myers
New York: Scholastic, 1988. 286p. (1, 2)

Richie Perry, seventeen, is out of high school and in the Vietnam War. He might have gone on to City College—but money has always been scarce, and now he can send some home to his mom and little brother in Harlem. Richie tells his story, of the camaraderie that develops among the men during the "hours of boredom and seconds of terror," and of the fighting, the narrow escapes, being wounded, and surviving. At first, the war seems something far away, and then guys he knows are killed, even Lieutenant Carroll. To save his own life, Richie guns down a young Vietcong soldier, but getting accustomed to this role is difficult. There are jokes, there is fear, and then there is guilt when someone else is not going to get to go home. Richie and his good friend Pee Wee are lucky.

Comment

This grippingly realistic account shows the day-to-day lives of young soldiers in Vietnam. The events at home—the demonstrations and draft card burnings—and the attempts to make peace are mentioned, but they seem unreal to the teenage soldiers as they struggle to make sense of their being in Nam. The bantering and fooling around, which make daily life tolerable, are in contrast to the fear, the pain, the confusion, the carnage (accidental or purposeful), the courage, and the attempt to understand, which the author describes in the vivid language of young soldiers. This graphic account of life "in the trenches" of Vietnam will contribute to young readers' understanding of the general feeling of ambiguity regarding the Vietnamese conflict.

Suggestions for Reports or Activities

1. What lay behind the United States' involvement in the Vietnamese conflict? Based on what you have read in the novel, your text, and other sources, discuss the official U.S. government position.

2. From what you have found out in the book, who served in Vietnam? That is, whose war was it?

3. Can you notice any changes in Richie as a result of his experiences? Discuss.

4. What do you suppose happened to Richie and Pee Wee after they came home? Write what you think in a short epilogue to the story.

Fragments   Jack Fuller
New York: Morrow, 1984. 210p. (1, 2)

During the peak of the war in Vietnam, two young men join the United States military. One enlists by choice; the other is drafted out of college. Neumann, the charismatic leader and natural fighter, and Morgan, the pensive pessimist, bond together in the struggle for survival during their year of combat. As they become more involved in the horrors of Vietnam, however, a shocking turn of events threatens their friendship as well as their lives.

Comment

Told from the point of view of Morgan, this novel makes vivid his participation in a war that he does not understand and cannot justify. The book thus provides a glimpse of what it is like for an eighteen-year-old to leave college, enter the army, and be forced to grow up immediately. Neumann exhibits another side of American youth, that of a volunteer who dedicates himself to his own success and that of his companions in a totally new and alien environment. The complex friendship that develops contrasts the personalities of the two young men and sets the scene for an enlightening look at the Vietnam War.

Suggestions for Reports or Activities

1. Locate a Vietnam veteran in your community: a neighbor, family member, teacher, or person referred to you by your local vet-

erans' organization. Ask him or her to tell you some stories about serving in Vietnam. Compare these to the tales included in this book.

2. Analyze the reasons for the reactions of Neumann and Morgan to the task of readjusting to the "world." Which of them had the easier time? Why?

3. Speculate about why Neumann and Morgan became such close friends despite their many and obvious differences. What needs did each have that the other was able to fill?

Freedom's Blood   James D. Foreman
New York: Franklin Watts, 1979. 114p. (2, 3)

By the summer of 1964, Michael Schwerner has been working in Meridian, Mississippi, for nearly six months, encouraging local blacks to register and vote. In the company of a new college student recruit, Andrew Goodman, and a native black Mississippian, James Chaney, Mickey drives to the rural town of Longdale to set up a freedom school in a church. Finding that the church has recently been burned to the ground and its members beaten, the three young men decide to hold the school on benches amid the ashes. Then they head for Meridian. They never make it.

Comment

Freedom's Blood is a fictionalized account of three civil rights workers who were murdered at the very beginning of "Freedom Summer," which brought 600 Northerners to the South. A vivid reconstruction of their motivations, their fears, their hopes, and their faith in law and basic human goodness makes their short lives transcend their brutal deaths. Knowing how the story ends does not diminish the suspense of the fateful drive.

Suggestions for Reports or Activities

1. Read a contemporary newspaper account of the debates in Congress related to the Civil Rights Acts of 1964 and 1968 or the Voting Rights Act of 1965. Were there any references, either positive or negative, to the activities of Northern civil rights workers in the South? Discuss.

2. What did your nearest large-city newspaper have to say when the deaths of Schwerner, Goodman, and Chaney were discovered? Who was to blame?

3. Write the letter of farewell to his wife, Rita, that Mickey Schwerner might have written if he had had time. What feelings (besides his love for her) might he have expressed, knowing that he was about to die?

Freedom Songs   Yvette Moore
New York: Orchard, 1991. 168p. (1, 2)

In 1963 Sheryl Williams and her family go down South at Easter to visit her mother's folks in Mississippi. They find their relatives torn between the desire not to make life harder for themselves by objecting to their mistreatment at the hands of local whites and the call to stand up as free citizens who have the right to vote. Sheryl is especially impressed by her uncle Pete, less than six years older than she, who is determined to help his people get educated in order to be truly free. What happens to Pete and his friends, and to Sheryl and hers when she returns to Brooklyn, determines the fate of many others at the beginning of the struggle for civil rights in the 1960s.

Comment

This moving story describes the violence directed at the Southern Freedom Riders from the point of view of young people in the North who, while not directly affected, nonetheless want to help. The physical courage of the one group is balanced by the energy and focus of the other. Sheryl changes from being a young person interested in clothes and her status in school to one who discovers her gifts as an artist, an organizer, and a young woman.

Suggestions for Reports or Activities

1. Read about the "Freedom Summer" of 1963. Who organized the voting drive? Who built and staffed the schools? Where did the young people come from and where did they live? Did any white people participate?

2. Compare the open kinds of prejudice and discrimination in the South and the more subtle kinds in the North at the time of this story. Give some examples, from the book or from other sources known to you.

3. Compose the letter from Debra Jean to Sheryl that she might have written while she and her sister Brenda were in jail. What were her thoughts and fears? How did she feel about what she and her friends had done?

The Girl on the Outside   Mildred Pitts Walter
New York: Scholastic, 1982. 147p. (2, 3)

In 1957, in the town of Mossville in an unnamed Southern state, nine black students have enrolled at the all-white high school for the first time. Eva Collins has agreed to be one of them, although she's scared about what might happen to her. Sophia Stuart, about to enter her senior year, is furious about the disruptions that she imagines the black students will bring to "her" school. Sophia and her friends agree simply to ignore the interlopers, while Eva and her group carefully plan what to wear and how to behave. Then the governor calls out the National Guard to "protect citizens of the state": Does this mean the Guard will assist the black students to enter, or bar them at the door? Angry whites from neighboring states crowd the streets around the school as they wait to find out which way the National Guard will move.

Comment

This fictionalized account is based on the efforts to integrate Central High School in Little Rock, Arkansas, in September 1957. Elizabeth Eckford, one of the nine black students who had enrolled, was prevented by the National Guard from entering the school. A white woman named Grace Lorch sat beside Elizabeth and helped her onto a city bus. An author's note at the end of the book explains what happened afterwards, when President Dwight D. Eisenhower federalized the Arkansas National Guard and sent troops from the 101st Airborne Division into the city.

Suggestions for Reports or Activities

1. Read about the integration of Central High School in Little Rock, Arkansas. How did it happen that Elizabeth Eckford tried to enter the school alone? What became of her and the other eight black students in later life?

2. Imagine that you were in Eva's place, as she sat on the bench waiting for the bus, tormented by an angry mob. What would you have been thinking? What feelings would you have had? What would you want most?

3. What is the status of racial integration in American schools today? Find out how many public school systems have mostly integrated schools. Compare this statistic with those for 1950 and 1975. Write a paragraph speculating about the reasons for the trend that you have uncovered.

Journey of the Sparrows   Fran Leeper Buss (with Daisy Cubias)
New York: Dutton, Lodestar, 1991. 155p. (1, 2)

María, her little brother Oscar, and her pregnant older sister, Julia, have crossed illegally into the United States locked in a crate. Since their father and Julia's husband were killed by the militia in El Salvador, it is not safe for them to stay in their country. The children's mother and infant sister Teresa are waiting in Mexico till the baby becomes strong enough to flee also. Meanwhile, María feels responsible for the family, since she is the only one who has learned to read and write. Arriving in Chicago in the middle of winter, the youngsters rely on the help of other immigrants in obtaining food, shelter, jobs, and support, especially when Julia goes into labor. When their mother is deported to El Salvador, María has to figure out how to rescue Teresa and get them both back safely across the border.

Comment

This story makes vivid the lack of security felt by people living in a country without a competent and reliable civil authority. They fear for their lives if they stay, and yet there is nowhere they can legally go. That there are people in the United States working to legalize immigration from such areas is made clear; for now, however, their lives are in danger wherever they may be. María and her family personalize this dilemma as the reader follows the ups and downs of their brave adventure.

Suggestions for Reports or Activities

1. What is U.S. immigration policy toward Central American refugees? Which ones may be allowed to enter legally, and which may not? Compare the figures in recent years for legal and illegal immigration from Central America.

2. Compose one of the letters that María sent to her mother from Chicago. Tell what jobs the sisters have, how Oscar is getting along, and how Tomás and his family are helping.

3. Imagine another chapter to the story. How could the mother legally enter the United States and join her family?

Just Like Martin   Ossie Davis
New York: Simon & Schuster, 1992. 215p. (2, 3)

The year 1963 in the Southern United States is marked by violent death: Medgar Evers, Mississippi civil rights leader, is killed in

June; several black children die in a church bombing in Alabama in September; and President John F. Kennedy is murdered in Texas in November. In this story thirteen-year-old Isaac Stone, Jr., tries to emulate the nonviolent approach of Martin Luther King, Jr., despite the disdain of his widowed father, a Korean War veteran. When the father is beaten by police at a march in memory of the children who were killed and injured in the church bombing, young Isaac has to confront the possible limits of nonviolence in a racist community.

Comment

Set at the beginning of the Civil Rights movement in the United States, this tale illuminates the appeal of King's emphasis on nonviolence as the only way for the powerless to make an impact on those who control their very lives and livelihoods. That nonviolence is difficult to carry out becomes clear as Isaac's classmates try to make him fight the local bully, and drunken rednecks force the Stones' pickup truck off the road into a ditch.

Suggestions for Reports or Activities

1. Get a copy of the "I Have a Dream" speech which Martin Luther King, Jr., made at the March on Washington in 1963. Which is your favorite passage, and why? To what extent do you think King's dream has come true since that time?

2. Who was Medgar Evers and how did he die? What happened to his assailant? Find out what became of his widow and his children.

3. Part of this story is based on a real incident when four little girls died in the bombing of a Birmingham church. Look up the details of what happened and tell it in your own words. Include the names of the four girls and the name of the church.

Ludie's Song   Dirlie Herlihy
New York: Dial, 1988. 212p. (2)

When Marty leaves her home in the state capital in the early 1950s to spend a couple of weeks with her Aunt Letta and Uncle Ray in rural Georgia, she finds many customs that are strange to her. How come whites and coloreds can be friends when they're little but not when they're older? Why does Uncle Ray have two kinds of charge slips in his store? What happened to Ludie, the washerwoman's daughter, that disfigured and crippled her? Why won't the three white boys who beat up the black boy be punished? Twelve-year-old Marty affects the lives of many of the people in town as she finds the answers to her questions.

Comment

The flavor of small-town Southern life becomes sharp and vivid through this story. Even well-meaning whites appear trapped by local customs into behaving in cruel and thoughtless ways. At the same time, outsiders who single people out for their attention and attempted kindness are shown to bring unexpected harm to those whom they most want to help. The ideas of honor and justice come to be defined culturally rather than absolutely.

Suggestions for Reports or Activities

1. Marty's mother mentions things "happening in other parts of the country" with regard to black people. What was going on? What was the nature of the Supreme Court decision in 1954 on *Brown v. Board of Education of Topeka, Kansas?*

2. How do you think Ludie felt about her friendship with Marty, niece of the man who was responsible (even if indirectly) for her burning? Imagine that Ludie kept a journal, and write a page or two regarding her feelings about Marty and the memories she brought back of her Uncle Lonnie.

3. Write a letter from Thad to Marty dated about six months after he moved to Chicago with his mother. What would have struck him about the different ways black people in the North were treated at that time as compared with the South? Were the differences only formal (e.g., anybody could drink at any water fountain) or real as well?

Lupita Mañana   Patricia Beatty
New York: Beech Tree, 1981. 186p. (2)

Two Mexican teenagers, Lupita and her brother Salvador, are sent north by their mother to seek work in the United States. Called "Lupita Mañana" (Lupita Tomorrow) because she always says things will be better tomorrow, the plucky young girl undergoes many hardships on both sides of the border. Worst of all, perhaps, is losing her older brother to the lure of Yankee materialism; as the weeks go by, he contributes less and less of his wages to send back to Mexico for the support of his mother and younger siblings, until finally he is caught at a dance by the dreaded immigration officials *(la migra)*.

Comment

While America has in the past been proud to be a nation of immigrants, present-day immigration policy discourages so-called economic refugees from seeking their fortune within U.S. borders. As this book demonstrates, the decision to leave one's home and family is seldom an easy one; being subject to arrest and forcible exile almost guarantees that the illegal arrivals will be robbed and exploited by unscrupulous citizens. The story of Lupita and her brother personalizes the dilemma of those who would prefer to stay home with their families but see no choice other than to leave if they are to survive at all.

Suggestions for Reports or Activities

1. With the assistance of a reference librarian, find out how many immigrants (that is, people born outside the U.S.) were living in the United States in 1890 as compared to 1990. List the countries from which they came and each country's proportion of the total immigrant population.

2. What happened to Salvador in this story to drive him and Lupita apart? What did Lucio (Lucky) Ruiz and his friends offer that became more important to Salvador than helping his mother and little sisters and brother?

3. Speculate about what became of Lupita and Salvador after the novel ended. Did Salvador find his way back to Indio? If so, how? Did Lupita learn English and escape *la migra*? Explain what they were doing five years after the end of the book (when Salvador was 20 and Lupita 18) and how they got there.

Pageant Kathryn Lasky
New York: Four Winds, 1986. 221p. (2, 3)

November for the students at Stuart Hall, a conservative Indianapolis prep school, means rehearsing for the annual Christmas pageant. For Sarah Benjamin, one of only three Kennedy supporters in the school, November 1960 is the beginning of new awareness. The headmistress is furious because Sarah is wearing a "Kennedy for President" button on her shepherd's costume. Why not? wonders Sarah, but she has other questions. Should a Jewish student be a shepherd in a Christmas pageant? Through the next three years, from November to November, her tiny, tidy world begins to change. Her sister Marla goes away to college; her Aunt Hattie, bothersome and pushy, comes for a long stay. A promising date for the Christmas dance ends in disaster. The headmistress rejects her science project. But Sarah is beginning to know herself. Finally, one more pageant is just too much, and on a fateful November day in 1963, Sarah makes a bold move.

Comment

This coming-of-age story is set against the background of the sixties, beginning with the election of President Kennedy. The atmosphere of the time is vividly evoked, for example, in the broad vision of optimism in the "New Frontier" and the national mourning at the President's death. The author has also shown, through Sarah's reaction to the little black stableboy lawn statues and to her prom date's comments about blacks, the growing general concern over racial prejudice. Sarah's decision to join the Peace Corps reflects the idealism of college-age youth at that time.

Suggestions for Reports or Activities

1. What was the "New Frontier"? What were the larger goals of the Kennedy administration? What was accomplished?

2. Sarah decides to join the Peace Corps. What is the Peace Corps? What are the requirements to become a volunteer? Write a short paper on the Peace Corps then and now.

3. Why is the title *Pageant* appropriate for this book?

Park's Quest Katherine Paterson
New York: Dutton, Lodestar, 1988. 148p. (2, 3)

Parkington Waddell Broughton the Fifth is eleven years old, and he wants to know about the dead father whose name he bears but whom he does not remember. There are so many questions: Why did his father go back to Vietnam for a second tour? Why won't his mother talk about him? Is his grandfather, Parkington Waddell Broughton the Third, still alive? Finally he is allowed to visit the ancestral home in southern Virginia. There he discovers clues to his past, including those provided by a spunky Vietnamese girl named Thanh, who cries when she thinks no one is listening.

Comment

For today's young readers the Vietnam War era is as much a part of history as World War II. The unfolding of this story's mysteries brings alive some of the conflicts of the time and the varying ways in which people reacted to them; for example, Park and Thanh are both searching for their identities, while the adults wrestle with feelings of guilt for the death of Park's father. The impact of war and racism is felt by all.

Suggestions for Reports or Activities

1. Park searches for his father's name on the Vietnam Memorial. Describe the Memorial. Who designed it? When was it built? How many names are inscribed on it? What happens when new deaths from that conflict are discovered?

2. Thanh is one of the "Amerasian" children born to Asian women and fathered by American servicemen stationed in that region. Find out how many such children there are. Do their fathers sometimes take responsibility for them? If they don't, what happens to the children?

3. From all the clues given in this story, reconstruct the relationship of Park's parents and the reactions of Park's family to what was going on. Show in chronological order what happened from the time when Park IV and Randy got married to when Park V finally learned the truth.

To Stand Against the Wind   Ann Nolan Clark
New York: Viking, 1978. 136p. (3)

Eleven-year-old Em is now in America, with his grandmother and Old Uncle, and his older sister, Chi-Bah. It has been one year since the dreadful day that changed forever a family and their traditional way of life. Now, on the Day of the Ancestors, it is Em's task, as head of the family, to record memories of Vietnam and of what happened to loved ones. It is hard, but he must try. So he remembers and tries to write about the hamlet where his family lived for generations; about his parents and how the war gradually was everywhere around them; about his beloved water buffalo; and about Sam, the American reporter, who was his dear friend. He recalls it all, but on paper he can put only an old proverb learned from his father: "It takes a strong man to stand against the wind."

Comment

This story introduces readers to Vietnam before and during the war. It shows the Vietnamese as a gentle, thoughtful, disciplined people with a deep respect for their ancient traditions. Em's story emphasizes the Vietnamese belief in the importance of the family, respect for elders, knowing one's role, acceptance of fate. The horror of the killing of innocent villagers, the bewilderment and frustration of the American soldiers, and the dislocation of the war victims are vividly portrayed through Em's stories.

Suggestions for Reports or Activities

1. Some Vietnamese customs are described. Based on what you have learned from the book, write a short paper on the celebration of Tet or on the traditional arrangements for a wedding.

2. What was the Tet Offensive in the Vietnam War?

3. What is the meaning of the title, taken from a Vietnamese proverb?

4. If possible, talk to someone who came to the United States from Indochina as a result of the war. Ask if he or she would be willing to share some experiences.

The Watsons Go to Birmingham—1963   Christopher Paul Curtis
New York: Delacorte, 1995. 210p. (2, 3)

Ten-year-old Kenny tells about his family, known in their Flint neighborhood as the "Weird Watsons," in vivid and humorous language. When his older brother Byron seems to be out of control, the parents decide to take the children for a visit to their maternal grandmother near Birmingham, Alabama, and to leave Byron there for the summer and possibly longer. But while they are in Alabama, the church which little sister Joetta is attending is bombed. Four little girls are killed, and two others are blinded by the blast. But where is Joetta?

Comment

The Birmingham calamity is presented as the most significant and least comprehensible of the many adventures in the life of a small boy. Here these include befriending a poor Southern classmate newly arrived in the North; submitting to the bullying of his big brother; trying to cure his "lazy eye"; getting caught in a whirlpool; coping with the overdressing in winter imposed by his Southern-born mother; and dealing with a whiny little sister. Life goes on, marked by comedy as well as tragedy.

Suggestions for Reports or Activities

1. Read about the bombing on September 15, 1963, at the Sixteenth Avenue Baptist Church in Birmingham. What have you learned besides what is told in this book?

2. Find out more about the march in Washington, D.C., on August 28, 1963, in which Martin Luther King, Jr., delivered his speech featuring the phrase, "I have a dream." How many people attended? Who else spoke? What happened in Congress and the White House as a result? Has King's dream come true, even in part?

3. Provide biographical information about two or three of the following civil rights workers: Thurgood Marshall, John Lewis, Ralph Abernathy, Medgar Evers, Fannie Lou Hamer, Rosa Parks. Assess their impact on improvement of the conditions under which African-Americans live.

A Woman of Independent Means   Elizabeth Forsythe Hailey
New York: Viking, 1978. 256p. (1, 2)

This story is told entirely in the form of letters from Elizabeth Alcott Steed Garner, known as Bess, to members of her family, to friends, and to business associates. The first letter is to her fourth-grade sweetheart, later her first husband, and the last is to welcome her new great-grandchild. In between are covered nearly seventy years of history, political as well as personal. Through her letters the reader comes to know Bess and also to experience the major events of the period through their effect on her life and thinking.

Comment

Bess's perspective, as "a woman of independent means," should not be generalized too widely. Yet many of the events that affected her life touched the lives of Americans from other parts of the country and other social and economic levels as well. Wars were important, of course, but so were gradual changes in race relations, women's rights, and even American concepts of justice and fair play. Bess's development from a woman not only independent but unbearably domineering surely reflects in part the changing times in which she lived.

Suggestions for Reports or Activities

1. Bess, her daughter Eleanor, and her granddaughter Betsy all show their independence, but in different ways. Name some of these ways and tell how they reflect the changing values of the society of the time.

2. Find the part in the book where Bess writes an angry letter to Eleanor. Write a letter from Eleanor in response to her mother's complaints.

3. Bess mentions once that she cannot sell her house, which is in her name alone, because her husband Sam will not consent. Research the current laws of Texas to see if this situation would prevail today.

MORE CHALLENGING BOOKS FOR ADVANCED READERS

Going After Cacciato   Tim O'Brien
New York: Delacorte, 1978. 338p
    During the Vietnam War, a soldier named Cacciato walks away from combat to "go to Paris." His friend Paul Berlin, confined to an observation tower, fantasizes about following Cacciato to his destination. The story illuminates the constant inner conflicts of the American soldiers as a result of their fragmentary understanding of their role and purpose in Vietnam.

Invisible Man   Ralph Ellison
New York: Vintage, 1947. 568p.
    The struggle of blacks a decade before the Civil Rights movement is used to urge all to follow the wisdom of the author's former slave grandfather, "to keep up the good fight," in order to allow people to become fulfilled and the nation thereby to live out its possibilities. Also offered are inside views of sharecropping, life at an all-black college, hazardous working conditions, and the experience of living in substandard housing.

Author-Title Index

Rosemary K. Coffey is a former teacher and curriculum developer with the Pittsburgh, Pennsylvania, School District. She was one of the annotators for the first edition of this book and used it in an eighth-grade American history class. She is the author of *The Story of Pittsburgh,* a history of the city used by third graders enrolled in the city schools. Coffey is now a freelance writer and editor.

Elizabeth F. Howard, author of the first edition, is professor emerita at West Virginia University, where she taught courses in children's and young adult literature in the department of library science. As an active member of the American Library Association, Howard has served on numerous committees, including the Caldecott Award Committee, the ALA-Children's Book Council Liaison Committee, and the Teachers of Children's Literature Discussion Group. She is the author of several picture books for young children drawn from her African-American family history.